Ethics and the Golden Rule

It is commonly accepted that the golden rule – most often formulated as "do unto others as you would have them do unto you" – is a unifying element between many diverse religious traditions, both Eastern and Western. Its influence also extends beyond such traditions, since many non-religious individuals hold up the golden rule as central to their lives.

Yet, while it is extraordinarily important and widespread, the golden rule is often dismissed by scholars as a vague proverb that quickly leads to absurdities when one attempts to formulate it in clear terms. In this book, Harry J. Gensler defends the golden rule and addresses all of the major philosophic objections, pointing out several common misunderstanding and misapplications. Gensler first discusses golden-rule reasoning and how to avoid the main pitfalls. He then relates the golden rule to world religions and history, and to areas like moral education, egoism, evolution, society, racism, business, and medicine. The book ends with a discussion of theoretical issues (like whether all morality reduces to the golden rule, which the author argues against).

Ethics and the Golden Rule offers two introductory chapters, the first is simpler and the second more technical; a reader may start with either or both. One can then read any combination of further chapters, in any order, depending on one's interests; but Chapters 13 and 14 are technical and assume one has read Chapter 2. This is "a golden-rule book for everyone," accessible to a wide readership.

Harry J. Gensler, S.J., an American philosopher who has published twelve books on ethics and logic, has had a lifetime passion for the golden rule. His Web site http://www.harryhiker.com has more information on him.

Ethics and the Golden Rule

Harry J. Gensler

Routledge
Taylor & Francis Group

NEW YORK AND LONDON

First published 2013
by Routledge
711 Third Avenue, New York, NY 10017

Simultaneously published in the UK
by Routledge
2 Park Square, Milton Park, Abingdon, Oxon OX14 4RN

Routledge is an imprint of the Taylor & Francis Group, an informa business

Library of Congress Cataloging-in-Publication Data
Gensler, Harry J., 1945–
Ethics and the golden rule / By Harry J. Gensler.
p. cm.
Includes bibliographical references and index.
1. Golden rule. 2. Religious ethics. I. Title.
BJ1188.G45 2013
170—dc23
2013000419

ISBN: 978-0-415-80686-2 (hbk)
ISBN: 978-0-415-80687-9 (pbk)
ISBN: 978-0-203-15437-3 (ebk)

Contents

Part 3: Practice

Part 4: Theory

Preface

The golden rule (GR) says "Treat others as you want to be treated." GR is a global standard – endorsed by nearly every religion and culture – important for families and professionals across the planet for many centuries – and a key part of a growing global-ethics movement. But many academics see GR as vague and riddled with difficulties.

This book defends the golden rule. It first talks about GR reasoning and how to avoid the main pitfalls. Then it relates GR to world religions and history, and then to areas like moral education, egoism, evolution, society, racism, business, and medicine. It ends with theoretical issues (like whether all morality reduces to GR: I say no). This book is interdisciplinary but grounded in philosophy.

Two introductory chapters deal with GR reasoning, including misunderstandings and misapplications. Chapter 1 is simpler and Chapter 2 more technical; start by reading either or both. Then read any combination of further chapters, in any order, depending on your interests; but Chapters 13 and 14 are technical and assume Chapter 2. This is "a GR book for everyone," accessible to a wide readership.

I intend this book for various groups of readers. First are college students in ethics courses (moral philosophy/theology). How can this book serve them?

Students studying ethics, while searching for ideas to help them live better lives, are often relativistic about values. GR addresses both concerns – since GR is a very practical tool for moral living and a global norm that can be defended rationally. In addition, students will enjoy the book's clear and concise writing, interesting examples, and boxes for key ideas. And the wide range of topics will appeal to the special interests of individual students.

Teachers should first assign Chapter 1 or 2 or both, depending on the course level. Then they can assign any combination of other chapters, in any order, depending on which topics they want to cover. The book is ideal for having students write papers that connect GR with special interests (e.g., education, business, biology, activism, or religion). Use the index to find parts of the book that relate to specific areas, and then see which bibliography items are mentioned for further reading. Or explore my GR Web page. Or search the Web for "Golden Rule" followed by other terms (but be forewarned that you'll find both wisdom and foolishness).

Teachers can use this book as their sole text or as one of several texts – perhaps also using books on ethical theory, history of ethics, applied ethics, religious ethics, or world religions. Some might pair this present book with my *Ethics: A Contemporary Introduction* (2011), which gives a simple introduction to some main issues of contemporary moral philosophy.

But again, this is "a GR book for everyone," not just students, but also general readers and specialists in various areas. If you skim the book, or its index or bibliography, you'll see that people are interested in GR from many angles – such as activism (including peace, discrimination, and economic justice); applied ethics (including business and medicine); biology (especially evolution); cultural and historical studies (Chinese, African, American, etc., or intercultural); ecology; ethical theory; law and politics; literature; moral education; psychology and sociology; and religious ethics and scriptural studies (Christian, Jewish, Muslim, Buddhist, etc., or interfaith). GR ties much together.

Readers should check out my http://www.harryhiker.com/gr Web page on the golden rule. This page, which is available in many languages, has much useful information on GR – including a short essay, several videos, a list of related books, tools for searching the Web for various GR topics, GR links, GR stories, and how to get GR shirts and other items.

I thank all who somehow contributed to this book. Particularly notable are Jeff Wattles (a GR expert whom I've collaborated with for two decades and who made suggestions after reading the whole text), Paul McKenna (a GR activist with whom I've often discussed GR), Tom Carson (a distinguished ethicist who has supported this project), T. Frank Kennedy and the Jesuit Institute of Boston College (for funding me for a year during which my chief task was to reflect on earth's greatest moral principle), Andy Beck (my Routledge editor who pushed me to make this the best book it could be), and my sister Carol Ann Tuttle (who deserves much of the credit if any of this is readable by a wider audience). These are all wonderful people. Many others, far too many to mention here, contributed in some way.

I became a GR junkie in 1968, after hearing a talk by the Oxford philosopher R.M. Hare. The book that you're holding developed out of forty-five years of reflection on the golden rule. I hope that it leads to a better understanding of earth's most important moral idea.

Harry J. Gensler
http://www.harryhiker.com

CHAPTER 1
Simpler Introduction

There are two introductory chapters: this one is simpler,
while Chapter 2 is longer and more technical. Read either or both.
Then read any combination of further chapters, in any order; but
Chapters 13 and 14 are technical and assume Chapter 2.

The golden rule (GR) says "Treat others as you want to be treated." The idea
is global. It's common to all major world religions; Confucius, Hillel, Jesus,
and many others used it to sum up how to live. For centuries across the planet,
it's been important in families and professions, and in thinkers and cultures,
both religious and non-religious. Today it's part of a growing global-ethics
movement.

GR touches many areas of life. Later we'll connect it to world religions, history, moral education, egoism, evolution, society, racism, business, medicine,
and so on. But first we'll consider how GR reasoning works.

1.1   A simple idea?

I'll start with a story (Grimm Brothers 1812). There once was a grandpa who
lived with his family. As Grandpa grew older, he began to slobber and spill his
food. So the family had him eat alone. When he dropped his bowl and broke it,
they scolded him and got him a cheap wooden bowl. Grandpa was so unhappy.
Now one day the young grandson was working with wood. "What are you
doing?" Mom and Dad asked. "I'm making a wooden bowl," he said, "for when
you two get old and must eat alone." Mom and Dad then looked sad and
realized how they were mistreating Grandpa. So they decided to keep quiet
when he spills his food and to let him eat with the family.

The heart of GR is *switching places*. You step into another's shoes. What
you do to Grandpa, you imagine being done to you. You ask, "Am I willing
that if I were in the same situation then I be treated that same way?"

GR seems simple. We want others to tell us the truth and not steal from us,
so this is how we treat them. But GR's loose wording can be confusing to apply
and can give strange results. We need to understand GR more clearly.

I put my attempt at a clearer wording on a t-shirt (see http://www.harryhiker.com/gr). The top has "the golden rule" and symbols for eight major world religions. The bottom has my GR formula. Most who react to my formula nod in approval. It's intended to help us apply GR to difficult cases. I call it "Gensler's GR" (or "Gold 1," since I accept other GR formulas). Note the same-situation clause:

Treat others only as you consent to being treated in the same situation.

Gold 1: Gensler's GR	Treat others only as you consent to being treated in the same situation.

Gold 1 commands consistency. It demands a fit between my *act* toward another and my *desire* about how I'd be treated in the same situation. GR doesn't replace other moral norms or give all the answers. GR doesn't say specifically what to do (and so doesn't command bad actions if we have flawed desires). Instead, it forbids an inconsistent combination:

- I do something to another.
- I'm unwilling that this be done to me in the same situation.

← Don't
← combine
these.

GR, far from being a vague platitude, is a precise consistency test. Suppose I force Grandpa to eat alone. I switch places in my mind: I imagine that *I'm* forced to eat alone in the same situation. Do I condemn this same act done to me? Then I condemn how I treat Grandpa. *I condemn how I treat another, if I condemn the same act when I imagine it done to me in the same situation.*

Switching places is a golden idea that's global and beautifully simple. It promotes justice, consideration, cooperation, and unity. But alas, there are ways to mess up the GR reasoning, and I call these "GR fallacies." So I'll now present five GR fallacies and illustrate each with a story.

1.2 Literal GR fallacy

(1) The literal GR fallacy assumes that everyone has the same likes, dislikes, and needs that we have.

There once lived a monkey and a fish. The monkey followed GR, always trying to treat others as he wanted to be treated. But he sometimes applied GR foolishly. Now one day a big flood came. As the threatening waters rose, the monkey climbed a tree to safety. He looked down and saw a fish struggling in the water. He thought, "I wanted to be lifted from the water." And so he reached down and grabbed the fish from the water, lifting him to safety on a high branch. Of course that didn't work. The fish died.

The monkey applied GR literally: *treat others as you want to be treated*. He wanted to be taken from the water, so he took the fish from the water. He didn't consider how monkeys and fish differ. Being taken from the water saves a monkey but kills a fish. So the monkey applied GR foolishly.

Here's another example. I visit my sister Carol at her house. In the morning, I wake energized and like to chat. But Carol absolutely hates early chatting, since she needs to wake up before she can deal with others. Should I chat with Carol? The literal GR says yes: "If I want Carol to chat with me, then I'm to chat with her." But this is inconsiderate, since her needs differ from mine.

Or suppose I'm a waiter, and I hate broccoli (which I do). Becky orders broccoli (which she likes). Should I serve her broccoli? Not by the literal GR, which says: "If you want Becky not to serve you broccoli, then don't serve her broccoli." Becky would be upset, and I'd likely be fired.

So it may be wrong to treat others *in their situation* as I want to be treated *in my situation* – since their situation may be different. Does this show that GR is flawed? Many think so. They contend that GR wrongly assumes that everyone's the same (in likes, dislikes, needs, and so on). Since we're not all the same, they conclude, GR is simplistic and flawed. I think, rather, that this literal understanding of GR is flawed. Fortunately for us, the island with a foolish monkey also had a wise monkey.

1.3   Kita, a wise GR monkey

Kita was a wise GR monkey. She learned that fish die when taken from water. When the flood came, she considered taking a fish from the water. But she imagined herself in his situation. She asked, "Am I now willing that *if I were in the same situation as the fish*, then I be taken from the water?" She answered, "Gosh no: this would kill me!" So she left the fish in the water.

We are to treat others only as we consent to being treated *in the same situation*. The same-situation clause is important. We imagine ourselves having all the other's qualities – including likes, dislikes, needs, and so on. So Kita asks: "Am I now willing that if I were in the same situation as the fish, then I be taken from the water?" And she says "No, that would kill me."

The same-situation clause also helps our other cases. With Carol, I ask, "Am I willing that if I were in the same situation as Carol (who absolutely hates early morning chatting), then someone chat with me in the morning?" I answer no; so I won't chat with her. With Becky, I ask, "Am I willing that if I were in the same situation as Becky (who loves broccoli and ordered it) then I be served broccoli?" I answer yes; so I can serve her broccoli.

By a marvelous coincidence, "Kita" is also an acronym (Know-Imagine-Test-Act) for some main elements for using GR wisely:

> K. Know: "How would my action affect others?"
> I. Imagine: "What would it be like to have this done to me in the same situation?"
> T. Test for consistency: "Am I now willing that if I were in the same situation then this be done to me?"
> A. Act toward others only as you're willing to be treated in the same situation.

When Kita considered taking the fish from the water, she tried to *know* how her action would affect the fish. She *imagined* being in the fish's exact place and having this same thing done to her. She *tested* her consistency by asking: "Am I now willing that if I were in the same situation as the fish, then I be taken from the water?" Finally, she *acted* on GR (leaving the fish in the water).

Memorize the wording of the GR question: *"Am I now willing that if I were in the same situation then this be done to me?"*

My favorite historical GR example is a civil rights speech by President John Kennedy (1963), during the first black enrollment at the University of Alabama. While Kennedy didn't know about GR monkeys, his speech followed Kita. He first got people to *know* how blacks were treated as second-class citizens (in areas like voting, education, and employment). He had whites *imagine* themselves being treated as second-class citizens on the basis of skin color. To *test* their consistency, he asked whether they'd be content to being treated that way. Finally, he urged *acting* on GR: "The heart of the question is whether all Americans are to be afforded equal rights and equal opportunities, whether we are going to treat our fellow Americans as we want to be treated."

The heart of morality is GR. And the heart of GR is switching places. What we do to Grandpa (or blacks, gays, or whomever we mistreat) we imagine being done to ourselves. And to avoid the literal GR fallacy, we can imagine ourselves in the other's exact place (having their likes, dislikes, needs, and so on).

1.4   Soft GR fallacy

> (2) The soft GR fallacy assumes that we should never act against what others want.

There once was a baby squirrel named Willy. Being curious but ignorant of electricity, he wanted to put his fingers into electrical outlets. Now Momma Squirrel thought about stopping him. But she asked, "If I were in Willy's exact place, then would I want to be stopped?" She answered no: if she were in his exact place, then she too would be a curious baby squirrel, ignorant of electricity, wanting to put fingers into outlets, and she wouldn't want to be stopped. Following GR foolishly, she didn't stop him. So Willy put his fingers into an outlet and was electrocuted.

Foolish Momma Squirrel asked the GR question wrongly, in a way that forced her to follow Willy's desires. She should have asked about her *present reaction to a hypothetical case*: "Am I now willing that if I were in Willy's situation then I be stopped from putting my fingers into electrical outlets?" She would have answered yes. She's willing that if she were a baby squirrel in his exact place then she be stopped. And she's grateful (now!) for when her parents, showing tough love, stopped her from doing this when she was young.

Sometimes we need to act against what others want. We may need to stop a baby who wants to put fingers into electrical outlets, refuse a salesperson who wants to sell us overpriced products, fail a student who doesn't work, forcibly defend ourselves against an attacker, or jail a dangerous criminal. And yes, we're now willing that if we were in their situation then we be treated that way. GR lets us act against what others want, as long as we're now willing that if we were in their situation then we be treated similarly.

1.5 Doormat GR fallacy

> (3) The doormat GR fallacy assumes that we should ignore our own interests.

There once was a woman named Frazzled Frannie. Frannie wanted to follow GR. But she thought GR makes us always do what others want (the previous fallacy). So she said yes whenever anyone asked a favor. People took advantage of her, asking "Please loan me $50,000" and "Could you watch my children while I vacation for three months?" Frannie always said yes; she thought saying no violates GR and makes you a bad person. Soon Frazzled Frannie had no life. She became a doormat for others, serving their every whim, ignoring her own interests. She shriveled up and became cranky.

For every Frannie there's a dozen Frannie-wannabes, who sometimes say no but feel guilty about this. Both groups misunderstand GR. GR doesn't force us to do what others want, or say yes to unreasonable requests. GR lets us say no, if we're willing that others say no to us in similar circumstances.

GR should build on self-love and extend this to others. It isn't supposed to destroy self-love and make you a doormat. GR works best if you love yourself and care about how you're treated. If you lack a healthy self-love, you need to build this up – by seeing yourself and your good points more positively, for example, and not fixating on your defects. If you're a doormat, repeat to yourself, "As others have needs and rights that ought to be respected, so too do I." Take comfort that most of us have the opposite problem: we treat others, not ourselves, as doormats.

1.6   Third-parties GR fallacy

> (4) The third-parties GR fallacy assumes that we should consider only ourselves and the other person.

There once was a student named Pre-law Lucy. Lucy realized that she needed good grades to get into law school. But she was lazy. Now one day Lucy had a bright idea. She'd plead her case to her professor: "Please give me an undeserved A in this course so I can get into law school! This will help me and not hurt you – so there's no GR objection to this."

Alas, Lucy ignored third parties. If she's accepted, then another student will be rejected. Imagine yourself being rejected because a less qualified student gets in dishonestly. And if Lucy becomes a lawyer, then we've likely added another lazy and dishonest lawyer. Imagine having to deal with such a lawyer.

The *generalized GR* has us satisfy GR toward each affected party: "Act only as you're willing for anyone to act in the same situation, regardless of where or when you imagine yourself or others." If your action affects X, Y, and Z, you must be willing that it be done regardless of your place in the situation. The affected parties may include future generations. This leads to the *carbon rule*: "Keep the earth livable for future generations, as we want past generations to have done for us."

1.7   Easy GR fallacy

> (5) The easy GR fallacy assumes that GR gives an infallible test of right and wrong that takes only seconds to apply.

There once was a woman named Electra. Electra wanted to follow GR, but she got her facts wrong. She thought severe electrical shocks were pleasant. So she shocked others and, yes, she was willing that she be shocked in their place. She followed GR but acted wrongly.

While Electra satisfied GR consistency, she can be faulted for not getting her facts straight. Applying GR wisely requires more than just sitting down in ignorance and asking how we want to be treated. To lead reliably to right action, GR must build on *knowledge* and *imagination*. But even if we're misinformed, GR doesn't command specific wrong acts – because it doesn't command specific acts. Instead, GR forbids inconsistent combinations.

Here's a second example. There once was a coal-mine owner named Rich. Rich was very rich, but paid his workers only a miserly $1 a day. He was asked if he'd be willing to be paid only $1 a day in their place. He said yes, and so was consistent. But he said yes only because he thought (wrongly) that his workers could live tolerably on this much. If he knew how little $1 buys, he wouldn't have answered that way. Rich needed to get his facts right. He might have tried going to the store to buy food for his family with only $1 in his pocket.

Now suppose that Rich decides to run his mine by the golden rule. What would he do? Following Kita, he'd do four things.

(K) Rich would gain *knowledge*. He'd ask, "How are my company policies affecting others – workers, neighbors, customers, and so on?" To know this, Rich would need to spend time talking with workers and others.

(I) Rich would apply *imagination*. He'd ask, "What would it be like to be in the place of those affected by these policies?" He'd imagine himself as a worker (laboring under bad conditions for a poor salary), or a neighbor (with black smoke coming into his house). Or he'd imagine his children being brought up under the same conditions as the workers' children.

(T) Rich would *test* his consistency by asking: "Am I now willing that if I were in the same situation (as my workers, neighbors, or customers) then I be treated that same way?" If the answer is no, then his actions clash with his desires about how he'd be treated in a similar situation – and he must change something. Changing company policies requires creativity. GR doesn't tell Rich what alternative policies to consider. Instead, it gives a way to *test* proposed policies. Any acceptable policy must be one he can approve regardless of where he imagines himself in the situation: as owner, worker, neighbor, or customer. The final solution will likely be a compromise that's minimally acceptable (but not ideal) from everyone's perspective.

(A) Rich would *act* on GR: "Treat others only as you consent to being treated in the same situation." Yes, it's a simple formula. But applying it wisely requires *knowledge* and *imagination* – which may be difficult. Our knowing and imagining will never be perfect. But the fact that we'll never do something perfectly doesn't excuse us from trying to doing it as well as we reasonably can.

1.8   Consistency requires GR

Why does consistency require that we follow GR? Suppose I make Grandpa eat alone but am unwilling that I be treated that way in the same situation. Why is that inconsistent?

GR rests on two consistency requirements: that we be *impartial* (in the sense of making similar evaluations about similar actions, regardless of the individuals involved) and *conscientious* (in the sense of living in harmony with our moral beliefs). If I'm impartial and conscientious, then I'll necessarily follow GR. The argument for this is difficult but gives a deeper insight into GR.

Suppose I'm consistent. Then I won't make Grandpa eat alone unless I believe that this act is all right – and thus believe that it would be all right to do to me in the same situation – and thus am willing that it be done to me in the same situation. Hence, if I'm consistent, then I won't do something to another unless I'm willing that it be done to me in the same situation.

So my GR formula can be based on an abstract consistency argument. Similar reasoning justifies many GR variations. So we might consider someone else we care about (maybe our daughter) on the receiving end of the action. Or we might give consistency conditions, not for *doing* something, but for *wanting* something or for *holding a moral belief*. GR can be, and historically has been, expressed in many ways. GR is a family of related ideas.

It's also important that GR can be, and historically has been, put into a wide range of frameworks (religious, philosophical, or scientific), which give GR a further context and justification. GR is a point of unity in a diverse world.

1.9 Further chapters

This book has four parts:

1. "Golden Rule Reasoning" has two chapters, 1 and 2; read either or both. Chapter 2 is more academic and has more about GR objections.
2. "Religion and History" has three chapters: GR in world religions (Chapter 3), a dialogue on GR and religion (4), and a GR chronology that reviews 3000 years of reflection on GR (5).
3. "Practice" has four chapters: moral education (6), egoism and evolution (7), racism and other discrimination (8), and applied ethics (about business, medicine, animals, etc.) (9).
4. "Theory" has five chapters: positive and negative GRs (10), more GR questions (11), GR in many philosophies (12), GR approaches of Hare and Carson (13), and more GR objections (14).

Again, read any further chapters, in any order; but Chapters 13 and 14 are technical and assume Chapter 2.[1]

---

[1] Sections 1.1–1.7 are based on talks I gave in 2011 at Scarboro Missions in Toronto (11 May) and at the NAIN (North American Interfaith Network) conference in Arizona (25 July keynote).

CHAPTER 2
Harder Introduction

> There are two introductory chapters: this one is longer and more technical, while Chapter 1 is simpler. Read either or both. Then read any combination of further chapters, in any order; but Chapters 13 and 14 are technical and assume Chapter 2.

The golden rule (GR) says "Treat others as you want to be treated." Other phrasings include "Do unto others as you'd have them do unto you," "Do as you'd be done by," and "Don't do to others what you want not done to yourself." GR calls for a harmony between my *act* toward another and my *desire* about how I'd be treated in the same situation.

This book is a fairly comprehensive treatment of the golden rule. We'll defend GR philosophically, connect it with world religions and history, and apply it to practical areas like moral education and business.

This chapter is about *GR reasoning*. We'll first note that GR is wildly influential across the globe (and considered *gold*) but largely ignored in academic circles (and considered *garbage*). Then we'll look at problem areas.

2.1 Gold or garbage?

The golden rule for centuries has been important all over the world, in different cultures and religions, and in professions and families.

All major religions accept GR. Confucius, Hillel, Jesus, and many others used it to sum up how to live. The Parliament of the World's Religions in 1993 overwhelmingly supported GR as the basis for global ethics and the "irrevocable, unconditional norm for all areas of life" (Küng and Kuschel 1993: 23f).

Conscientious professionals often appeal to GR. A business person might say, "I try to treat customers as I desire that I'd be treated." A nurse might say, "I care for patients as I hope that I'd be cared for if I were sick." A teacher might say, "I teach students as I wish that I'd have been taught."

GR is popular among politicians. President Barack Obama used it in over twenty speeches; here are two examples (see also Obama 2006):

> The only time I ever saw my mother really angry is when she saw cruelty, when she saw somebody being bullied or somebody being treated different-ly because of who they were. And, if she saw me doing that, she would be furious. And she would say to me: "Imagine standing in that person's shoes. How would that make you feel?"

> If there is one law that we can be most certain of, it is the law that binds people of all faiths and no faith together. It's no coincidence that it exists in Christianity and Judaism; in Islam and Hinduism; in Buddhism and human-ism. It is, of course, the golden rule – the call to treat one another as we wish to be treated.[1]

His Republican predecessor, George W. Bush, in at least eighteen speeches used some variation of this GR phrasing: "Love your neighbor just like you'd like to be loved yourself."[2] GR is non-partisan.

A British TV station created a new "ten commandments" (Spier 2005), sur-veying 44,000 people about the most important norms for living. GR was by far the most popular norm: "Treat others as you want to be treated."

Searching the Web for "golden rule" reveals many Web pages, including my http://www.harryhiker.com/gr page. GR is growing in popularity.

GR is less popular in academic circles. Courses in moral philosophy or moral theology typically ignore GR or mention it only briefly. Marcus Singer began an article about GR by saying (1963: 293):

> The golden rule has received remarkably little philosophical discussion.... Considering its obvious importance and its almost universal acceptance, this ... is unfortunate, and also somewhat surprising.

The only philosophy dissertations on GR up to now were Alton 1966 and Gensler 1977.[3] Jeff Wattles 1996: 6, in a groundbreaking first scholarly book in English on GR since the 17th century, noted that:

> Many scholars today regard the rule as an acceptable principle for popular use but as embarrassing if taken with philosophic seriousness. Most professional ethicists rely instead on other principles, since the rule seems vulnerable to counterexamples, such as the current favorite, "What if a sadomasochist goes forth to treat others as he wants to be treated?"

---

[1] I searched http://www.whitehouse.gov for "golden rule" and for "do unto others" in August 2012. The quotes are from http://archives.cnn.com/transcripts/0808/28/ec.04.html (beginning) and http://www.presidentialrhetoric.com/speeches/05.17.09.html.
[2] Search http://georgewbush-whitehouse.archives.gov for "like to be loved." A general Web search for Bush's GR gives references mainly to him.
[3] Most Gensler items in the Bibliography discuss GR, including a technical book on formal ethics (1996, ch. 5), a logic textbook (2010, ch. 11), and an ethics textbook (2011a, ch. 8).

When I wrote this present book, my fellow academics often asked about it. Imagine this conversation. Professor asks, "What is your book about?" I say, "The golden rule." Professor then snickers inside, thinking, "You mean that silly kindergarten saying that doesn't apply to the complex problems of the real world?" Now Professor is too polite to say this out loud. His mother long ago used GR to instruct him against rudeness, and this is still with him. But his behavior suggests what's in the back of his mind: "The golden rule – what a silly principle for a grownup philosopher to write a book on!"

Not all academics think so little of the golden rule. But most do. Most think that GR is unclear and full of problems. If we take the vague GR and try to formulate it clearly, it quickly leads to absurdities. So GR is dismissed as a folksy proverb that self-destructs when analyzed carefully.

So is GR *gold* (as the world thinks) or *garbage* (as many academics think)?

2.1a Literal GR

What does "Treat others as you want to be treated" mean? Let's try taking it as the *literal golden rule* (or *Pyrite 1*, where pyrite is fool's gold):

Pyrite 1: the literal GR

> If you want X
> to do A to you,
> then do A to X.

Objection 1: different circumstances

> If you're in *different circumstances* from the other person (for example, you have different likes and dislikes), GR can command bad actions.

To derive an instance, substitute a person for X and an act for *do-A*, and re-phrase to keep it grammatical. So Pyrite 1 logically entails "If you want Jones to be polite to you, then be polite to Jones" – and "If you want Jones not to hit you, then do not hit Jones." Pyrite 1 works well if you and X are in *similar circumstances* and you have *good desires* about how you're to be treated. If either condition fails, Pyrite 1 can tell you to do crazy or evil things.

Consider this *different circumstances* objection. Suppose you have a bad appendix and want Dr. Davis to remove it. Then Pyrite 1 absurdly tells you: "*If you want Davis to remove your appendix, then remove her appendix.*" Pyrite 1 assumes that how you want to be treated in *your situation* is how you should treat others in *their situation* – even if their situation is very different.

Here's another example. I'm a waiter, and I hate broccoli (which I do). Becky orders broccoli (which she likes). Should I serve her broccoli? Not by the literal GR, which says: "If you want Becky not to serve you broccoli, then don't serve her broccoli." Becky would be upset, and I'd likely be fired. Pyrite 1 seems to assume that the other person's tastes are the same as mine.

Or suppose I visit my sister Carol at her house. In the morning, I wake energized and like to chat. But Carol absolutely hates early chatting, since she needs to wake up before she can deal with others. Should I chat with Carol? The literal GR says yes: "If I want Carol to chat with me, then I'm to chat with her." But this is inconsiderate, since her needs differ from mine.

Or you're a little boy who loves fighting, and you'd love to have your little sister fight with you. She's peaceful and hates fighting. Should you fight with her? Pyrite 1 says yes: "If I want my little sister to fight with me, then I'm to fight with her." Pyrite 1 here is violent and inconsiderate.

Here's another objection to GR (don't worry about why it's 3):

Objection 3: your flawed desires	If *you have flawed desires* about how you're to be treated, GR can command bad actions.

Suppose you eat bad broccoli and catch the dreaded broccoli-itis disease, which makes you want everyone to hurt you. Pyrite 1 tells you: "*If you want your friend to hurt you, then hurt her.*" But you do want your friend (and everyone else) to hurt you; thus by Pyrite 1 you're to hurt her (and everyone else). So Pyrite 1 can tell a person with flawed desires to do bad things.[1]

Pyrite 1 assumes that our desires about how we're to be treated are fine and guide us well on how to treat others. But our desires may be flawed. Maybe we have mental problems and want everyone to hurt us. Or maybe we have immoral desires and want Rob to help us to rob banks; then Pyrite 1 tells us to help him to rob banks. Or maybe we're misinformed and want others to give us severe electrical shocks (which we think are pleasurable); then Pyrite 1 tells us to give others such shocks. Since our desires about how we're to be treated may be flawed, they aren't a reliable guide on how to treat others.

Since Pyrite 1 can tell us to do crazy things, it's only fool's gold. It also fails the Wattles (1996: 6) GR test for GR interpretations: "Would you want to be treated according to a rule construed in this way?"[2]

Some who use GR in their lives are impatient with GR objections and say they know how to avoid the problems. They may be right. But still it's important to study the objections, because (1) many reject GR on this basis; (2) GR should lead us to take seriously the views and objections of others; (3) a clear GR formula that avoids the objections may help others to use GR; and (4) without understanding the objections, we'll never really understand GR.

---

[1] The first GR objection was perhaps from Augustine (400a & 400b), who about 400 AD pointed out that we may want bad things done to us (e.g., we may want others to get us drunk) – and so by GR we ought to do these bad things to others. He suggested taking GR in effect to mean "Whatever *good things* you want done to yourself, do to others." This makes GR harder to apply and doesn't handle the different-circumstances problem. So I prefer other solutions.

[2] Pyrite 1 says to treat X *as you want X to treat you.* A Pyrite 1a variation says to treat X *as you want to be treated* (not necessarily by X, perhaps by someone else). Both have similar problems.

2.1b   Same-situation clause

GR urgently needs a same-situation clause.

Here's a fable about the literal GR. There once was a flood involving a monkey and a fish. The monkey climbed a tree to escape the rising flood waters. He looked down and saw a poor fish struggling against the current. Because he cared about the fish, he reached down and grabbed him from the water, lifting him to safety on a high branch. But the fish died after being taken from the water. The foolish monkey applied GR too literally; he wanted to be taken from the water himself, so he took the fish from the water.

Now there was also a wise GR monkey, named Kita, who knew that fish can't survive out of water. Kita saw a fish, imagined herself in its place, and asked "Am I now willing that if I were in the same situation as the fish, then I be taken from the water?" She answered, "Gosh no: this would kill me!" So Kita left the fish alone.

In applying GR, we need to *know* the other's situation, which may differ from ours: the other may have different likes, dislikes, and needs. We need to *imagine* ourselves in the other's situation. And we need to ask, "How do I desire that I be treated *if I were in that situation*?"

The same-situation clause helps with the other cases:

- I want Dr. Davis to remove my appendix. Should I thus remove hers? No, since I desire that if I were in her situation (with a healthy appendix) then my appendix not be removed by a patient ignorant of medicine.
- I'm a broccoli-hating waiter, and Becky who likes broccoli orders it. Does GR prevent me from serving her broccoli? No, since I'm willing that if I were in her situation (loving the stuff) then I be served it.
- I want people to chat with me in the morning, but my sister Carol hates this. Should I chat with her? No, since I desire that if I were in her situation (hating early chatting) then people not chat with me.
- I'm a violent little boy who loves to have others fight with me. Should I fight with my peaceful little sister who hates fighting? No, since I desire that if I were in her situation (hating violence) then people not fight with me.

Adding a same-situation clause improves GR greatly.[1]

---

[1] Francis of Assisi (c. 1220: 134) was the first I know to use a same-situation clause: "Blessed is the person who supports his neighbor in his weakness as he would want to be supported were he in a similar situation." Robert Golobish, a Franciscan, sent me this quote. Benjamin Camfield, who published a GR book in 1671, wrote (p. 61): "We must suppose other men in our condition, rank, and place, and ourselves in theirs"; Boraston 1684, Goodman 1688, and Clarke 1706 used similar clauses. Wattles 1996: 35 says: "When we say, 'Do not treat others as you do not want others to treat you,' there is the unspoken assumption 'in (essentially) the same situation.'" Wattles and I differ in strategy. He keeps the GR wording as it is but applies GR in subtle ways to avoid objections; I rephrase GR. We have the same goal, to understand GR.

How should we go about reformulating GR? Should we just tinker with the wording until we get it right? It's better to apply a deeper understanding. GR, I contend, is a child of two parents: IMPARTIALITY and CONSCIENTIOUSNESS. GR inherits its same-situation clause from IMPARTIALITY.

Impartiality, as I use the term, requires that we *make similar evaluations about similar acts, regardless of the individuals involved*. If we're impartial, then we'll evaluate an act based on what it's like – and not based on who plays what role in the situation; so we'll apply the same standards to ourselves that we apply to others. I violate impartiality if I make conflicting evaluations about acts that I regard as *exactly similar* or *relevantly similar*.

Here's a Good Samaritan example (Luke 10:30–5). Suppose that, while jogging, I see a man who's been beaten, robbed, and left to die. Should I help him, perhaps by making a phone call? I think of excuses why I shouldn't. I'm busy and don't want to get involved. I say, "It would be all right for me not to help him." But then I consider an exactly similar reversed situation, where our properties are switched.[1] I imagine myself in *his* exact place; so I'm the one who's been beaten, robbed, and left to die. And I imagine him in *my* exact place; so he's jogging and sees me in my sad state. I ask myself, "Would it be all right for this man not to help me in this reversed situation? Surely not!" But then I'm inconsistent. What's all right for me to do to another must be all right for the other to do to me in an imagined exactly similar reversed situation.

In the actual world, no two acts are exactly similar. But I can always *imagine* an exactly similar act. If I'm about to do something to another, to test my impartiality I can *imagine* what it would be like for this to be done to me in an exactly similar situation. Impartiality forbids the combination on the left:

Impartiality forbids combining these:	GR forbids combining these:
• I believe: "It's right for me to do A to another." • I believe: "It's wrong for A to be done to me in the same situation."	• I do A to another. • I'm unwilling that A be done to me in the same situation.

The left box is about *impartiality*: making similar *evaluations* about similar acts. The GR analogue, by contrast, forbids combining an *act* toward another with a *desire* about how I'd be treated in the same situation. Both are good principles. And both take "(exact) same situation" the same way; we are to imagine the two acts having all the same properties in common.

[1] Instead of switching *every* property in my mind, I could switch just those *relevant* to evaluating the act. If I'm unsure whether a property is relevant, I could switch it anyway – just to be safe. This has me imagine a *relevantly similar* action.

In this section, it would be more technically precise to speak of *switching universal properties* instead of just *switching properties* – so being injured and having blue eyes would be switched, but not being me or being Harry Gensler; §2.7 has more details.

My example uses an *imagined* second case. But we can use an *actual* second case, if there's one handy. Suppose I cut X off in traffic and I think this is OK. Later, Y cuts me off and I think this is wrong. But I ask, "Why would cutting-someone-off be right for me to do but wrong for another to do?" Since I find no reason, I conclude that the two acts are *relevantly similar*. But then I violate impartiality, which forbids the combination on the left:

Impartiality forbids combining these:	GR forbids combining these:
• I believe: "It's right for me to cut X off." • I believe: "It's wrong for Y to cut me off." • I believe: "These two acts are relevantly similar."	• I cut X off. • I'm unwilling that Y cut me off. • I believe: "These two acts are relevantly similar."

I violate impartiality, since my three beliefs don't fit together. I must reject at least one belief. I could hold that both actions are wrong, or that both are right, or that one act was right, but not the other, because of such and such differences. So, while impartiality doesn't say specifically what to believe, it guides me on how to work out my beliefs in a consistent way.

The GR analogue involves an *act* toward another and a *desire* about how I'd be treated in a similar situation. We can express this GR as "Don't act to do A to another while you're unwilling that A be done to you in a situation that you regard as relevantly similar." Both boxes take "relevantly similar" the same way: two acts are *relevantly similar* if the reasons why one fits in a given moral category (good, bad, right, wrong, or whatever) also apply to the other.

In deciding whether two actions are *relevantly similar*, we appeal to antecedent moral beliefs about which factors give reasons for a given moral appraisal. Impartiality and GR push us to apply these reasons in the same way to our actions and to another's actions. But since the appeal to relevantly similar cases can get slippery, it's often cleaner to appeal to *imagined exactly similar cases* – and so I'll emphasize these more.

Thus we can apply impartiality and GR to imagined cases or to actual cases. *Poetic justice* occurs when you later have the same thing actually done to you. So the Good Samaritan may later be helped in a similar way.

Impartiality requires a same-situation clause. It doesn't violate impartiality to say "It's right for me to drive but wrong for my sister to drive" – since there may be important differences between the cases (maybe I'm sober but she isn't). Impartiality needs a clause about the acts being relevantly or exactly similar. GR needs this too, which is why Pyrite 1 is pyrite.[1]

---

[1] We can mix the elements in each pair of boxes. So this is inconsistent: "I do A to another but I believe it's wrong for A to be done to me in the same situation." And so is this: "I believe it's right for me to do A to another but I'm unwilling that A be done to me in the same situation."

2.1c The GR question

We need to be careful about something else. GR is about my *present desire about a hypothetical case*. It isn't about what I'd desire if I were in the hypothetical case. Ask the first question, not the second:

<u>Am</u> I <u>now</u> <u>willing</u> <u>that</u> <u>if</u> I were in the same situation then this be done to me?	~~If I were in the same situation, would I then be willing that this be done to me?~~

The difference is subtle. Let me try to clarify it.

Suppose I have a two-year-old son Willy, who puts his fingers into electrical outlets. I try to discourage him from this, but nothing works. I see that I need to stop him when he does it. But can I stop him without violating GR? In deciding this, I should ask the first question, not the second:

<u>Am</u> I <u>now</u> <u>willing</u> <u>that</u> <u>if</u> I were in Willy's place in the same situation then I be stopped?	~~If I were in Willy's place in the reversed situation, would I then be willing to be stopped?~~
This has "willing that if." It's about my present adult desire about a hypothetical case.	This has "if" before "willing." It's about the desire I'd have as a small child.

With the first question, I imagine this case: *I'm a two-year-old child who knows nothing about electricity; I want to put my fingers into electrical outlets and I want not to be stopped from doing this.* As an adult, I say "I *now* desire that if I were in this situation then I be stopped from putting fingers into an outlet." Thus I can stopped Willy without breaking GR, since I'm willing that I would have been treated the same way in the same situation. I might even tell my parents: "Thanks for stopping me in this situation!"

On the other hand, if I were in Willy's place, and thus judged things from a two-year-old mentality, then I'd desire not to be stopped. That's what the stopped-out question is about. If we express GR using this, then I'd break GR if I stopped Willy. But this is absurd and leads to fried children. The GR question needs to deal with my *present desire about a hypothetical case*. I satisfy GR because I'm now willing that I would have been stopped in this situation.

Many people ask the GR same-situation question wrongly. The distinction is crucial when we deal with one who is less rational (e.g., drunk, senile, or in a coma). Suppose a friend at your party wants to drive home despite being drunk and confused. You tell her no; and you're willing that if the situation were reversed (and you were drunk and confused) then you be told the same thing. You might even say: "If I ever insist on driving home drunk, please stop me!" In applying GR here, ask the first question, not the second:

| Am I now willing that if I were drunk in this situation then I be told that I can't drive home? | ~~If I were drunk in this situation, would I then be willing to be told that I can't drive home?~~ |

With the second question, drunk and confused desires give the norm of how to treat your friend. To use GR correctly, say "*I'm willing that if.*" Ask this: "*Am I now willing that if I were in the same situation then this be done to me?*"

Here's another example. You're a judge, about to sentence a dangerous criminal to jail. The criminal protests and appeals (incorrectly) to GR: "If you were in my place, you'd want not to be sent to jail; so by GR you can't send me to jail." You should respond: "I can send you to jail, because I'm now willing that if I were in your place (as a dangerous criminal) then I be sent to jail." You could add, "If I do such things, then please send me to jail too!"[1]

Pyrite 2 goes with the bad crossed-out question and suffers from Objection 2:

Pyrite 2: a faulty same-situation GR   Objection 2: X's flawed desires

| Given that if you were in X's exact place (in the reversed situation) then you'd want A done to you, then do A to X. | If *X has flawed desires* (about how he wants to be treated), GR can command bad actions. |

Suppose X has flawed desires. For example, X is little Willy (who wants to be allowed to put his fingers into electrical outlets), or a drunk (who wants to be allowed to drive home), or a dangerous criminal (who wants to be set free so he can harm others). If you were in X's exact place, then you'd have the same flawed desires. Then by Pyrite 2, you should act according to these desires (and let Willy put his fingers into electrical outlets, or let the drunk drive home, or let the criminal go free). But these actions are wrong. Sometimes we need to act against what others want. GR lets us do this, as long as we're now willing that if we were in the same situation then we be treated similarly. We might say: "If I ever insist on driving home drunk, please stop me!"[2]

---

[1] Immanuel Kant (1785: 97) used this criminal objection against GR; others followed, including defenders of slavery who wanted to discredit GR (§§8.5 & 14.3c). R.M. Hare was perhaps the first to apply the distinction between our two questions to GR (1963: 108). He noted that "Do unto others as you *would* have them do unto you" obscures the issue (1972b: 44). See also Hare 1981: 95f, Hoche 1982: 76–9, and Carson 2010: 139f.

[2] Shifting to Pyrite 2a won't help: "Given that if you were in X's exact place *except that you're rational* then you'd want X to do A to you, then do A to X." People often need to be treated in certain ways because they're irrational. For example, I may need to confront X about being irrational. If I were in X's place but rational then I wouldn't want to be confronted about being irrational; so, by Pyrite 2a, I shouldn't confront X. So the solution in the text is better.

GR inherits its *present desire about a hypothetical case* question from its CONSCIENTIOUSNESS parent.

Conscientiousness, as I use the term, requires that we *keep our life (including actions, intentions, etc.) in harmony with our moral beliefs.* Suppose I believe that one *ought* never to kill a human being for any reason. If I'm *conscientious*, then I'll never intentionally kill a human being, I'll resolve not to kill for any reason (even to protect myself or my family), and I won't want others to kill for any reason. Similar requirements cover beliefs about what is "all right" ("permissible"). If I'm conscientious, then I won't do something without believing that it would be *all right* for me to do it. And I won't believe that something is *all right* without consenting to the idea of it being done.

The conscientiousness norm says "Avoid inconsistencies between your moral beliefs and how you live." It forbids inconsistent combinations like these:

• I *believe* I ought to do A. • I don't *act* to do A.	• I *believe* act A is wrong. • I *act* to do A.	• I *believe* everyone ought to do A. • I don't *act* to do A.

Conscientiousness gives a consistency tool to criticize moral principles. Let's call "All short people ought to be beat up, just because they're short" *shortism.* Now shortism commits us to these two conditionals:

> (1) If I were short, then I ought to be beat up.
> (2) If I were short, then beat me up.

If I accept shortism, then, to be consistent, I must accept these. Accepting (1) is *believing* that if I were short then I ought to be beat up. Accepting (2) is *desiring* that if I were short then I be beat up; this is a *present desire about a hypothetical case*, like GR uses.

2.1d GR requires consistency

Pyrite 3 adds a *present desire about a hypothetical case*:

Pyrite 3: an almost correct GR	Objection 3: your flawed desires
If you want it to be that if you were in X's exact place (in the reversed situation) then A would be done to you, then do A to X.	If *you have flawed desires* about how you're to be treated, GR can command bad actions.

Pyrite 3 still suffers from Objection 3. Suppose you're a masochist and want everyone to hurt you. You desire that, if you were in Xavier's place in the reversed situation, then you be hurt. Then Pyrite 3 tells you to hurt Xavier.

Think of an evil action that you could do to another. Imagine that you're so deranged that you desire that, if you were in the other's place, then this action be done to you. Then Pyrite 3 would tell you to do this evil action.[1]

My solution is to rephrase GR so it forbids an inconsistent combination *but doesn't say specifically what to do*:

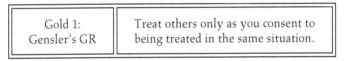

- I do something to another.
- I'm unwilling that this be done to me in the same situation.

← Don't
← combine
these.

This consistency GR won't tell you to hurt Xavier (a specific action), even if you have flawed desires. A more complete solution would also say how to criticize flawed desires (§2.2). But for now it's enough to formulate GR so it won't tell you to do bad things, even if you have bad desires.

This prose version is my central GR formula, with three key features:

Gold 1: Gensler's GR	Treat others only as you consent to being treated in the same situation.

- a same-situation clause,
- a present desire about a hypothetical case, and
- a *consistency form* that forbids an action–desire combination.

We need these features to avoid absurd implications and insure that GR follows from impartiality and conscientiousness.

Two examples show how Gold 1 works with flawed desires. (1) There once was a woman named Electra who got her facts wrong. Electra thought severe electrical shocks were pleasant. So she shocked others and, yes, she was willing that she be shocked in their place. She followed GR but acted wrongly. While Electra satisfied GR consistency, she can be faulted for getting her facts wrong. Applying GR wisely requires more than just sitting down in ignorance and asking how we want to be treated. To lead reliably to right action, GR needs to build on *knowledge* and *imagination*. But even if we're misinformed, GR doesn't command specific wrong acts – because it doesn't command specific acts. Instead, GR forbids inconsistent combinations.

(2) There once was a coal-mine owner named Rich. Rich was very rich but paid his workers only a miserly $1 a day. He was asked if he'd be willing to be paid only $1 a day in their place. He said yes, and so was consistent. But he said yes only because he thought (wrongly) that his workers could live tolerably on

[1] Shifting to Pyrite 3a won't help: "If *you believe that if you were in X's place then A ought to be done to you,* then do A to X." Pyrite 3a commands you to do evil action E to X if your moral beliefs are deranged (you believe that if you were in X's place then E *ought* to be done to you).

this much. If he knew how little $1 buys, he wouldn't answer that way. Rich needed to get his facts straight; he might have tried going to the store to buy food for his family with only $1 in his pocket. Here Rich satisfied GR consistency but acted wrongly, because he was misinformed. GR consistency needs to combine with other elements, like knowledge and imagination.

Let's consider three consistency examples, to see better how consistency principles work. Then we'll get back to GR.

I've had a beard on and off for much of my life. I sometimes meet people who say things like "All bearded people are crazy." I like to challenge their consistency. So I ask, "Did Jesus Christ and Abraham Lincoln have beards?" They say yes. I ask, "Were they crazy?" They say no. Then I say, "You contradicted yourself." You can't reasonably combine these three beliefs:

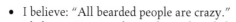

- I believe: "All bearded people are crazy."
- I believe: "Jesus and Lincoln are bearded people."
- I believe: "Jesus and Lincoln aren't crazy."

← Don't
← combine
these.

If you hold all three, you must give up one. A consistency challenge doesn't say exactly what to believe. It just says, "The things you accept don't fit together – so you must change something."

Or suppose that Donna wants to become a doctor. She realizes that, to do this, she needs to study hard and get good grades. But she doesn't act accordingly. Donna violates this ends–means consistency imperative:

- I have the goal of becoming a doctor.
- I believe that achieving this goal requires that I study hard.
- I don't study hard.

← Don't
← combine
these.

Since her goals, beliefs, and actions don't fit together, she must change something. Maybe her doctor-goal is unrealistic and should be rejected; or maybe she just needs to carry out the means. Consistency doesn't say what to change.

Here's a simple imperative about consistent willing:

- I resolve to eat nothing.
- I eat this granola bar.

← Don't
← combine
these.

This forbids a combination but doesn't say exactly what to do. If my medical exam requires that I not eat, then I should do the resolving and avoid the eating. If my resolving is an unhealthy way to diet, then maybe I should do the eating and avoid the resolving.

Gold 1, on the left, likewise forbids a combination but doesn't say exactly what to do (and so doesn't tell us to do bad actions if we have flawed desires):

<table>
<tr>
<td>Gold 1 forbids an
inconsistent combination:</td>
<td>Deductive model of GR reasoning
(the desire wording can vary):</td>
</tr>
<tr>
<td>

- I do something to another.
- I'm unwilling that this be done to me in the same situation.

</td>
<td>

If you have this desire about A being done to you, then do A to X.
You have this desire about A being done to you.
∴ Do A to X.

</td>
</tr>
</table>

Gold 1 has a *consistency model of GR reasoning*. If we violate GR consistency, it needn't be that our action is wrong. It could be that our action is right and *we should be willing* that this thing be done to us in the same situation.

Pyrite 1–3 use a *deductive model*, on the right. This can prescribe bad actions if we have flawed desires. Flawed desires might, for example, be immoral (like wanting others to cooperate with you in doing evil), come from an unhealthy psychological condition (like wanting everyone to hurt you), or come from wrong information (like thinking that severe electrical shocks are pleasurable). And this model can lead to contradictions in multi-party cases, where you desire conflicting things depending on which place you consider yourself in (§14.3e). We fix these problems if we see GR as a consistency norm that forbids a combination but doesn't prescribe or forbid specific actions.[1]

So how is Gold 1 derivable from IMPARTIALITY and CONSCIENTIOUSNESS? Suppose you want to steal Detra's bicycle. And suppose you're impartial (make similar evaluations about similar acts) and conscientious (have your moral beliefs and how you live in harmony). Then you won't steal her bicycle unless you're also willing that your bicycle be stolen in the same situation. Here's a chart showing the steps involved:

---

[1] We could rescue the deductive model by rewording GR to say: "If you have this desire about A being done to you *and your desire isn't flawed*, then do A to X." Then we'd add this premise: "*Your desire about A being done to you isn't flawed*" – so it isn't immoral, based on an unhealthy psychological condition, or based on false information. While this works, the added premise makes GR harder to apply, since we must check whether our desire is morally proper (which requires antecedent moral norms and makes GR a less important addition to these norms), based on an unhealthy psychological condition (and that idea needs clarification), or based on false information (and even a morally and psychologically mature person can have false information). So GR gets messy. The consistency model is cleaner; it doesn't try to build everything into GR but rather sees GR as a consistency component that needs to be combined with other components (like knowledge and imagination).

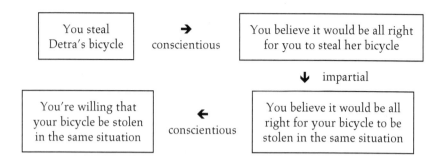

Here's a less graphical version. If we're impartial and conscientious, then:

> We won't *do* A to X unless we believe that our doing A to X would be *all right*.
> We won't believe that our doing A *to X* would be all right unless we believe that it would be all right for A to be done *to us* in the same situation.
> We won't believe that it would be *all right* for A to be done to us in the same situation unless we're *willing* that A be done to us in the same situation.
> ∴ We won't do A to X unless we're willing that A be done to us in the same situation.

So if we're impartial and conscientious, then we'll follow GR: we won't do A to X unless we're willing that A be done to us in the same situation. If we assume that we *ought* to be impartial and conscientious, then it follows that we *ought* to follow GR. So GR is a *theorem*, provable from the impartiality and conscientiousness requirements.

As a consistency norm, GR isn't a direct criterion of right and wrong, and isn't a rival to moral norms like "We ought not to steal." GR works at a different level. GR is more like "Don't contradict yourself" or "Don't accept a premise without accepting what logically follows from it." GR's role isn't to *replace* other ethical theories but to *supplement* them – by giving a consistency tool that's often useful. Most ethical theories recognize the role of consistency and so should be able to accept GR on this basis.

2.1e Gold, not garbage

So is GR *gold* or *garbage*? As opposed to what many academics think, we can explain GR in a clear way that avoids the absurdities:

Gold 1: Gensler's GR	Treat others only as you consent to being treated in the same situation.

Understood correctly, GR is pure gold; we'll appreciate this more as we move through this book. GR is gold (valuable) because it captures so much of the spirit behind morality. It counters self-centeredness and helps us to see the point of moral rules. It's psychologically sound and personally motivating, engages our reasoning instead of imposing answers from the outside. It promotes cooperation and mutual understanding. It criticizes culturally taught racist or sexist moral intuitions. It concretely applies ideals like fairness and concern. And the core idea is a global wisdom, common to most religions and cultures. So GR makes a good one-sentence summary of morality.

GR also can be gold *if we live and apply it wisely*, even if we word it poorly. Many people *live* GR more subtlely than how they *say* it.

2.2 Applying GR wisely: Kita

Kita (Know-Imagine-Test-Act) gives four main elements for using GR wisely:[1]

K. Know: "How would my action affect others?"
I. Imagine: "What would it be like to have this done to me in the same situation?"
T. Test for consistency: "Am I now willing that if I were in the same situation then this be done to me?"
A. Act toward others only as you're willing to be treated in the same situation.

Suppose that Rich, who pays his workers a miserly $1 a day (§2.1d), decides to run his coal mine by the golden rule. How could he apply GR wisely?

(K) Rich would gain *knowledge*. He'd ask, "How are my company policies affecting others – workers, neighbors, customers, and so on? What problems do my policies create for people?" To know such things, Rich would need to spend time talking with workers and others.

As we form our moral beliefs, we need to be informed. As far as reasonably possible, we need to know circumstances, alternatives, and consequences. To the extent that we're misinformed or ignorant, our thinking is flawed. We also need to know alternative moral views and arguments for or against them; our thinking is less rational if we're unaware of opposing views. We also need self-knowledge. We can to some degree neutralize our biases by understanding how they originated. For example, some are hostile toward a group because they were brought up this way; their attitudes might change if they understood their hostility's source and broadened their experience.

---

[1] These elements can be based on GR. Since we want others to use *knowledge* and *imagination* when deciding how to act toward us, we need to use these too. The question *tests* whether we're following GR. And the *act* element is just GR itself.

Dialogue, while not mentioned by Kita, is needed to get the facts, imagine another's situation, and uncover inconsistencies (see Habermas 1983). While Kita covers some key elements of responsible decision making, there are other elements too (Gensler 1996: 149–57).

We can never know *all* the facts. And we often must act quickly and can't take time to research a problem. But we can act out of greater or lesser knowledge. Other things equal, a more informed judgment is a more rational one.

(I) Rich would apply *imagination*. He'd ask, "What would it be like to be in the place of those affected by my company's policies?" He'd imagine himself as a worker (laboring under bad conditions for a poor salary), or a neighbor (with black smoke coming into his house). Or he'd imagine his children being brought up under the same conditions as his workers' children.

As we form moral beliefs, we need to exercise imagination. As far as reasonably possible, we need to be vividly and accurately aware of what it would be like to be in the place of those affected by our actions. This differs from just knowing facts. So besides knowing facts about poor people, we also need to appreciate and envision what these facts mean to their lives. Movies, literature, and personal experience can help us visualize another's life.

Imagining another's place is a common human experience (Katz 1963). A child pretends to be a mother or a soldier. A chess player asks, "If I were in my opponent's place, how would I respond to this move?" A writer dialogues with an imagined reader who misunderstands and raises objections. A teacher asks, "How would I respond to this assignment if I were a student?" Imagining another's place is especially important for applying GR.

We can do imagination better or worse. The mine owner will never perfectly understand what it's like to be in the place of his workers and their families. But, with effort, he can grow in this area and become better at it. The fact that we'll never do something (like moral decision making) perfectly doesn't excuse us from trying to do it as well as we reasonably can.

Believers can see this Kita procedure as an attempt to imitate God's wisdom. Only God can know perfectly how an action affects another and understand perfectly what it would be like to be in another's place. We struggle in these areas, knowing that our wisdom will always be incomplete. Kita reflects our attempt to know what a perfectly knowing and loving God would want.

(T) Rich would *test* his consistency using the GR question: "Am I now willing that if I were in the same situation (as that of my workers, neighbors, or customers) then these company actions be done to me?" If the answer is no, then his *actions* toward others clash with his *desire* about how he'd be treated in a similar situation – and so he must change something.

If Rich changes company policies, he'll need *creativity* to find alternatives. He might listen to ideas from others, after first helping them to feel free to share ideas. He might learn what other companies and cultures do. He might imagine what policies make sense from a worker's perspective, explain current policies to a child, write an essay listing options, take a long walk, or pray about it. Any acceptable policy must satisfy GR; he must be able to approve of it regardless of where he imagines himself in the situation: as owner, worker, neighbor, or customer. The final solution, while maybe not satisfying everyone fully, needs to be at least minimally acceptable from everyone's perspective.

(A) Rich would *act* on GR: he'd act toward others only as he's willing to be treated in the same situation. Yes, it's a simple formula. But it may require difficult preparatory work on *knowledge, imagination,* and *creativity.*

Flawed desires (about how we'd be treated in a similar situation) can stall GR. And so sometimes we need to make our desires more rational. Many think desires can't be appraised as rational or irrational. Richard Brandt 1970 rightly disagrees. He proposes that a *rational desire* is one that would survive *cognitive therapy*: a maximal criticism in terms of logic and vivid exposure to facts.

Suppose you hate the very idea of eating yogurt. Maybe you never tried it; but you were falsely taught that it has bad germs, tastes awful, and is eaten only by weird people. Then your aversion would likely diminish if you understood its origin, learned more about yogurt, and actually tried it.

Or suppose you dislike Xs because your family hated Xs, called them names, taught false stereotypes about them, and had you meet only a few atypically nasty Xs. Your aversion to Xs would likely diminish if you understood its origin and broadened your experience and knowledge. Such cognitive therapy can be useful to help us conquer prejudices and apply GR more wisely. We'll appeal to it later, in discussing racism and masochism (§§8.2 & 14.3g).

My favorite historical GR example is a civil rights speech by President John Kennedy (1963) during the first black enrollment at the University of Alabama. His speech exemplifies Kita: Know-Imagine-Test-Act. Here's part of it:

> If an American, because his skin is dark, cannot eat lunch in a restaurant open to the public, if he cannot send his children to the best public school available, if he cannot vote for the public officials who represent him, if, in short, he cannot enjoy the full and free life which all of us want, then who among us would be content to have the color of his skin changed and stand in his place? Who among us would then be content with the counsels of patience and delay? ... The heart of the question is whether all Americans are to be afforded equal rights and equal opportunities, whether we are going to treat our fellow Americans as we want to be treated.

Kennedy also stressed the inconsistency between American ideals ("All men are created equal") and practice (black soldiers are denied basic rights but fight and die for freedom). His Civil Rights Act passed in 1964, after his death.

2.3   Further GRs and relatives

Many GR formulas (not just Gold 1) are good principles and derivable from IMPARTIALITY and CONSCIENTIOUSNESS. The golden rule is a family of related formulas. No one formula exhausts GR.

Section 2.1b gave a GR variation about *relevantly similar* actual cases. This variation gives a duty instead of an imperative:

Gold 2: a duty GR	You *ought* to treat others only as you consent to being treated in the same situation.

This one deals with desires instead of actions:

Gold 3: a GR about desires	Don't combine *desiring* something to be done to another with being unwilling that this be done to you in the same situation.

These give consistency conditions for using moral terms:

Gold 4: a GR about consistently using "all right"	Don't believe that it would be *all right* for you to do A to X unless you're willing that A be done to you in the same situation.

Gold 5: a GR about consistently using "ought"	Don't believe that you *ought* to do A to X unless you want A to be done to you in the same situation.

Or we could imagine someone else we care about (for example, our daughter) on the action's receiving end.[1] Since these and other variations can combine, there are at least 6,460 correct GRs (Gensler 1996: 101–4, see also Terry 2012). So "the" golden rule is a family of principles rather than a single principle.

Related principles can help us recognize duties to ourselves. Suppose you have so much concern for your children that you never think of your own needs; you're inconsistent if you aren't willing that your children live that way when they grow up. Or you go through college putting little effort into it; you're inconsistent if you don't consent to the idea of a daughter of yours doing this. Or, because you lack courage and a sense of self-worth, you refuse to seek treatment for a drug habit that's ruining your life; you're inconsistent if you aren't willing that your younger brother do this in a similar situation. The *self-regard principle* says: "Treat yourself only as you're willing to have others (especially those you most care about) treat themselves in the same situation."

Many people have too little concern for themselves. Various factors (like

---

[1] So we can say "Treat others as you want *yours* to be treated" or "Treat others as you want *you or someone you love* to be treated" (Thompson 1905: 164 and Carson 2010: 131).

laziness, fear, habit, and lack of self-appreciation or discipline) can drive us into actions that benefit neither ourselves nor others; consider how we hurt ourselves by overeating, selfishness, laziness, or overwork. Our consistency norms recognize the importance of concern both for others and for ourselves.

GR and self-regard *switch persons*. We also can *switch times* and imagine that we *now* experience future consequences. *Future-regard* says: "Treat your-future-self only as you're willing to have been treated by your-past-self in the same situation." More crudely: "Don't do what you'll later regret." For example, maybe you cause yourself a future hangover by drinking; but, when you imagine yourself experiencing the hangover *now*, you don't consent to the idea of your having treated yourself this way. Or you cause yourself a future jail sentence by stealing; but when you picture yourself suffering these consequences *now* because of your past actions, you don't consent to these actions. In both cases, you're inconsistent and violate future-regard.

This *carbon rule* switches both persons and times: "Keep the earth livable for future generations, as we want past generations to have done for us."

How does GR apply to actions that affect several parties? Suppose I own a store and need to hire just one worker. Alice and Betty apply, and I must choose between them. Here I must satisfy GR toward each party. So if I pick Alice (who's more qualified) instead of Betty, then I must be willing that I *not* be picked if I were in Betty's situation. Combining two Gold 1s, we get:

Gold 6: a three-party GR	Don't act in a given way toward X and Y without being willing that this act be done when you imagine yourself in X's place and being willing that this act be done when you imagine yourself in Y's place.

The *generalized GR* goes further:

Gold 7: a generalized GR	Act only as you're willing for anyone to act in the same situation, regardless of where or when you imagine yourself or others.

This includes GR (you're in the place of someone affected by your action), self-regard (someone you care about is in your place), and future-regard (you're at a future time experiencing your action's consequences).

Reasonable moral beliefs need to be consistent, informed, imaginative, and maybe more things. Consistency requires GR, impartiality, conscientiousness, logical consistency in beliefs, ends–means consistency, self-regard, and future-regard. Consistency forbids *combinations* (of beliefs, actions, resolutions, or whatever) instead of saying exactly what to believe or do. Consistency norms specify a broader norm: "Be consistent in thought and action."

2.4   GR fallacies

At least six fallacies can corrode golden-rule thinking.[1]

(1) The *literal GR fallacy* assumes that everyone has the same likes, dislikes, and needs that we have. So we treat others *in their situation* exactly how we want them to treat us *in our situation*. But on the contrary, we often need to grasp another's uniqueness, imagine being in their shoes (which includes their likes and dislikes), and ask: "Am I now willing that if I were *in the same situation* then this be done to me?" Many problems come from neglecting the same-situation clause. (§§1.2–3, 2.1a–b, & 14.1–2)

(2) The *soft GR fallacy* assumes that we should never act against what others want. So we always yield to the desires of others. But on the contrary, we sometimes need to stop a two-year-old who wants to put fingers into electrical outlets, refuse a salesperson who wants to sell us overpriced products, fail a student who doesn't work, forcibly defend ourselves against an attacker, and jail a dangerous criminal. And yes, we're now willing that if we were in their situation then we be treated that way too. (§§1.4 & 2.1c)

(3) The *doormat GR fallacy* assumes that we should ignore our own interests. So we let others take advantage of us. But on the contrary, we need to consider everyone's interests, including our own. GR lets us say no to others, as long as we're willing that others say no to us in similar circumstances. GR tries to harmonize self-love and other-love, without destroying either; it builds on self-love and extends this to others. (§§1.5, 2.3, & 14.3g)

(4) The *third-parties GR fallacy* assumes that we should consider only ourselves and the other person. But on the contrary, we also need to consider third parties. So a judge should consider that freeing a dangerous criminal may bring harm to future victims. We need to satisfy GR toward everyone affected by our action – acting only in ways that we find acceptable, regardless of where or when we imagine ourselves or others in the situation. (§§1.6 & 2.3)

(5) The *easy GR fallacy* assumes that GR gives an infallible test of right and wrong that takes only seconds to apply. We just ask ourselves how we desire that we be treated in the same situation. Sorry, life is more complicated than that. To lead reliably to right action, GR consistency needs to build on things like knowledge, imagination, creativity, rationalized desires, and a healthy self-love; these can take much time and effort. (§§1.7 & 2.2)

(6) The *too-simple-or-too-complex GR fallacy* assumes that GR is either so simple that our kindergarten GR is enough for adult decisions or so complex that only a philosopher can understand it. But on the contrary, GR is *scalable* (which is computer talk for "expandable"). You can teach GR to little children ("Don't hit your little sister – you don't want us to hit you, do you?"), but

---

[1] Other fallacies confuse GR with "Treat others as they treat you" (repayment and retaliation), "Treat others well so they'll treat you well" (self-interest), or "People will treat you as you treat them" (empirical claim); see also §11.2 Q2.

adults can use it in complex decisions (like how to run a coal mine in a way that respects everyone's rights and interests).

Robert Fulghum (1990: 6f) wrote an essay called "All I really need to know I learned in kindergarten." Here's an excerpt (my italics):

> Share everything. Play fair. Don't hit people. Put things back where you found them. Clean up your own mess.... The *golden rule* and love and basic sanitation.... Take any of those items and *extrapolate it into sophisticated adult terms* and apply it to your family life or your work or your government or your world and it holds true and clear and firm.

In kindergarten, you learned many things, including 2+2=4 and the literal GR. What you learned is a great beginning. But you must extrapolate the math further into sophisticated adult terms to do the company budget, and you must develop GR further to apply it to complex adult problems, like how to run a company in a way that respects everyone's rights and interests. Your kindergarten GR has major flaws if you import it unchanged into the adult world:

- Any smart philosopher can demolish your GR in thirty seconds.
- Your GR thinking may be of low level and suffer from fallacies.
- You may get so confused and frustrated applying your GR to adult problems that you reject it as unworkable and unrealistic.
- Your world will be deprived of benefits that mature GR thinking can bring.

Our GR needs to grow as we mature, or else we may trash it as a "silly kindergarten saying that doesn't apply to the complex problems of the real world."

2.5   Religions and philosophies

So far, I've discussed how to phrase GR to avoid absurdities and how to apply it wisely. I've been silent about why we should follow GR and what larger worldviews can explain GR. We need these, but not so early in the book.

GR can be part of diverse frameworks. When a Buddhist talks about GR, you may hear about karma, peace of mind, reincarnation, the no-self view, and nirvana. From a Christian, you may hear about God as Love and Father, how we're brothers and sisters of one family, Christ's example, and how gratitude to God impels us to love our neighbor.

At a meeting on GR in world religions (Neusner & Chilton 2008 & 2009), a speaker used an airplane example: if you're assigned a seat that splits a family, you might use GR to conclude that you should offer to switch seats, so the family can sit together. After that, others were inspired to use airplane examples. Mine was this. Motivated by GR, I offer to switch my seat to let a family sit together. A Buddhist does the same thing. And suppose we both formulate

GR the same way. Then is our GR thinking the same? Not necessarily. If we push it further, there may be differences: the Buddhist may talk about karma and reincarnation, while I talk about Christian things. Suppose the plane has many people of diverse religions and philosophies who, motivated by GR, offer to switch their seats. Is their GR thinking the same? The formula and Kita procedure may be the same, while GR's context may be very different.

Just as GR is part of diverse religions, so too it can be part of diverse philosophies. What do you think ethics is based on? *Self-evident principles?* Then you can see GR (or the consistency axioms from which it follows) as self-evident. *A rational procedure?* GR uses facts, imagination, and consistency. *God's will?* Almost every religion teaches GR. *Cultural conventions?* Almost every society endorses GR. *A social contract for mutual advantages?* GR promotes cooperation and helps resolve conflicts. *Social usefulness?* GR has this. *Personal feelings?* Many have feelings that support GR. *Self-interest?* Many find that living GR brings self-respect and better treatment from others, and helps us avoid painful inconsistency and self-condemnation.

It's important that GR can be part of diverse frameworks. We live in an increasingly diverse world. How can we get along, when people have such different ways of looking at things, reflecting different religions, philosophies, and cultures? GR offers a global moral framework that diverse groups can share, but for different reasons. GR is a point of unity in a diverse world.

2.6   The rest of this book

This book has four parts:

1. "Golden Rule Reasoning" has two chapters, 1 and 2; read either or both. This present chapter is more demanding, while Chapter 1 is easier.
2. "Religion and History" has three chapters: GR in world religions (Chapter 3), a dialogue on GR and religion (4), and a GR chronology that reviews 3000 years of reflection on GR (5).
3. "Practice" has four chapters: moral education (6), egoism and evolution (7), racism and other discrimination (8), and applied ethics (about business, medicine, animals, etc.) (9).
4. "Theory" has five chapters: positive and negative GRs (10), more GR questions (11), GR in many philosophies (12), GR approaches of Hare and Carson (13), and more GR objections (14).

Again, read any further chapters, in any order; but Chapters 13 and 14 are technical and assume Chapter 2.

2.7   Technical appendix (difficult)

Gold 1 rests on the idea that *we ought to be consistent in thought and action*. This section mentions related technical points. If you're overloaded, skip this section. Or if you want more than what's here, see Gensler 1996 (more philosophical) or Gensler 2010: 290–335 (more logical).

I'll start with three points about consistency. (1) Our duty to be consistent is subject to certain implicit qualifications (Gensler 1996: 19–23), since there may be cases when we're unable to be consistent in certain ways (perhaps because of emotional turmoil or the inability to grasp complex logical relationships) or cases when being inconsistent in a minor way will have very bad consequences (maybe migraine headaches or Dr. Evil destroying the world). In practice, these qualifications aren't very important.

(2) This chapter leaves open *why* we ought to be consistent. While most thinkers accept a consistency duty, they justify it differently – for example, as a self-evident truth, a social convention, or a pragmatic norm to avoid confusion.

(3) When I call impartiality and conscientiousness "consistency norms," I mean that they forbid certain combinations that are *somehow* objectionable – whether logically (based on the meaning and logical implications of words), ethically, religiously, or pragmatically. This chapter leaves this open too, since various thinkers may understand these matters differently (ch. 12–13).

Recall our explanation of conscientiousness (§2.1c):

> *Conscientiousness*, as I use the term, requires that we *keep our life (including actions, intentions, etc.) in harmony with our moral beliefs.* Suppose I believe that one *ought* never to kill a human being for any reason. If I'm *conscientious*, then I'll never intentionally kill a human being, I'll resolve not to kill for any reason (even to protect myself or my family), and I won't want others to kill for any reason. Similar requirements cover beliefs about what is "all right" ("permissible"). If I'm conscientious, then I won't do something without believing that it would be *all right* for me to do it. And I won't believe that something is *all right* without consenting to the idea of it being done.

This explanation requires that key terms be taken in certain ways.

"*Believing that I ought now to do A* commits me to *acting now to do A*." Here "ought" must be used in an evaluative, all-things-considered sense. When I say "I ought to wear a tie at work," I may be just describing company policy instead of giving my own evaluation; if so, my statement doesn't commit me to acting accordingly. And a *prima facie* duty (a duty that may be overridden by other duties) doesn't commit me to action. Suppose I say: "Insofar as I promised to take you to the movies, I ought to do this (*prima facie* duty); but insofar as my wife needs me to drive her to the hospital, I ought to do this instead (*prima facie* duty). Since my duty to my wife is more urgent, my all-things-considered duty is to drive my wife to the hospital." Here the *prima facie* duties don't commit me to action, but the all-things-considered duty does. The *action* I'm committed to is *intentional action* (acting with the intention of doing the thing).

"*Believing that A ought to be done* commits me to *wanting A to be done*." Here "want" (or "desire," which I use equivalently) must be used in a volitional, all-things-considered sense. Suppose that, while I hate going to the dentist, I make an appointment to go. Do I *want* to go to the dentist? I don't want it in an emotional sense (I don't feel like going), but I do want it in a volitional sense (my will directs me to go). Our consistency norms require the volitional sense. Or suppose I have *some desire* (a *prima facie* desire) not to do A, even though my all-things-considered desire is to do A. Our consistency norms require that the all-things-considered desire go with the all-things-considered ought.

"All right" (or "permissible") in our consistency norms is also to be taken in an evaluative, all-things-considered sense.

"*Believing that act A is all right (permissible)* commits me to *consenting to act A being done*." Now what does this "consenting" (or "willingness" that the action be done, which I use equivalently) involve? I see it as a kind of legislating in our minds about which actions we *permit* (*allow, consent to, are willing to have done*). Such *permitting* has these features:

- For any specific act A that I've made up my mind about, I might permit doing A, or permit omitting A, or permit both.
- If I do A or want A to be done, then I must in consistency permit A.
- If I both permit doing A and permit omitting A, then I can consistently decide either way about what to do or want.
- Permitting is volitional and all-things-considered. I may permit act A in an all-things-considered way, even though I object to some aspects of A.
- Instead of *permit, consent,* or *be willing,* we can say *approve, allow, agree to, condone,* or *tolerate* – in some senses of these terms. The opposite is to inwardly *condemn, object to, disapprove, forbid, protest, prohibit,* or *repudiate.*

Recall our bicycle example. Stealing Detra's bicycle (intentional action) commits you to believing that this act is *all right* (in an evaluative, all-things-considered way), which commits you to believing that the reversed-situation act is *all right* (in this same way), which commits you to *be willing* (in a volitional, all-things-considered way) that this reversed-situation act be done.[1]

I sometimes speak of GR as calling for a harmony between *my act* (toward another) and *my desire* about how I'd be treated in a similar situation. Here

---

[1] See also Boonin 2003 (who criticizes *consenting*), Carson 2010: 129–56 (who emphasizes *not objecting*), Wallace 2007 (who emphasizes *resenting*), and our §14.3a. *All right* and *consenting* need to be qualified the same way; so if I judge A to be *all right* relative to the total facts (or to the agent's data), then I must also *consent* to A being done relative to the total facts (or to the agent's data).

"desire" is used in a broad sense to cover *consenting* (as just described) as well as *desiring* in a narrow sense (as described a few paragraphs back).

My consistency theory's more rigorous form uses three axioms, the first two adapted from R.M. Hare (§13.1). Axiom 1 is *universalizability*, which says that whatever is permissible (obligatory, wrong, etc.) in one case would also be permissible (obligatory, wrong, etc.) in any exactly or relevantly similar case, regardless of the individuals involved.[1] Axiom 2 is *prescriptivity*, which links judgments about what is obligatory/permissible to imperatives ("Do this") and permissives ("You may do this"). Axiom 3 is *rationality*, which says that we ought to think and live consistently with logic plus universalizability and prescriptivity. I take universalizability and rationality to be self-evident truths and prescriptivity to express a self-evident logical entailment; but other views are possible (ch. 12–13).

This is a rough outline. For details, see Gensler 1996 & 2010: 290–335. The latter puts the consistency theory into symbolic logic, as a formal system. Gold 1 in symbols is "$\sim(\underline{u}{:}A\underline{u}x \cdot \sim\underline{u}{:}(\exists F)(F^{*}A\underline{u}x \cdot \blacksquare(FA\underline{x}u \supset MA\underline{x}u)))$" and its 35-step proof is a thing of great beauty.

---

[1] The more precise wording for "permissible" (similar forms work for other terms) goes: "If act A is permissible, then there's some universal property (or conjunction of such properties) F, such that: act A is F, and in any actual or hypothetical case any act that's F is permissible." Here a *universal property* is a non-evaluative property describable without proper names (like "Gensler" or "Boston") or pointer terms (like "I" or "this"). An *exactly reversed situation* switches all the universal properties. See Gensler 1996: 69–92 & 2010: 324f.

CHAPTER 3
Many Religions and Cultures

St. Mary's was the name of the street in Detroit where I grew up. St. Mary's was also the name of my grade school and parish church. Almost everyone on my block was Catholic. No one was Jewish, Muslim, or Buddhist. Everyone was white. I don't recall immigrants or gays. Almost everyone I knew had the same race, religion, and ethnicity.

My family had nothing against people who were different, such as blacks. When we traveled to the South, which still had laws enforcing segregation, we insisted on the right of blacks to full equality. But we didn't know any blacks. Blacks lived in another part of town, as did Jews. Buddhists and Muslims lived in another part of the world.

My values came from the family, neighborhood, school, and church – all reflecting the strict Catholicism of the 1950s before the second Vatican Council. Presumably I was taught the golden rule; but I don't recall this, and GR wasn't important to me until I went to graduate school in 1968 (§13.1). While I was taught decent values, I wasn't in touch with the full range of humanity.

While America was said to be a melting pot, the vegetables kept separate identities in homogeneous neighborhoods. For a while, Catholics of different ethnic groups (Irish, German, and so on) preferred to have their own parishes. When my German-Irish father proposed to my Polish mother (both Catholics), he faced opposition from his relatives, who wanted him to stay with his own kind. The opposition faded when both sides got to know each other and discovered they weren't so different. So gradually there was more mixing.

If we fast-forward to the 21st century, the change is remarkable. Advances in transportation, communication, and the Internet have shrunk the planet. These, with immigration and multinational companies, have produced an unprecedented mixing of peoples and cultures. Today most neighborhoods are integrated. We all have friends, and even relatives, of diverse races, religions, ethnic groups, or sexual orientations. Diversity has replaced homogeneity.

How can diverse people learn to live together? How can our multicultural world find common values? The answer is that, despite some sharp differences (for example, about arranged marriages), good people from diverse groups tend to have some deep values in common. One shared value is the golden rule. Insofar as we agree on this, and put this agreement into practice, we have a good chance to learn to live together harmoniously. Accordingly, we need to understand, celebrate, and practice this common value.

Is it important that we do so? Indeed, it's difficult to find anything more important. What most divides the world is hatred, terrorism, and war between religious groups who profess the golden rule. As I write this, a Christian pastor is planning a "burn a Qur'an" day. Would he want Muslims to plan a "burn a Bible" day? Yes, good people from diverse groups share some deep values. But less enlightened people from diverse groups share some deep *disvalues*, like divisiveness and stereotypes. Those who spread division are much the same, whether they be Christian, Muslim, Jewish, or something else.

Earlier chapters analyzed GR reasoning but avoided deeper religious and philosophical questions. We eventually need to ask these questions and find answers that make sense to us. GR needs to be part of a larger framework. Indeed, GR fits amazingly well into many different frameworks.

This chapter discusses what the world's religions say about GR and about concern for others, which GR deals with in a specific way; philosophies get covered in ch. 12. I'll begin with Abrahamic religions (embraced by over half the planet) and then turn to non-Abrahamic religions (especially eastern ones). Then I'll discuss GR interfaith global-ethics movements and raise further issues about GR and world religions.[1]

In studying other religions, we need the right GR attitude (Troll 2008): "Try to understand the other's faith as you would like your own faith to be understood." I want people, when they approach my Christian faith, to:

- listen carefully, be fair, show respect, and not distort;
- not generalize from a few bad cases (don't say that *all* Christians are evil just because a *few* are);
- not compare the best of their faith with the worst of mine;
- give Christianity the benefit of the doubt (so don't take a passage like Luke 14:26, "Unless you hate your father and mother you cannot be my disciple," literally when most Christians don't take it that way);
- neither deny nor exaggerate differences between their faith and mine.

Likewise, I'll try to understand other faiths fairly.[2]

If you search the Web for "golden rule religions," you'll find many pages listing GRs from various religions. Such pages are becoming more numerous, as people discover that GR is common to most religions. This is wonderful.

Here we'll try to understand GR's role in many religions, which requires looking at larger selections from sacred texts. Often the Web lists don't make clear how to find a specific GR saying. For example, a reference that just says "from the Mahabharata" isn't helpful, since this Hindu epic is huge – my translation has 5479 pages! Here I've tried to give standard references (book,

---

[1] On GR in world religions, see Rost 1986, Neusner & Chilton 2008, and Wattles 1996. There are many lists of GRs in the world's religions; Paul McKenna's poster on this has sold 100,000 copies worldwide (http://www.scarboromissions.ca/Golden_rule/poster_order.php).

[2] Sohaib Saeed 2010, a Muslim, has additional GR-based interfaith-dialogue suggestions.

chapter, verse, or whatever) so interested readers can look them up. I've often provided Web links; if these disappear, try searching the reference, for example "Sanhedrin of the Babylonian Talmud 56a."

References to the Christian Bible are easy to work with. If you search the Web for "Matthew 7:12," you'll find many sites that give this verse in different translations. In giving passages from sacred texts, I don't uniformly follow any specific translation. Instead, I try to find several translations and then express the passage clearly in modern American English.

3.1   Abrahamic religions

Judaism, Christianity, and Islam trace their origin through Abraham. Such *Abrahamic religions* accept one supreme personal God who created the world out of love for us and revealed himself and his will through sacred writings.

Abrahamic believers, however they see morality philosophically, add a religious dimension: *morality is God's will for us*. We can be moral because God created us in his image and likeness, with the abilities to *know* right from wrong and to *choose* between the two. Morality is serious, objective, and part of our personal relationship to God. Right living has religious motives, both higher (unselfish love and gratitude) and lower (punishments and rewards), and pushes us toward our destiny of eternal happiness with God.[1]

Abrahamic believers endorse GR and concern for others. Most try to follow these values. But some (and this includes Jews, Christians, and Muslims) forget these core values and instead spread hatred and division.

3.1a   Judaism

Judaism was the original Abrahamic religion. Christianity and Islam build on its ethical ideals and notions about God.[2]

Jews have an identity based on history. They descended from Abraham, were freed from Egyptian slavery, and enjoyed a golden age under King David in the promised land. They were captives in Babylon, struggled under the Roman Empire, and scattered into many lands. After centuries of persecution leading to the Holocaust, they created the modern state of Israel.

Central to Judaism is the Torah ("Law"), or the first five books of the Bible (Genesis, Exodus, Leviticus, Numbers, and Deuteronomy – all ascribed to Moses). Jewish scriptures also have prophetic books (like Isaiah and Amos) and other writings (like Proverbs and Psalms). Also important is the Talmud, where rabbis comment on the Torah through stories, proverbs, and sermons.

---

[1] Mayton 2009: 167–203 discusses Abrahamic morality. Interfaith Declaration 1993 expresses an agreement between Jewish, Christian, and Muslim leaders on international business ethics.

[2] On GR in Judaism, see Alexander 2005, Goldin 1946, Jospe 1990, Küng & Homolka 2009, Neusner & Chilton 2008: 9–25 & 55–64, Telushkin 2006–9 & 2010, and Wattles 1996: 42–51.

Rabbis found 613 commandments in the Torah. The Ten Commandments (Exodus 20 and Deuteronomy 5) list our most important duties:[1]

Duties to God	1.	I am the Lord your God who brought you out of slavery in Egypt. You shall not have other gods before me.
	2.	You shall not make or worship idols.
	3.	You shall not take the Lord's name in vain.
	4.	Keep holy the Sabbath.
Duties to family	5.	Honor your father and mother.
	7.	You shall not commit adultery.
	10.	You shall not covet your neighbor's wife.
Duties to everyone	6.	You shall not kill.
	8.	You shall not steal.
	9.	You shall not bear false witness.

Non-Jews were seen as bound by only seven commandments: to set up a just legal system and not to blaspheme, worship idols, commit adultery, murder, steal, or eat a living animal's flesh; Gentiles following these seven Noahide Laws (laws binding on Noah's descendents) were considered just.[2]

The prophets, who boldly denounced injustice, show another side of Jewish morality. Isaiah 1:11–7 criticizes those who follow rituals while ignoring the needs of orphans and widows. Similarly, Amos 2:5f proclaims that God will punish his people for their injustices, for selling the just man for silver and the poor man for a pair of shoes.

The golden rule appears in a Talmudic story about Rabbi Hillel (c. 30 BC–10 AD). A Gentile came to Rabbi Shammai, stood on one foot, and promised to convert to Judaism if the rabbi taught him the whole Torah while he stood on one foot. Shammai got angry and sent the Gentile away. But Hillel, when asked the same thing, responded with GR: "What is hateful to yourself, do not do to another. That is the whole Torah. The rest is commentary. Go and learn."[3] Hillel gives GR as summarizing the Torah, which, with 613 commandments, needed a summary. Some Jews call GR "the Torah on one foot."

A more recent rabbi (Goldin 1946: 273f) says that this is the best known rabbinic story and familiar in Jewish circles. He sees Hillel's reply as brilliant. Hillel first expresses the Torah's spirit, its central thesis, in a neat and inspiring

---

[1] Traditions divide and number these differently; here I follow a system common in Judaism. Rabbis also divide and number the 613 commandments differently. To get a list, search for "613 commandments of the Torah" on the Web. Some rules sound strange. For example, Deuteronomy 22:11 forbids wearing clothes with a wool-linen combination (common today for summerweight suits). Some Jews today take this rule seriously while others see it as obsolete.

[2] From Sanhedrin of the Babylonian Talmud 56a (http://www.come-and-hear.com/sanhedrin /sanhedrin_56.html). Most other religions would accept these commandments.

[3] Shabbat of the Babylonian Talmud 31a (http://www.come-and-hear.com/shabbath/shabbath_31 .html). The cover of Telushkin's (2010) book on Hillel shows a Gentile standing on one foot.

epigram. Yes, everything in Judaism goes toward this GR goal. But this goal needs concrete means to promote it, which the Torah provides.

Hillel gives a *negative* GR (ch. 10): "What you want *not* done to yourself, *don't* do to others." This also had occurred a century earlier in a Jewish book not part of the official Jewish Bible, Tobit 4:16: "See that you never do to another what you would hate to have done to yourself."[1]

The official Jewish Bible has GR-like passages. King David once fell in love with Bathsheba and indirectly brought about her husband's death (2 Samuel 12:1–13). Prophet Nathan confronted the king about his wrongdoing by telling him a story where someone else did something similar. When David responded "That man did wrong!" Nathan exclaimed "You've condemned yourself!" Then David (who saw that the actions were relevantly similar) realized his error.[2] This story hints at another GR saying: "Don't do what you blame others for doing." (More precisely: "Don't combine doing A with believing that it would be wrong for another to do A in similar circumstances.")

Another GR-like passage is Exodus 23:9 (and Deuteronomy 10:19): "Do not oppress a foreigner, for you well know how it feels to be a foreigner, since you were foreigners yourselves in the land of Egypt." This suggests:

- that we can better imagine ourselves in another's place if we reflect on our similar experiences (as when *we* were foreigners);
- that in deciding how to act toward another, we should imagine the same thing being done to us (so we imagine ourselves as foreigners being oppressed);
- that we shouldn't oppress a foreigner without consenting to the idea of our being oppressed in the same situation.

Leviticus 19:18 is the most important GR-like passage: "Love your neighbor as yourself." Many rabbis saw this as the Torah's central norm. For us, it raises two key questions. First, what is its scope? Does it mean "Love *your fellow Jews* as yourself"? Or does it mean "Love *everyone* as yourself"? The universal reading fits better with what the Torah says about how to treat non-Jews. We just mentioned Exodus 23:9, about not oppressing foreigners. Leviticus (19:33–5 & 24:22) says we are to do foreigners no wrong, treat them as natives, love them as ourselves, and have the same law for them as for natives. Deuteronomy (10:19 & 24:14–22) says we are to love foreigners, be open to hiring them, give them just wages, and let them have after-harvest crop portions. All of this supports the universal "Love *everyone* as yourself" reading.[3]

---

[1] Sirach 31:15, from about the same time, has "Judge the needs of your guest by your own."

[2] 2 Samuel 14:1–13 & 1 Kings 20:38–42 have similar examples.

[3] The Torah made an exception for war enemies, like Amalekites; see Exodus 17:14–6, Numbers 31:1–18, and Deuteronomy 25:17–9. *New Encyclopedia of Judaism* 2002 (article on "love of neighbor") says that some rabbis taught that "Love your neighbor" doesn't apply to how to treat idolaters. If I give Judaism the benefit of the doubt here, I'll see the Torah as having a universal love norm – but also (as often happens when higher ideals first appear) as having elements inconsistent with this. The Torah displays various stages of moral and religious development.

MANY RELIGIONS AND CULTURES 39

A second question is how "Love your neighbor as yourself" relates to GR ("Do unto others"). There are two plausible views here.[1] The *equivalence* view claims that both say the same thing. One might argue for this as follows:

> "Love your neighbor as yourself" is equivalent to "Take your self-love as the model of how to treat others."
> "Take your self-love as the model of how to treat others" is equivalent to "Treat others only as you're willing to be treated in the same situation." (How else could we make sense of using self-love as a model?)
> ∴ "Love your neighbor as yourself" is equivalent to "Treat others only as you're willing to be treated in the same situation."

GR would then spell out the meaning of "Love your neighbor as yourself."

In contrast, the *complementarity* view sees GR and the love norm as different. GR is about *procedure*; when combined with knowledge and imagination, it gives a way to help us decide how to act. "Love your neighbor" is about *motivation*; it means "Act to do good and not harm to your neighbor – and this for the sake of your neighbor." Both ideas work well together:

> Love-your-neighbor provides the highest *motivation* for following GR. We might follow GR from lower motives (like self-interest or conformity) or higher motives (like genuine love for others). If we follow GR from love, we follow it because we care about others for their own sake. This brings us closer to moral perfection. Love provides GR with the highest motivation.

> GR gives a *procedure* to operationalize love-your-neighbor. Suppose we want to love others; how do we apply this love? GR (with Kita) shows how to translate love into action. If we love our children in the GR way, for example, we'll try to *know* them (including their needs and desires) and *imagine* ourselves in their place. And we'll treat them only in ways we're willing to be treated ourselves by a parent in the same situation.

So love provides a motivation (caring for others for their own sake) and GR provides a procedure to translate this into action.

The equivalence and complementarity views both seem sensible and consistent with the Bible. I know of no objective way to decide between them. I do, however, prefer the complementarity view, which I see as giving a richer way to think about how the two norms connect.[2]

---

[1] Many say the two norms are equivalent. Thomas Aquinas (*Summa Theologica* I-II, q. 99, a. 1) says that "Do unto others" analyzes and is implicit in neighborly love; Telushkin 2006–9 says something similar. Hanfling 1963 and Waterman 1945 say the two norms are distinct but complementary. Stanglin 2005 thinks they are distinct and that GR (which he takes in the literal way I criticized earlier) is flawed. See also Donagan 1977 and Wattles 1996: 64–6.

[2] Or we might take "Love your neighbor" as a comprehensive normative theory (utilitarian or otherwise, §14.2). Then the consistency GR, while not equivalent to "Love your neighbor," could be used (when combined with knowledge, imagination, and rationalized desires), to defend it.

3.1b Christianity

Christianity builds on Judaism. Distinctive to Christianity is the belief in Jesus Christ (c. 4 BC–27 AD) as the Son of God. And so we now turn to Jesus's teachings, focusing on gospel passages that connect with GR.[1]

Jesus's inaugural Sermon on the Mount, which is still the best introduction to Christianity, is Matthew ch. 5–7. It starts with beatitudes: blessed are the poor in spirit, the meek, promoters of justice, peacemakers, the merciful, and so on – for all will be rewarded. Then there are radical demands. Have, not just pure outer behavior about anger and lust, but also pure inner dispositions. Love neighbors *and* enemies: do good to those who hate you. Care about divine, not human, approval and rewards. Pray to our Father, free yourself from worries, trust God. Don't be judgmental; evaluate yourselves by the same standards that you evaluate others. As you treat others, so will God treat you. And so *treat others as you want to be treated* (GR), for this sums up the Law and the prophets (the Jewish scriptures). Finally, put these teachings into practice.

GR is the sermon's punch line, the summary idea: "Therefore, treat others as you want to be treated, for this sums up the Law and the prophets" (Mt 7:12). GR connects with other parts of the sermon:

- Jesus rejects "An eye for an eye, and a tooth for a tooth" (Mt 5:38) – and thus also rejects the vengeful "Treat others as they treat you" rival of GR.
- "Love your enemies and do good to those who hate you" (Mt 5:44) makes clear the universal scope of love and GR.
- "Our Father who art in heaven, hallowed be thy name" (Mt 6:9): praying together to a common father, we recognize that we're all brothers and sisters – and so should treat others as brothers and sisters.[2]
- "Forgive us our trespasses as we forgive those who trespass against us" (Mt 6:12): we can't sincerely pray this unless we forgive others as we ourselves want to be forgiven (a GR about forgiveness).
- "Why do you see the speck in your brother's eye but not the beam in your own eye?" (Mt 7:3–5): this suggests a related GR form, that we aren't to do what we complain about when others do it. (More precisely: "Don't act to do A while believing that it's wrong for others to do A in similar circumstances.")

God will do to us as we do to others:

[1] Wierzbicka 2001: 191–202 discusses issues about GR in Matthew's gospel – like the historicity of Jesus's statement, whether Jesus reacted to Hillel, whether Jesus's positive GR was original and important, how central GR was to Jesus's teachings, and whether Jesus rejected GR (Dihle 1962 and others propose this, seeing GR as egoistic, but see §§7.3 & 14.4 Obj. 30–31). Other studies include Alexander 2005, Allison 1987, Betz 1995, Easton 1914, Jeremias 1961, Little & Twiss 1978: 179–206, Manek 1967, Meier 2009, Neusner & Chilton 2008: 76–87, A. Perry 1935, Topel 1998, Tullberg 2011, and Wattles 1996: 52–76 & 182–9.

[2] Along these lines, Wattles 1996: 183 calls the golden rule "the principle of the practice of the family of God" and rephrases it as "Treat other persons as brothers and sisters, as sons and daughters of God, as you want others to treat you."

- "Blessed are the merciful, for they shall obtain mercy" (Mt 5:7).
- "If you forgive others, then God will forgive you; but if you don't forgive others, then God won't forgive you" (Mt 6:14f; see also 18:21–35).
- "Judge (condemn) not, that you may not be judged; for God will judge you by the same measure that you judge others" (Mt 7:1f).
- Many other verses deal with rewards and punishments (Mt 5:3–12, 20–26, 29f, 46f; 6:1–6, 16–21, 33; and 7:11).

So in the afterlife we'll receive the same treatment that we've given others.[1] When Mt 7:12 says "Therefore, treat others as you want to be treated," the "therefore" hints at an ends–means argument: if you want a certain treatment yourself, then, to get this, you must treat others that way too.

It may disappoint that Jesus appeals to self-interest (reward and punishment) instead of something higher (like unselfish love for God and neighbor). But the gospels have to appeal to a wide range of people and thus provide lower motives as well as higher ones. Jesus sneaks in "Be perfect, as your heavenly Father is perfect" (Mt 5:48) and in other places there are higher motives, like being grateful to God who has first loved us and modeling ourselves after the self-giving love for us of Jesus on the cross.

Here are three further points from Matthew's gospel. (1) Jesus often uses consistency arguments when disputing with opponents, for example about Sabbath regulations (Mt 12:1–8, 10–3; 15:1–9; and 23:23f). Since GR is a consistency principle, this roots GR more firmly into how Jesus argued.

(2) The good or evil that we've done to others counts in the last judgment as having been done to Jesus: whatever you did to even the least person in the world, you did to me (Mt 25:31–46). This hints at a GR variation, where we imagine someone we care about on the receiving end of the action. Here we're to treat others as if they were Jesus.

(3) Jesus was asked to give the Torah's greatest commandment (Mt 22:35–40). He gave Deuteronomy 6:5, to love the Lord our God with our whole heart and soul and strength. He added, from Leviticus 19:18, to love our neighbors as ourselves. So the most important things in life are to love God and love our neighbor. He added that these sum up the Law and the prophets. He had previously given GR as summarizing the Law and the prophets (Mt 7:12). So how do the two love norms relate to GR? Augustine claimed that they're derivable from GR: since we want both God and neighbor to love us, by GR we're to love both God and neighbor.[2]

Luke's gospel has a teaching similar to Matthew's, but arranged and worded differently. Luke 6:17–49 presents Jesus's inaugural sermon as being shorter and on a plain (not a mountain); but it has the same essentials: beatitudes, love your enemies, God will treat us as we treat others, GR (Luke 6:31), and an

---

[1] This may remind us of the *karma* of eastern religions. In Christianity and monotheistic forms of Hinduism, God brings it about that you get the kind of treatment that you've given to others. In many forms of Buddhism, however, this repayment operates by a law of nature.

[2] Augustine 400a. (See also §3.1a and Wattles 1993: 81 and 1996: 47 & 203.)

exhortation to put these ideas into practice. Luke also has Jesus give the two love norms (Luke 10:24–37). But now there's a follow-up example, a story about the Good Samaritan helping a Jew who had been beaten, robbed, and left to die. The point is much like "Love your enemies": our neighbor is everyone, even a member of a group that we've been taught to hate.

John's gospel, while not mentioning GR, talks much about love. Jesus gives a new commandment that's more demanding than GR: that we love one another as Jesus loves us; there's no greater love than to lay down your life for another, as Jesus did for us (John 15:12f).

Let me answer three questions that some Christians might raise.

> (Q1) As a Christian, I enjoy what you say about Jesus. But I must protest the nice things you say about other religions, which are from the devil, and their followers, who follow Satan.

You need to study the gospels more. Jesus lived in an interfaith environment and often praised those of other faiths. Those outside the Judeo-Christian tradition portrayed positively in the gospels include the Wise Men from the East (perhaps Hindus) who visited the infant Jesus (Mt 2:1–12), the Roman Centurion whose servant Jesus cured (Mt 8:5–13), the demented Gentile who lived among the pig-raisers (Mt 8:28–34 & Lk 8:26–39), the Ninivites who reformed their lives after Jonah confronted them (Mt 12:39–41), the queen of the South who visited Solomon (Mt 12:42), the Canaanite woman (Mt 15:22–8 & Lk 7:25), Pilate's wife (Mt 27:19), the Roman Centurion at Jesus's death (Mt 27:54 & Lk 7:2–9), the Gentile widow that Elias visited (Lk 4:26), Naaman the Syrian leper who was cured (Lk 4:27), the Good Samaritan who helps a stranger (Lk 10:24–37), and the Samaritan leper who was cured and gave thanks (Lk 17:12–9). All are praised or presented positively; they're not called "followers of Satan." Remember too that Jesus taught us to be non-judgmental (Mt 7:1f) and to love everyone, even enemies (Mt 5:43f).

> (Q2) As Christians, don't we see moral knowledge as coming only from the Bible – and thus as impossible for non-believers or those of other faiths?

No, this view clashes with Christianity, for three reasons. (1) The early parts of the Bible talk about people who knew right from wrong, even though the Bible wasn't yet written. (2) Most of the good people outside the Jewish faith who were praised by Jesus (Q1) had moral knowledge without getting it from the Bible. (3) Paul speaks about Gentiles who lack the biblical law but have the moral law written on their hearts (Romans 2:14f). So the Bible teaches that it isn't the only source of moral knowledge.

> (Q3) Is GR part of Christianity's "natural law" tradition?

Yes, many Christian thinkers over many centuries have seen GR as the central norm of the "natural law" that's built into our reason and accessible to people of every religion and culture (see the ch. 5 chronology).

3.1c   Islam

Muhammad (570–632), Islam's founder, was born in what is now Saudi Arabia. In his travels, he learned about Judaism, Christianity, and polytheism. In Mecca in 610, the Angel Gabriel purportedly began revealing the Qur'an to him and missioned him to convert his people from immorality and paganism. In 622, he traveled north to Medina to escape persecution. His influence grew, partly through military conquest, and Arabia became Muslim.[1]

"Islam" means "submission to God's will." The one supreme God revealed himself through Muhammad (the last and greatest prophet), Jesus (who was a prophet but not God), and the Jewish prophets. The Qur'an is the highest revelation; also important are the Hadiths (sayings or actions of Muhammad or his companions), which clarify the Qur'an. Based on these, Muslims forbid killing, adultery, stealing, lying, and disrespecting parents. We are to help those in need, whether Muslim or non-Muslim, and pardon anyone who injures us. Pure intention is emphasized. In waging war, permitted only to defend ourselves or protect oppressed Muslims, we must minimize force, treat prisoners humanely, not show anger, and not injure innocent civilians.

While the Qur'an lacks the phrase "Love your neighbor as yourself," it says this in different words: "Show kindness and do good to parents, relatives, and orphans – to the near neighbor and the distant neighbor who is a stranger – to the companion by your side and the traveler that you meet" (Qur'an 4:36). And it has a GR-like saying: "Woe to those who cheat: they demand a fair measure from others but they do not give it themselves" (Qur'an 83:1–3). The Islamic GR occurs in three Hadiths, which attribute it to Muhammad: "None of you is a true believer unless he wishes for his brother what he wishes for himself" (Bukhari 1:2:12, Muslim 1:72f, and An-Nawawi 13).

Does "brother" in the Islamic GR refer just to "brother Muslims," or does it also include "brother humans" (as Saeed 2010 argues)? There are reasons for preferring the universal "brother humans":

- *Common Word* (2009: 27), expressing a wide consensus by Muslim leaders, claims that Christianity and Islam agree on GR and love-your-neighbor and understand them the same way – which would include a universal GR.
- As mentioned earlier, the Qur'an gives duties toward non-Muslims.
- Ibn Arabi (1165–1240, quoted by Neusner & Chilton 2008: 107) saw GR as applying to all creatures: "All the commandments are summed up in this, that

[1] On GR in Islam, see An-Na'im 1991 & 2008, Neusner & Chilton 2008: 99–115, Rost 1986: 96–110, and Saeed 2010. Sites http://www.quranexplorer.com and http://islamworld.net have texts. Michel 2010 has a very positive assessment of Islam from a Catholic theologian.

whatever you would like the True One to do to you, that do to His creatures."

Based on these, and on my principle to give other faiths the benefit of the doubt, I take the Islamic GR to apply to our treatment of everyone.

Imam Ali (c. 600–60), Muhammad's relative and an important leader, said:

> What you prefer for yourself, prefer for others; what you find objectionable for yourself, treat as such for others. Don't wrong anyone, just as you would not like to be wronged; do good to others just as you would like others to do good to you; that which you consider immoral for others, consider immoral for yourself. (Nahj al-Balaghah, Wasiyya to al-Hasan b. `Ali, #31, quoted in Chenai 2008: 215)

Shuja Sh. Ali (a Muslim seminarian in Qom, Iran) sent me this quote.

Today there's turmoil about values in the Muslim world. Should Islam adapt better to the modern world and Western values? Many conservative Muslims say no. They see the West as godless and decadent. They want to preserve a union of church and state that enforces Islamic law and forbids giving up Islam. Most conservative Muslims are peaceful. But a few extremists resort to terrorism, as in the attack on the U.S. of 11 September 2001. It would be wrong to conclude that all Muslims are terrorists – just as it would be wrong to conclude from Protestant and Catholic terrorism in northern Ireland that all Christians are terrorists. It also would be wrong for the West to ignore criticisms that even moderate Muslims make against the West: for example, that it sides too much with Israel against Palestinians; that it often ignores Muslim sensibilities, as in how it acts in the holy land of Saudi Arabia; or that it's obsessed with material things, sex, and individual freedoms. These criticisms may contain much truth.

Many liberal Muslims, although critical of the West, want to adapt more to the modern world. They believe in freely elected governments, equality for women, and the right to choose and exercise one's religion (Majid 1998 and An-Na'im 1991 & 2008). These Muslims think democracy and human rights fit Islam's essential message. And they emphasize how Islam is like other religions and how different faiths need to understand and learn from each other.

Islamic-Christian relations recently moved to a new phase. What started this was a talk by Pope Benedict XVI (2006) on faith and reason. The pope briefly referred to a remark made in 1391, as part of an Islamic-Christian debate, by Byzantine emperor Paleologus: "Show me just what Muhammad brought that was new, and there you will find things only evil and inhuman, such as his command to spread by the sword the faith he preached." Benedict didn't accept or reject the remark – that wasn't his point. His point was that Paleologus assumed that *acting unreasonably contradicts God's nature*. This was what Benedict wanted to discuss. The anti-Islam remark was used to lead to the point about reason and God's nature.

The anti-Islam remark shocked many. While Benedict didn't endorse the remark, he mentioned it without repudiating it. Many surmised that he agreed with it. Was Benedict anti-Islam? Or just careless? Or was he trying to shake up Islamic-Christian relations for the good (which was the ultimate effect)?

Reactions came quickly. Many criticized the pope, some defended him, some thought critics overreacted, and some added more anti-Islam remarks. The wisest reaction was a letter of 11 October 2006 (*Common Word* 2006) signed by 38 Muslim leaders and scholars throughout the world, written to correct misconceptions, point out Muslim-Christian similarities, and call for dialogue. This became in 2007 a longer letter to the pope and 26 other Christian leaders, signed by 138 Muslim leaders. This later became a book (*Common Word* 2009) featuring the 2007 letter, now endorsed by over 300 Muslim leaders and 460 organizations, with responses from over 60 Christian leaders (including Benedict). The tone is positive, puts away petty divisions, and exemplifies the GR attitude mentioned earlier: "Understand the other's faith as you would like your own faith to be understood."

Common Word says that Muslims and Christians, who together make up over half the world's population, need to live together in peace and justice. It appeals to the two love norms (of God and neighbor) that both groups share. Islam has "So invoke the Name of your Lord and devote yourself to Him with a complete devotion" (Qur'an 73:8) and "None of you has faith until you love for your neighbor what you love for yourself" (the Islamic GR). The document also endorses the right to choose one's own religious beliefs and claims that this too is part of the Qur'an (2:256): "Let there be no compulsion in religion." This brought relief to many and the hope that all Islamic countries might respect religious freedom.

The pope responded positively (*Common Word* 2009: 229–36). Without denying differences, he emphasizes that both groups worship the one God and must show mutual respect and solidarity. He mentions the Islamic GR and love norms. So the pope's snafu led to the two faiths coming closer together. One can only hope that this new spirit of mutual respect and understanding will trickle down to Muslims and Christians throughout the world.

Recall 11 September 2001, when a few Muslim terrorists killed nearly 3,000 people in the U.S. I expected a GR response from my country, but it didn't happen. What would a GR response look like?

Applying GR wisely involves Kita (Know-Imagine-Test-Act). First, we need to *know* how our actions affect others. Why were so many Muslims (and not just the terrorists) angry with America? What were their perceptions, feelings, sensitivities? Could there be things that America was doing wrong? Understanding must come first – preferably a mutual understanding. Then we'd *imagine* ourselves in their place and *test* for GR inconsistencies. Finally, we'd *act* on policies that we can endorse regardless of where we imagine ourselves in the situation. Preferably, both sides would do all this. The GR approach is slow and requires effort; but it's the only way to a just and lasting peace.

Instead, we gave an ultimatum and then used violence. We did little to understand the other side. We said: "We're good, the extremists are evil, and we must defend ourselves." The extremists *were* doing evil,[1] we were doing a *mix* of good and evil, and we'd defend ourselves better by promoting mutual understanding. Violence should only be a last resort. Returning force for force, instead of first trying GR, encourages further retaliation. And it goes against central teachings of both Christianity and Islam.

3.1d   Other Abrahamic religions

An *Abrahamic* religion, again, is one that traces its origin through Abraham. The main examples are Judaism, Christianity, and Islam. Another example, Samaritanism, is mentioned in the gospels but today has only a few members; it accepts one God and the Torah.

Thomas Jefferson and many early Americans were Deists; they accepted God but rejected revelation and organized religion. Jefferson liked the Bible's moral teaching, but he didn't see it as divinely inspired; his Jeffersonian Bible had just the gospel verses he agreed with, including GR (Jefferson 1804: 13). Searching http://www.deism.com shows that many Deists today are devoted to GR as "rule number one." While calling Deism "Abrahamic" is stretching the term, Deism's beliefs do come historically through Abraham.

Mormonism was founded by Joseph Smith (1805–44) and is strongest in Utah.[2] GR occurs in the Book of Mormon (3 Nephi 14:12) as well as the Christian Bible, which Mormons also accept. A Web search revealed that many Mormons are strongly committed to GR.[3]

The Bahá'í faith, with members across the world, is Abrahamic. Bahá'í was founded in Persia (now Iran) by Prophet Bahá'u'lláh (1817–92). According to Bahá'ís, there is one God and ultimately just one religion. God revealed himself through prophets that include Abraham, Moses, Krishna, Buddha, Zoroaster, Christ, and Muhammad. The latest is Bahá'u'lláh, but more will come. Humanity is one family, men and women are equal, prejudice must be eliminated, and world peace must be upheld by a world government.[4]

Bahá'í scriptures say much about love and GR. Bahá'u'lláh's *Epistle to the Son of the Wolf* has this passage:

---

[1] Http://ammanmessage.com/media/911-Islamic-Condemnation.pdf has a long collection of strong "Islamic statements against the terrorism of 9/11." Sites http://ammanmessage.com and http://acommonword.com are useful to counter negative stereotypes against Muslims.
[2] There's controversy on whether Mormonism, Christian Science, and the Unification Church are Christian. If they aren't, then at least they're Abrahamic.
[3] The Book of Mormon is at http://scriptures.lds.org, while http://www.mormon.org has general information about Mormonism.
[4] On GR in Bahá'í, see Rost 1986: 115–55 & 175–9. Http://reference.bahai.org/en has texts.

Be generous in prosperity, and thankful in adversity. Be worthy of the trust of your neighbor, and look upon him with a bright and friendly face. Be a treasure to the poor, an admonisher to the rich, an answerer to the cry of the needy.... Be fair in your judgment, and guarded in your speech. Be unjust to no man, and show all meekness to all men. Be as a lamp unto them that walk in darkness, a joy to the sorrowful, a sea for the thirsty, a haven for the distressed, an upholder and defender of the victim of oppression. Let integrity and uprightness distinguish all your acts....

It also has GR: "If your eyes be turned towards justice, choose for your neighbor that which you choose for yourself."

The Bahá'í have seven temples throughout the world, and I've often visited the one just north of Chicago. This beautiful temple is open to all faiths. It has Bahá'u'lláh quotations that highlight God's greatness and love, and the oneness of humanity and religion. The information center has posters with quotations from Bahá'u'lláh (the second with GR):

O ye children of men! The fundamental purpose animating the Faith of God and His Religion is to safeguard the interests and promote the unity of the human race, and to foster the spirit of love and fellowship among men.

The children of men are all brothers, and the prerequisites of brotherhood are manifold. Among them is that one should wish for one's brother that which one wishes for oneself.

The Bahá'í faith captures well what is common to the Abrahamic religions.

Christian Science was founded by Mary Baker Eddy (1821–1910). Her 1885 *Science and Health* puts GR as the last of six tenets of Christian Science: "To do unto others as we would have them do unto us."

The Unification Church was founded by Sun Myung Moon (1920–) and is strongest in Korea. It emphasizes GR, including its global, interfaith dimension and our need to live for others (A. Wilson 2007).

3.2   Non-Abrahamic religions

Religions that didn't originate through Abraham are more diverse. They may believe in one God, many gods, or no gods. So the theology varies. What is common is GR and concern for others. We'll start with the religions of India.

3.2a   Hinduism

Hinduism, India's traditional religion, is the world's third largest religion, after Christianity and Islam. Hinduism started before recorded history and has no known founder. It's colorful and complex, with vast scriptures, complicated spiritualities, and many gods (which are often taken to represent different aspects of one supreme God). Hindus tend to be tolerant of doctrinal differences, believing that ultimate reality is beyond our ability to put into words.[1]

Hinduism has the whole GR package – the positive and negative forms and the claim that GR sums up how we're to live:

> One who practices the religion of universal compassion achieves his highest good.... One who regards all creatures as his own self, and behaves towards them as towards his own self ... attains happiness.... One should never do to another what one regards as hurtful to one's own self. This, in brief, is the rule of righteousness.... In happiness and misery, in the agreeable and the disagreeable, one should judge of effects as if they came to one's own self. (Mahabharata bk. 13: Anusasana Parva, §113)

GR applies to our treatment of all creatures, including animals (who may be humans reincarnated). Here are further GR-like statements:

- Good people do good to others without expecting any good in return.... Good people, understanding their own feelings, can understand the feelings of others. (Mahabharata bk. 2: Sabha Parva, §72)
- One who regards all creatures as his own self enjoys the fruits of the holy places. (Mahabharata bk. 3: Vana Parva, §82)
- One who casts an equal eye everywhere, regarding everyone as his own self and the happiness and misery of others as his own, is deemed to be the best. (Mahabharata bk. 6: Bhishma Parva, §30)
- One who is kind and who practices righteousness ..., who considers all creatures on earth as his own self, attains the Immortal Being; the true God is ever with him. (Songs of Kabir 65)

Four Hindu beliefs give GR a context. (1) There's a divine cosmic order about how to live (for example, to be truthful and chaste, and to treat others as you want to be treated). Violating this order brings harm to us and to others.

(2) There's *karma*, a moral law of cause and effect: you tend to get the treatment you give others. So you'll receive good if you give good to others, and you'll receive needless suffering if you give this to others. Hindu karma works in part through reincarnation; your soul after death returns to live in another human or animal body, higher or lower depending on your moral character. So the good or evil you do to others comes back to you, if not in this life then in the next. Many religions see life as a spiritual journey toward God; the Hindu journey covers several lifetimes. Doing evil sets us back, while doing good moves us forward, both in this life and in the next.

(3) In some mystical way we're all identical to our neighbor and to God. If I harm my neighbor then I harm myself, for my neighbor *is* myself.

---

[1] On GR in Hinduism, see Rost 1986: 25–31 and Neusner & Chilton 2008: 146–56. Http://www.sacred-texts.com/hin/maha and http://www.sacred-texts.com/hin/sok have texts.

(4) Our true happiness is the spiritual possession of God, who is within us. Spirituality is more than morality, but it must include moral intentions.

Hinduism has a caste system. In the Veda, the world was created from the dismembered god Purusha. Brahmins, made from the head, are leaders, intellectuals, and priests; they abstain from meat and alcohol. Kshatriyas, from the arms, are warriors. Vaisyas, from the thighs, do farming, ranching, and business. Sudras, from the feet, do physical labor. Untouchables (touching them contaminates upper castes) are lower and outside the caste system. Society works best if each group follows its proper function (as in Plato's *Republic*). Which caste one is born into depends on how one lived in a previous life; a good life moves you up, while a bad life moves you down. So those of lower caste are getting what they deserve, being punished for sins of a previous life. The caste system remains influential, even though India outlawed it in 1948.

Mahatma Gandhi (1869–1948) opposed British rule over India and the harsh treatment of the untouchables (whom he called "the children of God"). While a firm Hindu, Gandhi was influenced by other faiths and claimed to be also Jewish, Christian, Islamic, and Buddhist. He preached non-violent resistance to British rule. He was committed to truth, faith, vegetarianism, simple living, and universal justice and love toward all faiths, races, and castes. He said that we can't claim to have God on our side if we act immorally. He also said that we'll all end up blind and toothless if we all follow "An eye for an eye and a tooth for a tooth." He's called "the father of India" for helping to bring India's independence. He influenced the anti-apartheid movement in South Africa and Martin Luther King's non-violent resistance in the United States.

Hinduism gave the West karma, methods of prayer and spirituality, non-violent resistance, and yoga. When I did yoga this morning, the DVD instructor started with the traditional Sanskrit greeting "Namaste" ("I honor the Divinity in you which is also in me"), spoken with hands together and a bow.

India produced other religions. Jainism, which began in the sixth century BC and somewhat resembles Hinduism and Buddhism, emphasizes compassion, non-violence, and the sacredness of all life; here are GR passages:[1]

- A monk should ... treat all beings as he himself would be treated. (Jaina Sutras, Sutrakritanga, bk. 1, 10:1–3)
- Indifferent to worldly objects, a person should wander about treating all creatures in the world as he himself would be treated. (Jaina Sutras, Sutrakritanga, bk. 1, 11:33)
- As I feel every pain and agony from death down to the pulling out of a hair – in the same way, be sure of this, all other living beings feel the same pain and agony as I, when they are ill-treated in the same way. For this reason no living being should be beaten, treated with violence, abused, tormented, or deprived of life. (Jaina Sutras, Sutrakritanga, bk. 2, 1:48)

[1] On GR in Jainism, see Rost 1986: 32–6. Http://www.sacred-texts.com/jai has texts.

- As it would be to you, so it is to one you intend to kill. As it would be to you, so it is to one you intend to oppress. As it would be to you, so it is to one you intend to torment.... And so the righteous person ... does not kill nor cause others to kill. (Jaina Sutras, Akaranga Sutra, bk. 1, Lecture 5, 5:4)

Sikhism, which began 500 years ago, is strongly monotheistic and combines elements from Hinduism and Islam; here are GR-like passages:[1]

- Conquer your egotism. As you regard yourself, regard others as well. (Shri Guru Granth Sahib, Raag Aasaa 8:134)
- A true Guru is a friend to all; everyone is dear to Him. (Shri Guru Granth Sahib, Raag Wadahans 12:33)
- No one is my enemy, and I am no one's enemy. God, who expanded His expanse, is within all; I learned this from the True Guru. I am a friend to all; I am everyone's friend.... By His Grace, I am cured of the disease of egotism. (Shri Guru Granth Sahib, Raag Dhanaasaree 14:12)

When I once attended Sikh worship, t-shirts were sold saying *Karma*. Given karma, GR is only a small step – since then to get the treatment I want I must give others that same treatment.

3.2b   Buddhism

Siddhartha Gautama (c. 563–483 BC), who started Buddhism, was born a Hindu to a royal family in India. Being distressed by suffering he saw outside the palace, he became an ascetical monk, denying himself pleasure and eating almost nothing. Later he found this empty and turned to a "middle way" of moderation, shunning both luxury and self-denial. At age 35, he achieved *enlightenment* while sitting under a Bodhi tree, and henceforth was called "Buddha" (enlightened one). He attained wisdom, compassion, virtue, and freedom from hatred and desire. He remembered events from a previous life and saw how our deeds influence our next life. He achieved *nirvana*, so by not being reborn he'd avoid future suffering. But out of compassion for others, he returned to the world and taught his path to enlightenment.[2]

Buddhism teaches four noble truths: (1) Life involves suffering. (2) We suffer because we have unhealthy desires that we can't fulfill. (3) We can avoid suffering by avoiding these desires; this brings nirvana – a peaceful, happy existence now and the freedom from being reborn into another life after our death. (4) We can avoid suffering and achieve enlightenment through the

---

[1] On GR in Sikhism, see Rost 1986: 111–4. Http://www.sacred-texts.com/skh has texts. While many Web sites give the Sikh GR as "Treat others as you would be treated yourself," references are obscure and I haven't found this in the Sikh scriptures.
[2] On GR in Buddhism, see Neusner & Chilton 2008: 116–45 and Rost 1986: 37–41. Reilly 2008 reinterprets GR using Buddhist ideas.

eightfold path: living rightly about beliefs, intentions, speech, actions, work, effort, mindfulness, and concentration.

Buddhism teaches *karma*, that the good or evil we do to others will come back to us, now or in a future life. Its five precepts forbid killing or harming sentient beings, stealing, adultery, lying, and intoxicating drinks and drugs. Buddhism also teaches GR:

> Look where you will, there is nothing dearer to man than himself; therefore, as it is the same thing that is dear to you and to others, hurt not others with what pains yourself. (N. Canon Dhammapada 5:18, Rockhill 1883: 27)

This next passage similarly appeals to self-love:

> The King said to the Blessed One: "Just now I was with Queen Mallika. I asked her, 'Is there anyone dearer to you than yourself?' "'No, your majesty,' she answered. 'There is no one dearer to me than myself. And what about you, your majesty? Is there anyone dearer to you than yourself?' "'No, Mallika. There is no one dearer to me than myself.'" On realizing the significance of that, the Blessed One exclaimed: "Searching all directions, one finds no one dearer than oneself. In the same way, others are fiercely dear to themselves. So one should not hurt others if one loves oneself." ("Raja Sutta: The King," Pali Canon Tipata, Khuddaka Nikaya, Udana 5:1, http://www.accesstoinsight.org/tipitaka/kn/ud/ud.5.01.than.html)

Some Western thinkers similarly argue that if my concern for myself gives value to what happens to me, then your concern for yourself must give value to what happens to you. But then I should be concerned about both – my good and yours. Here's another such passage that exhibits GR reasoning:

> The disciple reflects: "Here am I, fond of my life, not wanting to die, fond of pleasure and averse to pain. If someone would deprive me of my life, it would not please me. If I, in turn, were to deprive another such person of his life it would not please him. For that state unpleasing to me must be unpleasing to him; and so how could I inflict that upon him?" As a result of such reflection he abstains from taking the life of creatures and encourages others so to abstain. (Samyuttanikaya 55:7, http://www.accesstoinsight.org/lib/authors/bodhi/wheel282.html)

GR connects with two important Buddhist virtues: peace of mind and compassion. The peaceful serenity suggested by Buddha statues goes well with these next passages, about how to respond to evil done to us:

> "He insulted me, hit me, beat me, robbed me" – brooding on this increases violence. "He insulted me, hit me, beat me, robbed me" – not brooding on this decreases violence. Violence increases through violence but decreases through non-violence. (Yamakavagga: Pairs, Pali Canon Tipata, Khuddaka

Nikaya, Dhammapada 1:3–5, http://www.accesstoinsight.org/tipitaka/kn
/dhp/dhp.01.than.html)

If a man foolishly does me wrong, I will return to him the protection of my
ungrudging love; the more evil comes from him, the more good shall go
from me. (Sermon on Abuse, like "Love your enemies," http://www
.sacred-texts.com/bud/btg/btg58.htm)

Treating others as bad as they treat us (revenge) divides people; it brings
violence and inner torment. Being forgiving and non-violent to others, as we
want them to be to us, unites people; it brings inner peace and serenity. This
next quote, from the Dalai Lama, is about compassion:

We all want to be happy and free from misery. In Tibet, the teachings of the
Buddha have been a strong and pervasive influence. From these we have
learned that the key to happiness is inner peace. The greatest obstacles to
inner peace are disturbing emotions such as anger and attachment, fear and
suspicion, while love and compassion, a sense of universal responsibility are
the sources of peace and happiness. (S. Johnson 1996: xiii–xiv)

The world-religions expert Karen Armstrong (2009: 370f) says that all major
religions teach *compassion* (in the root sense of "the ability to *feel with* the
other," com-passion = feeling with), and that compassion is the virtue (good
character trait) that corresponds to the golden rule.

Buddhism evolved different branches. Most branches don't believe in gods;
but some believe in many gods or one supreme God, and some see Buddha as
divine. Some branches have rational philosophies; others (like Zen) delight in
paradoxes, like the sound of one hand clapping. Some have belief systems,
while others are agnostic about beliefs. Some stress prayer, while others are
more secular. Some believe in one Buddha, while others believe in many
Buddhas or that all are called upon to become Buddha.

Some Buddhist branches believe in a self that continues through time (from
infant to child to adult) and in personal survival and heavenly bliss. Other
branches reject a genuine self, claiming that what we misleadingly call the
"self" is merely a collection of experiences.[1] So the Harry Gensler of ten years
from now will be a collection of experiences too, but it won't be *me* in any
significant sense. So why should "I" be concerned for "my" future pleasures
instead of for "yours"? This no-self (selfless) view undermines self-interest and
encourages an impersonal concern for good wherever it occurs.

Many from other faiths are impressed by Buddhist meditation, non-violence,
and a universal compassion that extends even to animals.

---

[1] Some Western thinkers have held similar things, including David Hume, William James, and
Derek Parfit. They have been opposed by thinkers like Roderick Chisholm and Richard Swin-
burne, who defend the belief in a self that literally persists through time.

3.2c   Confucianism

Confucius (c. 551–479 BC) greatly influenced Chinese thought. His *Analects* was one of the earliest books on ethics, coming before the *Nichmachean Ethics* of Aristotle (384–322 BC). While Aristotle gave definitions, alternative views, and complex reasoning, Confucius wrote as a sage – with proverbs, anecdotes, and brief dialogues. Both taught an elevated morality and set the tone for ethical thinking in their part of the world.[1]

Here are some ideas to ponder from Confucius's *Analects*:

- The wise consider justice, the unwise self-interest.
- You can still be happy if you have only coarse grain to eat, water to drink, and your arm for a pillow. Riches and honor without justice are like passing clouds.
- We can learn much from any two random people. We can imitate their good qualities and take their bad qualities as a warning.
- Goodness can't be out of reach since I attain it when I seek it.
- Rulers should ensure that a state has enough food, weapons, and trust. Weapons are the least important, trust the most important.
- The wise bring out the good in people, the unwise bring out the bad.
- Repay hatred with justice, and kindness with kindness.
- Demand much from yourself and little from others.
- Our lives degenerate if we love humanity but not learning.

Confucius says little about gods, karma, or the afterlife. He avoids paradoxical or mystical language. He focuses on how to develop concern for others.

When challenged to sum up his teaching, Confucius uses a negative GR:

> Tzu-kung asked, "Is there one word which can serve as the guiding principle for conduct throughout life?" Confucius said, "It is the word altruism (*shu*). Do not do to others what you do not want them to do to you." (Analects 15:23, in W. Chan 1963: 44)

Confucius uses 恕 (shu) for the GR virtue (good habit). "Shu" is sometimes translated as "reciprocity" or "fellow-feeling"; Holcombe 1904: 31 says that "shu" includes consideration for others, charity, forbearance, thoughtfulness for others, and mutuality of rights and interests. Confucius also says:

> A man of humanity, wishing to establish his own character, also establishes the character of others, and wishing to be prominent himself, also helps others to be prominent. (Analects 6:28, in W. Chan 1963: 31)

> [Humanity] is to love men. (Analects 12:22, in W. Chan 1963: 40)

GR occurs twice more in the Analects (5:11 & 12:2, in W. Chan 1963: 28 & 39).

[1] On GR in Confucianism, see W. Chan 1955, Dubs 1951a, Ivanhoe 1990, Jung 1969, Neusner & Chilton 2008: 157–69, Nivison 1996, Nussbaum 2003, Roetz 1993, Rost 1986: 47–53, Rowley 1940, and Wattles 1996: 15–26. Http://www.sacred-texts.com/cfu has Confucian texts.

In a work attributed to his grandson, Confucius repeats GR and gives four examples, noting that he's not always been able to live up to GR:

> What you do not wish others to do to you, do not do to them. There are four things in the way of the superior man, none of which I have been able to do: to serve my father as I would expect my son to serve me..., to serve my ruler as I would expect my ministers to serve me..., to serve my elder brothers as I would expect my younger brothers to serve me..., to treat friends as I would expect them to treat me. (Doctrine of the Mean 13:4, in W. Chan 1963: 101)

Classical Confucianism is more a philosophy than a religion. Some forms of Confucianism add gods, temples, worship, and venerating Confucius.[1]

Mo Tzu (c. 479–438 BC), who lived after Confucius, founded Mohism. Mo Tzu was more radical, insisting that we should have the same degree of love for all, not preferring our child's good to that of a stranger. He writes (from bk. 4 of the Book of Mozi (or "Mo Tzu") from http://ctext.org/mohism):

- Suppose that everybody in the world loves universally, loving others as one-self... When everyone regards other persons as his own person, who will rob? So there would not be any thieves or robbers.... If everyone in the world will love universally ... the world will be orderly.
- Universal love is to regard the state of others as one's own.... A person of universal love will take care of his friend as he does of himself, and take care of his friend's parents as his own. So when he finds his friend hungry he will feed him, and when he finds him cold he will clothe him.
- One who objects to universal love will yet prefer to put his trust in someone who practices it. So the objector shows his attraction to universal love in his actions – there is a contradiction between his word and his deed. So opposing universal love is incomprehensible.

The last example appeals to consistency.

3.2d   Taoism

Taoism (Daoism) for centuries in China was the chief rival to Confucianism and Buddhism. Taoism accepts many gods, is mystical and poetic, and emphasizes meditation and worship. It gave us acupuncture, Tai Chi, and Yin-Yang. While Laozi's popular Tao Te Ching book dates back to about the fourth century BC, it formulates a much older tradition.[2]

Tao (or Dao, pronounced "DOW") means "way" or "road." Tao is the unspeakable primal reality from which everything else comes. Tao isn't God, but

---

[1] My GR t-shirt (§1.1) uses 水 (the ideogram for "water") for Confucianism, as is often done; but Confucianism has no standard, universally recognized symbol.
[2] On GR in Taoism, see Rost 1986: 42–46. Http://www.sacred-texts.com/tao has Taoist texts.

that from which the gods and universe came. Tao Te Ching starts by saying that the Tao that can be put into words isn't the true Tao; then, paradoxically, it says much about Tao, using the word 82 more times.[1]

Our duty is to follow Tao. We do this by following nature and interfering as little as possible. So it's wrong to build a dam that blocks a river's natural flow to the sea. We need to live spontaneously and follow instinct. We do badly when we follow social convention or theory, as Confucius was seen as doing. The best rulers interfere little and are compassionate and flexible.

Despite appealing to spontaneity, Taoism has standard norms and virtues. It forbids killing, lying, stealing, and adultery. It has three great virtues: love (compassion, kindness); moderation (simplicity in life, which often includes abstaining from meat and alcohol); and modesty (humility). Tao Te Ching 13 & 49 have GR-like statements (in W. Chan 1963: 145 & 162):

- The only king worthy of governing is one who values and loves his kingdom as if it were himself.
- To those who are good to me, I am good; and to those who are not good to me, I am also good; and thus all get to receive good.

The later T'ai-Shang Kan-Ying P'ien has perhaps the clearest Taoist versions of love-your-neighbor and GR (Suzuki & Carus 1906: 12):

- With a compassionate heart, turn toward all creatures.
- Regard your neighbor's gain as your own gain and your neighbor's loss as your own loss.

The traditional Vinegar Tasters painting teaches how Taoists view their rivals. Confucius, Buddha, and Laozi are tasting vinegar. Confucius, with a sour face, sees the world as clashing with how we ought to live. Buddha, with a bitter face, sees life as full of suffering and unfulfilled desire. But Laozi, with a big smile, sees nature (Tao) as good and lives in harmony with it. This painting emphasizes the diversity of Eastern thinking and is good to counter those who simplistically contrast "the Eastern approach" with "the Western approach," as if all Easterners think the same and all Westerners think the same.

Japanese Shintoism accepts many gods. Here are some Shinto sayings:[2]

- Be charitable to all beings, love is God's representative.
- Do not forget that the world is one great family.
- Even the wishes of an ant reach to heaven.
- The heart of the person before you is a mirror. See there your own form.

---

[1] This is like Ludwig Wittgenstein's *Tractatus*, which gives a theory of reality but then says that the most important things (including his theory) cannot be put into words.
[2] While these sayings are often ascribed to Shintoism, I couldn't find their source in any general translation of the Shinto scriptures.

I like the mirror idea. I envision a smartphone app that shows, when we act toward another, a transformed video where the same thing is done to us.

3.2e   Other religions

Many see the first recorded GR as "Do to the doer to cause that he do," from ancient Egypt's "The Eloquent Peasant" story, about 1800 BC.[1] But the saying's translation is disputed and it takes much stretching to see it as GR.

Zoroastrianism, an ancient Abrahamic-resembling religion from Persia, has two main GRs: "That character is best that doesn't do to another what isn't good for itself" and "Don't do to others what isn't good for yourself."[2]

Many ancient Greek and Roman polytheists supported GR. The Chapter 5 chronology gives dozens of examples, from the Greek Homer (c. 700 BC) to the Roman Emperor Alexander Severus (222–35 AD).

Africa provides one of my favorite GR sayings. From the Yoruba people in Nigeria comes "One who is going to take a pointed stick to pinch a baby bird should first try it on himself to feel how it hurts."[3] Ogunyemi 2010: 35 & 40f has related Yoruba proverbs, along with originals in the Yoruba language:

- The kind-hearted are full of joy. (Compare with Buddhism.)
- The house of the kind-hearted does not burn down completely; it is that of the wicked that burns down completely. (Neighbors will give more help to a kind person, so the good you do will come back to you.)
- As sensitive to pain as are the rats' little ones, so also sensitive to pain are the birds' little ones.
- Whenever you break a stick in the woodland, you should consider what it would feel like if it were yourself who was thus broken.

The baby-bird proverb may have evolved from the stick proverb.

The Church of Scientology supports GR. Its founder, L. Ron Hubbard, in 1981 published an ethics guide, *The Path to Happiness*, with two GR chapters.

GR religions noted so far include Judaism, Christianity, Islam, Deism, Mormonism, Bahá'í, Christian Science, Unification, Hinduism, Jainism, Sikhism, Buddhism, Confucianism, Mohism, Taoism, Shintoism, Zoroastrianism, Greco-Roman polytheism, Yoruba, and Scientology. Section 3.3 adds Brahma Kumaris, Native Religions, Neo-Paganism, Theosophism, and Unitarianism. We need more research into other religions, especially tribal ones.

Augustine (400c), who in his early life went through various religions and

---

[1] The original source for this is J. Wilson 1956: 121. Http://www.jimloy.com/egypt/peasant.htm translates the hieroglyphics verse as "Give me justice for the wrong that was done to me" while http://www.rostau.org.uk/ep/EPAlign/Peasant/guest90.html has "Doer for the one who always does for you" or "Act for the one who acts for you." The passage is obscure.

[2] On GR in Zoroastrianism, see Neusner & Chilton 2008: 65–75; my quotes are from p. 68.

[3] While this is all over the Web, I couldn't find the original source. Wattles 1996: 9 & 193 gives further African and Native American GR sayings.

philosophies, recognized about 400 AD that GR was part of the wisdom of all nations. People today are rediscovering this same insight.

3.2f Atheism

Atheists (who say there's no God) and agnostics (who take no stand on God) often accept GR. These folks can feel neglected in interfaith-GR discussions. I recently got an e-mail from an atheist complaining (with some levity) about not having an atheism symbol on my GR t-shirt (§1.1):

> Why not an atheist GR shirt? Same rule for us, same logic, yes, just without the supernatural justifications. Any serious and thoughtful atheist likely supports GR in some form. Discussing ethics, morality, and religion without serious consideration of atheism leaves one, I think, with weak tea.

He was pleased when I told him that I'd have a section on atheism.

Atheists and agnostics can accept GR, but "without the supernatural justifications." They might accept GR as an intuitively self-evident principle, as part of a rational procedure, as a cultural convention, as a social contract for mutual advantage, as a socially useful rule, as reflecting their altruistic feelings, or as promoting their self-interest (§2.5 & ch. 12). Believers can accept GR on these grounds too; but they also have religious grounds. So GR can be a point of unity between believers (of all types) and non-believers.

3.3 Interfaith GR activists

An *interfaith GR activist* is one who goes beyond promoting GR in an academic context (as I do with my writing and teaching) to using GR to bring about change in the wider world, and especially in how various faiths relate to each other. Such activism can take many forms.

I noted earlier how multicultural the world is becoming. This mixing of peoples raises the question: "What do we have in common that can help us to live together?" People are increasingly finding part of the answer in GR. And they're encouraged and guided in this by *interfaith GR activists*. I'll here discuss three such activists from three different continents: Hans Küng from Europe (Germany), Paul McKenna from North America (Canada), and Mussie Hailu from Africa (Ethiopia). While there are many GR activists today (please forgive me for not mentioning more), these three are especially significant.

Hans Küng is a well-known Christian theologian. He wrote a GR global-ethics document that was approved by the Parliament of the World's Religions.[1]

---

[1] Küng & Kuschel 1993. See also Casanova 1999; Falk 1999; S. King 1995; Küng 1993, 1997, 2000, 2006; C. Lee 1995; Straus 1995; and Sullivan & Kymlicka 2007.

The first Parliament of the World's Religions, which met with the 1893 Chicago World's Fair, was the first formal, global meeting of Earth's religions. The parliament had a Christian Eurocentric bias and didn't include Tibetan Buddhists, Afro-Americans, or native Americans. But it was an important step. GR was prominent (Wattles 1996: 91 & 217n5f).

A century later, in 1993, the second Parliament of the World's Religions met in Chicago. Hans Küng was asked to write a global-ethics document to be voted on. Since Küng had no precedent for this, he was initially perplexed on what to do. He decided to write a draft on what was common to the religions and then revise it in light of reactions from many experts from different religions. The Parliament would discuss and vote on, but not modify, the document.

It wasn't easy to produce something that almost all could accept. The document had to compromise on whether to mention God (which Buddhists objected to, so "Ultimate Reality" was used instead), whether to support pacifism or women's rights, and so on. While some thought Küng's document was too Western, most thought it nicely expressed their own ideals. There was wide agreement on GR and the need for the document.

Küng's 20-page document is called "Towards a global ethic: An initial declaration." After sketching problems facing the world, it highlights the need for a *global ethic*: a consensus, not on everything, but on key norms that appeal to the religious and non-religious alike. One such norm is that every human being ought to be treated humanely. Another is GR:

> There is a principle which is found and has persisted in many religious and ethical traditions of humankind for thousands of years: What you do not wish done to yourself, do not do to others! Or in positive terms: What you wish done to yourself, do to others! This should be the irrevocable, unconditional norm for all areas of life, for families and communities, for races, nations, and religions. (Küng & Kuschel 1993: 23f)

There followed four commandments common to the various faiths:

- You shall not kill! Have respect for life!
- You shall not steal! Deal honestly and fairly!
- You shall not lie! Speak and act truthfully!
- You shall not commit sexual immorality! Respect and love one another!

These are explained in ways that all religions can accept. Finally, there is a call for all, whether religious or not, to follow their common ethic.

Every group overwhelming approved the document. It was signed by 143 representatives from Bahá'í, Brahma Kumaris, Buddhism, Christianity, Native Religions, Hinduism, Jainism, Judaism, Islam, Neo-Paganism, Sikhism, Taoism, Theosophism, Zoroastrianism, and Interreligious Organizations. Many religions had subgroups. So Judaism had Orthodox, Conservative, and Reformed signatures. Christianity had Orthodox, Protestant, Anglican, and

Roman Catholic signatures (the Catholics included Cardinal Bernadine of Chicago, Theodore Hesburgh of Notre Dame, Hans Küng of the University of Tübingen, a Vatican representative, religious sisters, and many others). And yes, the Dalai Lama signed the document along with over a dozen others who represented various branches of Buddhism.

And so, for the first time, representatives of the world's religions in 1993 formally agreed on a global ethic. This included GR (as "the irrevocable, unconditional norm for all areas of life"); the duty to treat everyone humanely; and commandments about killing, stealing, lying, and sexual immorality.

Paul McKenna, an interfaith lay minister with Scarboro Missions in Toronto, got interested in the golden rule in the 1980s while reading a book about world religions. This had a list, which he'd never seen before, of GR in many faiths. The list triggered a growing passion for GR, especially as a tool for unity. McKenna envisioned a poster that would display GR in various religions. The poster emerged in 2000. The earth is in the center. Continents are connected by longitude lines but not divided by national boundaries. Rays of yellow and blue radiate from the earth. Around the edge are symbols and GR sayings for 13 religions: Buddhism, Confucianism, Taoism, Sikhism, Christianity, Unitarianism, Native Spirituality, Zoroastrianism, Jainism, Judaism, Islam, Bahá'í, and Hinduism. A copy of the poster hangs in my office. It has sold 100,000 copies throughout the world, with copies in different languages and in many prominent places. The poster gives a powerful way to teach GR's global importance and presence in different faiths.

McKenna has had an impact that is both global and local. His http://www.scarboromissions.ca/Golden_rule is the most extensive GR site on the Web, with materials on GR workshops, GR meditations, GR school curricula, a GR movie (produced and directed by Tina Petrova), and much else. He also connects people across the world with a special interest in GR; I often get e-mails from him on GR. In Toronto, he's helped to create one-day interfaith GR retreats for high-school students; the students pray, sketch, sing, dance, and do skits about GR in different religions – emphasizing mutual understanding and respect for people who are different. When I visited Scarboro Missions in Toronto in August 2010, I saw that he had many people fired up about GR; I met with six who related their stories about how to apply GR, especially in educating children.

Why is the golden rule so special to McKenna? He's struck by GR's omnipresence. Since GR is common between peoples, religious and non-religious, from ancient times to the present, it has great moral authority. The rule is simple to understand (but not easy to live), universal (both in its occurrence and in its appeal as it challenges us to become better persons), and powerful (as it summarizes moral teachings about unity, non-violence, social justice, compassion, and cooperation between diverse groups). GR may be the best guide we have to help peoples of the world to live together in peace. To reflect on the golden rule is to reflect from the perspective of a universal wisdom.

If you search the Web for "golden rule," you'll find more and more people discovering GR and spreading the word. Multicultural mixing has moved many to look for values that express, not just the fashion of the moment, but what McKenna calls "a universal wisdom."

Mussie Hailu is an interfaith GR activist from Ethiopia. If you hear about the United Nations doing something with GR, or you see the leader of a country next to a GR poster, Hailu was likely involved.

Hailu uses interfaith dialogue to counter religious injustice and violence. He was a major force in creating the first interfaith organizations in Ethiopia. Later he was a founding member of URI, the United Religions Initiative (http://www.uri.org), which began as a UN analogue; if we can have *United Nations*, why can't we have *United Religions*? UN and URI often work together.

Hailu discovered McKenna's GR poster and spread it across Africa. He translated the poster into African languages and distributed perhaps 100,000 copies, including one to every African head of state. He sees GR as a path to peace, justice, and interfaith understanding.

Hailu pushed for an April 5 international golden rule day. This began in Ethiopia and was adopted by the United Nations and many countries. Having a GR day isn't, by itself, so important. There are many special days, and most have little impact. But it's a beginning, and it could evolve into something bigger. What could we do on a GR day? I envision interfaith GR services; parades featuring GR and various faiths; teachers instructing students about GR in world religions (which every schoolchild should know about); and talks and programs about GR (how it relates to evolution, for example, or how to apply it to business or sports or bringing up children). Today many of our celebrations involve just one faith, and this is fine; but a celebration that brings all faiths together would also be good to have. Sometimes divisive people get the most publicity, and a vibrant GR day could counteract this.

The number of interfaith organizations is growing (URI has 500 member organizations in 75 countries), and many emphasize GR. GR organizations include Paul Eppinger's Arizona Interfaith Movement (http://www.azifm.org); Karen Armstrong's Charter for Compassion (http://charterforcompassion.org), and Religions for Peace (http://religionsforpeace.org). Paul McKenna's http://www.scarboromissions.ca/Interfaith_dialogue/partners.php has further links. We see that GR is on the move.

I've come to know many of the GR people featured in this book, including Jeff Wattles, Paul McKenna, Mussie Hailu, and others. They are wonderful people and their example challenges me to become a better person.

3.4   Questions

(Q1) What is a *golden-rule saying,* what does it mean to say that GR is *in* a given religion, and is GR in *all* religions?

I take a *golden-rule saying* to be any saying fairly close to "What you want done (or not done) to yourself, do (or don't do) to others." Switching places is essential: we imagine the act done to us or to someone we love. So I don't see "Be kind to others" or "Love your neighbor" as GR sayings; but since they're related, I call them *GR-like* sayings. Whether "Love your neighbor *as yourself"* is a GR saying depends on how it's understood (§3.1a). I allow GR sayings to be applications (like "If you want others not to *cheat* you, then don't *cheat* them"), if the general rule is supported.

What about sayings that apply just to a limited group (like "Treat *those of your tribe* as you want to be treated")? For me, a *genuine GR saying* must apply to *everyone.* As groups develop, their morality often expands from applying to just a limited group to applying to everyone (ch. 8).

Sometimes it's disputed whether a religion has GR sayings. Wicca, for example, accepts "Do not harm" (often taken broadly to include "Do good") and karma (from which GR is only a small step). Some Wiccans see this combination as the Wiccan GR; but others say their religion has no GR.

GR could be in a given religion *explicitly* (in words) or *implicitly* (in how people live). Those who study indigenous or tribal religions sometimes say GR is *implicit* in such religions.[1] This makes sense, since people of such religions, when they hear GR, often take it to express how they try to live.

Finally, is GR present in *all* religions? While many religions have an explicit, clear, universal GR, it would be premature to conclude that such a GR is present in *all* religions. We need more research on indigenous or tribal religions, especially those less influenced by outside forces. I suspect that an explicit, clear, universal GR appears later, as human thought develops, but that at least the seeds of GR (perhaps an implicit GR limited to how tribal members are treated) is present in all, or nearly all, religions.[2]

(Q2) Won't this stress on what is common lead people to think that all religions are the same or that differences between them don't matter?

This is unlikely. To say that religions agree on GR isn't to say that they agree on all things. Consider the 1993 Parliament of the World's Religions. The

---

[1] Rost (1986: 21), who lived in Africa for 15 years, couldn't find a GR saying in many native African religions. But Azenabor 2008 argues that GR, even if not put into words, is a deep part of native African religions (see also Wiredu 1996: 29 & 41).

[2] Some groups that claim to be religions clearly reject GR. The so-called "World Church of Creativity" (Klassen 1991) has a "golden rule" that says "What is good for the White Race is the highest virtue; what is bad for the White Race is the ultimate sin." This isn't GR (Q1).

143 representatives who signed the global-ethics document all thereby agreed on some ethical essentials. But they continued to disagree on many other issues. After the meeting, the Vatican representative and the Dalai Lama didn't become indistinguishable. But they likely came to a deeper understanding of differences and a greater mutual respect.

(Q3) Shouldn't we Christians see our religion as "totally unique" instead of as "just one religion among many"?

As a Christian, I believe that Christianity is neither "totally unique" (since it shares much with other religions and took most of its Bible from Judaism) nor "just one religion among many." I believe that God can speak through other religions and that different religions can learn from each other. We saw earlier that Jesus in the gospels was often positive about people of other religions and praised them for their faith (§3.1b Q1).[1]

While I respect the beliefs of other religions, I'm sometimes perplexed about what personal attitude to take toward such beliefs. As a Christian, I accept the Creed and thus don't accept beliefs inconsistent with this. But much of what other religions teach – for example, that Buddha experienced enlightenment – is consistent with the Creed. As a Christian, I can hold that God enlightened and transformed Buddha, for his good and the good of his people. This doesn't clash with Christianity. Further beliefs about nirvana may clash; but some Buddhist views of nirvana are compatible with Christianity.

Practically all Christian thinkers say that God's greatness goes beyond what can be put into words. While Christian words help, God's greatness goes beyond them. So words from other traditions may help too.

(Q4) What can the various religious traditions teach us about GR?

---

[1] To learn about Christians who oppose interfaith activities, search for "Acts 4:12 Committee" on the Web. Acts 4:12 says that people are saved only under Jesus's name. Most commentators don't take this to mean that only those who *explicitly* accept Jesus will be saved. Instead they take it to mean that even those who don't explicitly accept Jesus, such as infants and non-Christians, can still in some way be saved through Jesus's power. Any interpretation of Acts 4:12 must account for passages like Acts 10:35, where Peter says, in the presence of the Roman soldier Cornelius, that those of every nation who fear God and act justly are acceptable to God.

Vatican II (http://www.vatican.va/archive/hist_councils/ii_vatican_council) was positive about other religions. *Nostra Aetate* 2 says: "The Catholic Church rejects nothing that is true and holy in these religions. She regards with sincere reverence those ways of conduct and of life, those precepts and teachings which, though differing in many aspects from the ones she holds and sets forth, nonetheless often reflect a ray of that Truth which enlightens all men." *Lumen Gentium* 16 says: "Those also can attain to salvation who through no fault of their own do not know the Gospel of Christ or His Church, yet sincerely seek God and moved by grace strive by their deeds to do His will as it is known to them through the dictates of conscience. Nor does Divine Providence deny the helps necessary for salvation to those who, without blame on their part, have not yet arrived at an explicit knowledge of God and with His grace strive to live a good life."

Let me sketch what I've gained from studying other traditions. First, what the other Abrahamic traditions (Jewish, Islamic, Bahá'í, etc.) say fits nicely with my beliefs. The Jewish scriptures are already part of my beliefs, the story about Hillel is helpful for those who complain that religion has too many rules, I like the Islamic stress on God's will and on GR also dealing with our desires, and I find Bahá'í inspirational. I also find useful Eastern teachings about GR. I like the high moral and spiritual tone of Hinduism, karma (which I accept in general terms), applying GR to animals (which the West needs to take seriously), the Buddhist stress on compassion and inner peace (which are part of Christianity too), and the wisdom of Confucius (which is compatible with Christianity). And GR's wide presence strengthens my Christian belief that we all have the moral law written on our hearts (Romans 2:14f).

> (Q5) Isn't it true that GR, while present in practically every religion, is considered significant only in Christianity and perhaps Confucianism?

Many Christians emphasize GR, while many others ignore it; Pope Benedict, for example, didn't mention GR in his letter on love or his book on Jesus in Matthew's gospel.[1] I don't know how important GR has been in other religions. People who don't appreciate GR need to understand it better.

I'm more concerned with the future. Representatives of the world's religions endorsed GR in their 1993 declaration (§3.3). For some of them, GR's value may have been a new discovery (despite GR being part of their religion). If so, then there's a growing appreciation for GR, as a common norm of great worth.

Here's an analogy. Suppose you have gold in your backyard but ignore it. Then you discover its value, and you say "What a wonderful thing I have!" Similarly a religion may have GR in its writings but not pay attention to it. Then it discovers its value, and it says "What a wonderful thing I have and others also have! May it help us to live together in peace and harmony!"

I'm a convert of another sort. While I've long appreciated GR, only recently have I emphasized its global and interfaith dimension. My 1969 GR master's thesis totally ignored this dimension and my GR doctoral dissertation (Gensler 1977: 1f) spent only two pages on it. To redeem myself a little, let me give a fine paragraph that I put into three books (Gensler 1996: 106, 1998: 112, and 2011a: 88) and later on the Web (http://www.harryhiker.com/gr):

> The golden rule, with roots in a wide range of world cultures, is well suited to be a standard that different cultures can appeal to in resolving conflicts. As the world becomes more and more a single interacting global community, the need for such a common standard is becoming more urgent.

This is now on over 75 Web pages (search for the first 12 words in quotes).

---

[1] Benedict 2005 & 2008. But Benedict mentions GR when discussing what Christians share with Muslims (Common Word 2009: 234) and with other groups (ch. 5: 2008).

(Q6) Do you really think different religions can use GR to get along?

Yes. Hard work may be needed to overcome prejudices, insensitivities, and hatreds. But the Kita way is clear: we need to *know* the other group, *imagine* ourselves in their place, *test* whether we're now willing that if we were in their place then we be treated as we treat them, and *act* on GR. If both sides follow this, they can learn to get along.

The major obstacle is divisive people who ignore what their religion says about GR and instead preach hatred towards other religions. Those who spread division are much the same, whether they be Jewish, Christian, Muslim, Hindu, or whatever. So harmony *between* religions requires a campaign *within* each religion to live GR toward those of other religions.

Some beliefs may lead to religious persecution despite GR. John Hick 1992: 157 mentions Christians who tortured others to accept their style of Christianity, based on the belief that these people would otherwise be damned to eternal torment. Given this belief (which virtually all Christians today reject as incompatible with God's love) the torturers could be willing that they be tortured under similar circumstances (to avoid eternal torment) and thus could be GR-consistent. As noted earlier, we need to get the facts straight before we apply GR. Here we need to get clearer on the nature of God, as loving.

> (Q7) Some religions teach a *positive* GR ("What you want done to yourself, do to others") while others teach a *negative* GR ("What you want *not* done to yourself, *don't* do to others"). These two forms are different; many think one form is flawed. But then the moral agreement between faiths is more apparent than real – and the interfaith GR is fake. (Anderson 2009)

This is an important objection to the interfaith GR. I later argue (ch. 10) that the positive and negative GR forms are logically equivalent and thus have identical logical implications. So both forms say the same thing.

> (Q8) GRs differ significantly between faiths. For example, Christianity's "Treat others as you want to be treated" is about *actions* while Islam's "Desire for others what you desire for yourself" is about *desires*. Actions differ from desires. (Wierzbicka 2001: 200–2)

The action and desire forms are different but complementary. Most people see morality as being about both actions and desires; if asked, they'd likely accept both GR forms. I argued earlier (§2.3) for both forms: Gold 1 is about actions while Gold 3 is about desires. GR is a family of related principles, not a single principle, and no one saying can exhaust GR.

GR formulas also have stylistic and cultural differences. One of my favorites is an African proverb: "One who is going to take a pointed stick to pinch a baby bird should first try it on himself to feel how it hurts." This proverb is vivid and concrete, not abstract and general. But it gives a lesson about how to treat not just baby birds but also humans and other sentient beings. So the proverb, while rooted in its own culture, is getting at a general truth.

It's unwise to emphasize subtle differences in wording between GRs of different traditions, especially since translations can vary significantly. So Matthew 7:12 is rendered as what we desire/want/wish/would/will that others do to-us/for-us/to-or-for-us. Chapters 1 and 2 took the general idea and then tried to express it carefully to make it as good an idea as possible.

Traditional religious GRs are folksy proverbs. They lack a same-situation clause and so lead to absurdities if taken literally (§§1.2–3 & 2.1a–b). This doesn't mean that these GR sayings are bad; it just means that we need to tidy up the wording if we want something that can be taken literally. Many people *live* GR more subtlely than how they *say* it (§2.1e).

> (Q9) Is your technically stated GR (Gold 1 in §§1.1 & 2.1d) plausibly attributed to Confucius, Hillel, and Jesus?

They had the basic insight but not the same words. Gold 1 expresses their basic insight with greater technical precision, so it can withstand objections and be applied more easily to difficult situations.

> (Q10) What groups most oppose a common GR across various religions?

The sharpest opponents are those who emphasize how religions differ and think that the emphasis on GR denies these differences. I'd respond that there are similarities and differences across religions, and to affirm one similarity isn't to deny the differences. Groups that differ greatly need to agree on some things, like GR, that can help them to live together in peace.

> (Q11) Isn't it cultural imperialism to use the Christian term "golden rule" to refer to similar teachings in other faiths?

According to Paul McKenna, a leader in this area, interfaith dialogue creates a shared vocabulary. Words like *karma*, *shalom*, and *tao*, from specific faiths, refer to things common to many faiths. This isn't cultural imperialism. *Golden rule*, which comes likely from Christians (but maybe from the pagan Severus – §11.3 Q2), is part of this shared vocabulary.

> (Q12) How does GR connect with the *faith and justice* mission of your Jesuit religious order?

GR is a *justice* norm that's rooted in my Catholic *faith* but also can be rooted in the faith (religious or otherwise) of everyone else on the planet. So GR, as the *interfaith-justice* norm, brings both ideas together.

(Q13) Why is GR so universal across humanity?

Various reasons can be given for GR's universality:

- Religious: God implanted GR in our hearts and revealed it in every religion.
- Biological: Evolution hard-wired GR into our genes and brains (§7.4).
- Psychological: Universal developmental stages lead to GR (§6.2).
- Sociological: Societies need GR to survive (§§7.2 & 8.1).
- Logical: GR forbids an inconsistency (ch. 1–2), and we all have a cognitive-dissonance drive to avoid inconsistency.

These explanations can work together.

(Q14) Why did God create a world with many religions but a common GR?

I don't know. Qur'an 5:48 suggests that God made us of different faiths to compete with each other in doing good. And a bumper sticker says "God is too big to fit into one religion." We all need to reflect on this question.

3.5   Composite GR message

Each verse has ideas from at least two faiths, as given earlier in this chapter:

Treat others as you want to be treated; what you want done (or not done) to yourself, do (or don't do) to another.
Love your neighbors; regard the joy or pain of another as your own.
Desire for others what you desire for yourself; let your heart be pure and your judgments fair.
Understand the feelings of others as you understand your own; the heart of another mirrors your own heart.
Love your enemies; if a foolish person does you wrong, respond with love.
Show peace or violence toward others, and they'll likely act that way toward you; the treatment you give is the treatment you'll get.
Fill your life with kindnesses, and you'll have joy; compassion brings contentment and inner peace.
Live as sons and daughters of one God; the world is one big family.

This nicely summarizes the GR message of the world's religions.[1]

---

[1] I got the idea for this from a paper by my student Ashley Marie Markiewicz. A good exercise is to take each verse and try to identify the faiths from which its elements are taken.

CHAPTER 4
A Socratic Dialogue

This chapter has a little dialogue that I wrote a few years ago. The dialogue summarizes my thinking about GR and puts it into a religious context. It also defends what is common to the world's monotheistic religions.

The dialogue's central figure, *Socrates*, shouldn't be too closely identified with the historical Socrates. The other figure, Aristides, is named after a second-century Athenian who may have been Christianity's first professional philosopher. Aristides defended Christianity to the Roman Emperor, who was persecuting Christians who, according to Aristides, "never do to others what they would not wish to happen to themselves."[1]

4.1 A consistency norm

Aristides: Where are you going, Socrates?

Socrates: I'm on my way to the forum. There's a sale on togas.

Aristides: Not so fast – I'd like to ask you some questions. Since you so often question others, can you object if others want to question you?

Socrates: Well no, assuming that the questioning is done in a similar way in similar circumstances. What do you want to ask me?

Aristides: Just this, Socrates. What is the most important principle about how to treat other people?

Socrates: You really like to ask big questions, don't you?

Aristides: I'm just following your example. Please don't evade answering.

Socrates: OK, the most important principle is the golden rule: treat others as you want to be treated. No other principle about how to treat others is more important than this.

Aristides: Indeed, there is much to commend the golden rule. Imagine how much better the world would be if we all followed it. People then seemingly wouldn't lie or steal or act cruelly toward others – since they surely don't want others to treat them that way.

---

[1] This dialogue is from Swindal & Gensler 2005: 523–31; footnotes are adapted. For more on Aristides, see Swindal & Gensler 2005: 41–6.

Socrates: Yes, and imagine what it would be like if rulers would ask how they themselves would want to be governed – and if nurses would ask how they would want to be treated while sick – and so on for others in society.

Aristides: Indeed, life would then be better for us all. Perhaps this is why the golden rule is so widely admired by the great masses of people.

Socrates: Yes, surely. Unfortunately the golden rule is sometimes more admired than followed. Have I answered your question to your satisfaction?

Aristides: No, I am disappointed with your answer.

Socrates: Why do you say that?

Aristides: Your answer is too ordinary; it is not the answer of an intelligent philosopher. Anyone with your expertise in criticizing ideas should see that the golden rule has serious defects.

Socrates: Like what?

Aristides: Suppose I am sick and want my doctor to remove my appendix; then, by the golden rule, I ought to remove my doctor's appendix. What could be sillier than that?

Socrates: I see your point. By the golden rule, I am to treat others as I want to be treated. So if I want my doctor to be polite to me, then I should be polite to her. And if I want her to remove my appendix, then I should remove her appendix. But the latter is silly.

Aristides: You understand my objection well. And I could give many further objections of a similar sort.

Socrates: I am impressed by the sharpness of your mind. Had I known of this, I would have answered in a more rigorous way.

Aristides: Please explain further.

Socrates: The popular masses have the golden rule, but they do not understand it correctly. They take it very literally, to mean something like "IF YOU WANT X TO DO A TO YOU, THEN DO A TO X," do they not?

Aristides: Yes, and this entails the absurdity: IF YOU WANT X TO REMOVE YOUR APPENDIX, THEN REMOVE X'S APPENDIX.

Socrates: The problem is that you, like the popular masses, take the golden rule too literally.

Aristides: Then how should I take it?

Socrates: Properly understood, the golden rule is a consistency principle. It forbids me to combine two things: (a) treating another in a given way, and (b) not being willing that I would be treated the same way in the same situation.

Aristides: Please explain further.

Socrates: Suppose your father is hard of hearing and you are deciding how loud to speak to him. How would you apply the literal golden rule to this case?

Aristides: I, with normal hearing, don't want my father to speak loudly to me; so I shouldn't speak loudly to him. This is silly, since it ignores differences in circumstances. Even if the other person is in a very different situation, I should treat him as I want to be treated myself, in my present situation.

Socrates: Exactly. Now how would you apply MY formulation?

Aristides: I'd imagine a reversed situation – where I have my father's properties, including not hearing well, and he has mine. Surely I'd desire that I'd be spoken to loudly in this situation; so I'd speak loudly to him.

Socrates: Exactly. And do you see that this role-reversal idea would also solve your appendix case, and many other problem cases?

Aristides: Yes, I see that your version, in which you imagine yourself in the other person's exact place (and thus having all the other person's properties) is a big advance. But it doesn't get around Immanuel Kant's objection.[1]

Socrates: And what is his objection?

Aristides: Suppose I am a judge about to sentence a criminal to jail. Now if I were in the exact place of the criminal then I wouldn't want to be sent to jail. So, by your golden rule, I shouldn't send the criminal to jail.

Socrates: Sorry, you misapplied my formulation. You shouldn't ask: "If I were in the exact place of this criminal (and thus had his desires about how he wants to me treated), then would I desire to be jailed?"

Aristides: Then what should I ask?

Socrates: You should ask: "Do I (now) desire that if I were in this criminal's exact place then I would be jailed?" A conscientious judge should be able to say YES to this – and desire that he would be jailed in a similar way if he acted as the criminal did.

Aristides: I think I grasp your point. But could you give me another example to make this distinction clearer?

Socrates: Suppose you have a two-year-old son who likes to put his fingers into electrical sockets – and the only way to stop him is by a spanking. Could you spank him, consistent with the golden rule?

Aristides: It seems not, since if I were in his exact place (and thus had the desires of a two-year-old), I wouldn't want to be spanked.

Socrates: You said it wrong again. Remember how we dealt with the case about the judge and criminal?

Aristides: OK Socrates, I understand it now. I should ask how I'm *now* willing that I'd be treated if I were in my son's exact place. Knowing what I do now, I surely desire that my parents would have spanked me in this situation – since this might save me from electrocution.

Socrates: Correct. The golden rule prescribes a consistency between my *present* actions and desires; it isn't about what I'd desire in different circumstances. The golden rule forbids me to combine two things: (a) treating another in a given way, and (b) not being willing that I would be treated the same way in the same situation.

Aristides: It's plausible that the golden rule is a consistency requirement; but how would you argue for this? Suppose I steal your toga, but I'm unwilling that if I were in your place then my toga be stolen. Why is this inconsistent?

Socrates: Does not consistency require that we make similar evaluations about similar cases (a requirement that I call "impartiality") – and that we keep

[1] Kant 1785: 97; see also §§1.4, 2.1c, 14.2, & 14.3c.

our moral beliefs in harmony with our actions, intentions, and desires (a requirement that I call "conscientiousness")?

Aristides: Yes. Impartiality and conscientiousness are kinds of consistency.

Socrates: Now suppose you are consistent and steal my toga. If you are conscientious, then you wouldn't do this unless you believed that this act was all right (permissible). And if you are impartial, then you wouldn't believe this unless you believed that it would be all right for the same thing to be done to you in the same circumstances. And if you are conscientious, then you wouldn't believe this unless you were willing that the same thing would be done to you in the same circumstances.

Aristides: So if I am conscientious and impartial, then I wouldn't steal your toga unless I'm willing that my toga be stolen in the same circumstances.

Socrates: Exactly.

Aristides: I must admit, Socrates, that your logic here is impeccable. And yet I have another question.

Socrates: Ask away.

Aristides: Can we deduce all our concrete duties from the golden rule – so that this rule is all we need for morality?

Socrates: No to both questions. First, we can't *deduce* our concrete duties from the golden rule. The rule, again, is a consistency principle – and thus a guide on how to be more consistent and hence more rational in our actions and moral beliefs; so it tells us to be consistent, but it doesn't tell us what to do or believe on concrete issues. Second, to apply the rule most adequately and rationally we need other things as well. We especially need knowledge about the case and the ability to imagine ourselves, vividly and accurately, in the place of the other person, on the receiving end of the action.

Aristides: This makes sense to me. And yet I have another question.

Socrates: The toga sale goes on for a few more hours. So ask away.

4.2 Morality and religion

Aristides: How does the golden rule connect with religion? Isn't it somewhere in the gospels?

Socrates: Yes, for example in Mathew 7:12, in the Sermon on the Mount, Jesus gives the golden rule to sum up the Jewish Bible ("the Law and the Prophets").

Aristides: Doesn't Jesus also use "Love your neighbor" to sum up the Jewish Bible? Then how do the two norms relate?

Socrates: The two are complimentary. "Love your neighbor" tells us to have concern for others, to promote their good and diminish their harm, and to do this for their own sake. Concern for others gives the highest motive for following the golden rule – which we might otherwise follow out of self-interest (treating others well so that they will treat us well) or habit or social conformity.

Aristides: But then how does the golden rule help "Love your neighbor"?

Socrates: "Love" is vague when we apply it to action. Suppose that you are a mother seeking to love your daughter – or the owner of a company seeking to love your employees. How do you do it? The golden-rule approach says: (1) get to know the people involved (here, your daughter or employees), especially their problems and how your actions affect them; (2) imagine yourself in their place; and (3) treat them only as you are willing that you would be treated in like circumstances. So the golden rule gives a useful way to apply "Love your neighbor" to concrete cases.

Aristides: OK, but how does all this relate to obeying God's will?

Socrates: God's will is that we follow the golden rule – and his will is the will of a being who is perfect in every way, including consistency, knowledge, and the ability to imagine the situation of another. So when we apply the golden rule in the way described, we are in effect trying to follow God's wisdom.

Aristides: Of course, our moral wisdom will always fall short of God's – since we are limited in our ability to be consistent, to know the facts, and to imagine ourselves in the place of another.

Socrates: You are exactly right.

Aristides: Just one more question. Is the golden rule unique to Christianity?

Socrates: Oh no; the golden rule is common to practically every religion and culture of the world. Confucius, Buddha, Zoroaster, the Rabbi Hillel, and others formulated it before Jesus did. As St. Paul said (Romans 2:15), the demands of the moral law are written on the hearts of people of all nations.

Aristides: Could atheists follow the golden rule?

Socrates: Yes, surely. Many atheists are good people and try to follow the golden rule; we believers have much common moral ground with such people.

Aristides: I recall your conversation with Euthyphro, where you said that morality is not based on religion. You maintained that something isn't good just because God desires it; instead, God desires good things because they are already good.

Socrates: Yes, I said something like that; but in those days I spoke of "the gods" instead of "God."

Aristides: Can religion add anything to morality and the golden rule?

Socrates: Certainly, religion can add a deeper dimension to every area of life. For example, believers hiking in the Grand Canyon will likely see it as manifesting the awesome power and beauty of the creator.[1] And believers doing science will likely see themselves as studying the work and plan of God.

Aristides: I see your general point. But could you focus more on the difference that religion makes to *morality*?

---

[1] I wrote the first draft of this dialogue while on a hiking trip, using a palm-sized computer in my backpack tent at night.

Socrates: First of all, believers see humanity as coming from a loving God with moral purposes – while non-believers see humanity as an accident in an amoral universe. So morality fits into the believer's worldview much better.

Aristides: Could you explain further.

Socrates: According to believers, we were created by an all-good, loving God – in his image and likeness – and destined to lead good and loving lives now and to enjoy eternal happiness with God in the hereafter. But God doesn't force this destiny on us; instead, he gave us free will, so we can choose to be loving and good – or to be selfish and bad.

Aristides: So for believers morality can take on a religious dimension?

Socrates: Yes. When I violate the golden rule, I'm not only being inconsistent and violating reason; I'm also going against why I was created in the first place. And I'm being an ungrateful jerk toward God, who has been so good to me and who, as the Father of us all, calls upon us to love one another.

Aristides: In contrast, the non-believer's morality seems so impersonal and impoverished.

Socrates: I would say that religion adds another dimension to morality, just as it does to other areas of life.

4.3 Science and religion

Aristides: There's another question, on a somewhat different topic, that I've wanted to ask you. I once heard you say that recent advances in science make atheism less plausible. Could you explain?

Socrates: First, recent science seems to give strong evidence for something that I taught in the *Timaeus* long ago [Swindal & Gensler 2005: 16] – namely that the universe had a beginning in time. It seems now that the universe started about 14 billion years ago with a "big bang" and has been expanding ever since.

Aristides: But isn't there also a multiple-big-bang theory, which says that the universe goes through an infinite cycle of expansions and contractions?

Socrates: Not many hold this today, since the force that would contract the universe would be gravity, and calculations show that the density of matter in the universe is probably not enough to make the contraction happen.[1] So our best current science supports the view that the universe is a one-shot process.

Aristides: But if the universe began to exist long ago, then surely something had to cause it to begin to exist – and what else could this be but a great mind?

Socrates: Yes, that seems plausible. Surely matter itself couldn't without circularity cause the beginning of the totality of matter (which is the universe); and so the only plausible cause would seem to be something like God.

Aristides: How does Mackie, your favorite atheist thinker, respond to this?

[1] Hawking 1998: 45–9.

Socrates: He says that atheists have two choices.[1] One choice is to say that science is wrong – and that the universe in fact had no beginning in time.

Aristides: So this approach would reject our best current scientific theory on the basis of one's religion (if we can call atheism a "religion")?

Socrates: Yes. The second choice is to say that the universe just popped into existence without a cause.

Aristides: This sounds implausible, although I can't prove it is impossible.

Socrates: Genesis says: "In the beginning, God created the heavens and the earth." Until the big bang theory, the atheistic alternative to this was: "There is no God, and the universe had no beginning – it always was and always will be."

Aristides: Atheists contended that a universe with no beginning or source was just as plausible as a God with no beginning or source. But science seems to show that the universe did in fact have a beginning.

Socrates: So atheists now, if they want to be scientifically up-to-date, have to instead say: "There is no God, but the universe about 14 billion years ago just popped into existence without any cause."

Aristides: This sounds far less plausible to me.

Socrates: But wait, it gets worse.

Aristides: Please explain how.

Socrates: Well, the physical laws and constants governing our universe have to be very precisely accurate in their values in order to make life possible. Steven Hawking gives this example: "If the rate of expansion one second after the big bang had been smaller by even one part in a hundred thousand million million, the universe would have recollapsed before it ever reached its present size."[2] Of course this would have prevented the evolution of life.

Aristides: So the expansion rate has to be correct to the 17th decimal place? This requires impressive engineering – or a remarkable coincidence!

Socrates: Other physical values that have to be "just right" for life to evolve include the gravitational constant "g," the strong nuclear force, the charge and mass of the proton, the speed of light, the energy of the electron, the density of ice, and the total mass of the universe. If we put random values into these constants, the resulting universe has an incredibly low chance of producing life.

Aristides: This strongly suggests that the universe was designed – and that the basic physical constants were set up by a very intelligent being who intended to produce life. But how do atheists respond?

Socrates: Again, they have two choices. One choice gives this alternative to Genesis: "There is no God, the universe about 14 billion years ago just popped into existence without a cause, and the basic physical laws and constants just happened (as a zillion-to-one coincidence) to be in the narrow range which would make life possible."

[1] Mackie 1982: 45–9. On the believer's side, see Craig 1994: 91–125.
[2] Hawking 1998: 126 (also 125–31). For more on the fine-tuning argument for God, see Collins 2006: 63–84, Flew 2007: 113–21, Gensler 2010: 111f & 2011b, Glynn 1997: 21–55, and Haisch 2006. Http://www.harryhiker.com/software has a computer-game version (Windows).

Aristides: This seems pretty implausible. What is their second alternative?

Socrates: Some atheists believe there are an infinity of parallel universes, each governed by a different physics; it was highly likely that some of these universes could produce life. Their alternative to Genesis says: "There is no God; but an infinity of parallel universes, each with a different set of basic physical laws and constants, just popped into existence without a cause; and our universe happens to be one of the very few of these that could produce life."

Aristides: This mental gymnastics makes my head spin! It all sounds crazy, although again I can't prove that it is impossible.

Socrates: Yes, I agree.

Aristides: So do you think that we should all base religion on science?

Socrates: No. While science can be a path to God, there are many such paths; others include feelings, religious instincts, and our search for meaning. But, since atheists often claim that their view is more scientific than old-fashioned religion, it is important to show that this is not so – and that scientific advances make atheism more difficult to hold than it was previously.

4.4 The problem of evil

Aristides: Please, just one more question. In light of all the suffering and evils in the world, how can you make sense of the belief that the world was created by a God who is all-powerful and all-good? Surely this isn't the sort of world that a perfect God would create.

Socrates: I'm not so sure that it isn't. Let me ask you a question. Suppose that you were a perfect God; what sort of world would you create?

Aristides: I don't know how to answer. Please give me some alternatives.

Socrates: Would you create the best of all possible worlds?

Aristides: Maybe there is no "best" possible world – just as there is no highest number. Maybe for each finite world there could be a better one. And maybe any decently good world requires free beings who are able to make a difference to the world, making it better or worse depending on how they choose; so then these free beings could, and perhaps would, bring evil into the world.

Socrates: Would you create a hedonistic paradise: a world with much pleasure and no pain, and a world in which our actions couldn't upset this?

Aristides: This sounds nice but not very meaningful. Since it wouldn't matter much how we acted, our actions wouldn't be significant.

Socrates: Would you create a world of great enjoyment, knowledge, and love – without suffering, ignorance, or hatred?

Aristides: How great is "great" here? There seem to be endless degrees of enjoyment, knowledge, and love – going along with the infinite gap between finite and infinite beings. And again, if our actions wouldn't matter much for the goods and evils of human life, then this world would seem to leave no significant function for human choice.

Socrates: Would you create a world where free beings can struggle meaningfully and lovingly against *evil*?

Aristides: I see the value of this. I am reminded of a story that I heard on the news. There was a divorcee on welfare with three children who were dying of an inherited disease. The woman could give up and drink away her problems – or struggle lovingly to make life as bearable as possible for her family. There is a chance for something of great value and beauty in a world where the freedom to love can make a significant difference.

Socrates: Yes, surely. It is hard to think of anything more precious.

Aristides: But again I am confused; I must admit that your question perplexes me. Please tell me, Socrates, how you would answer. If you were a perfect God, what kind of world would you create?

Socrates: I would create a world with two phases. The first phase would be a heroic struggle against evil (this present life); the second phase would be evil overcome (heaven). Each phase would incorporate values lacking in the other; but the two phases together would have a measure of completeness.[1]

Aristides: This sounds like the Christian idea of the cross and resurrection.

Socrates: Yes. And I believe that this is the kind of world that God did in fact create.

Aristides: I will have to reflect more on this and on the other matters that you have brought up; you gave me much to think about. But it is not fair to keep you longer. You'd better hurry to the forum before the stores close.

---

[1] The basic ideas here are from Hick 1977.

CHAPTER 5
A GR Chronology

> Early dates and attributions are uncertain. Quotes are often simplified or put into modern English. For more on an item, try the index or bibliography or a Web search. For more on GR history, I suggest Wattles 1996 and, if you read French, du Roy 2009 & 2012.

1,000,000 BC   The fictional Fred Flintstone helps a stranger who was robbed and left to die. He says "I'd want him to help me." GR thinking is born!

c. 1,000,000 BC–10,000 BC   Humans find that cooperative hunting works better. Small, genetically similar clans who use GR to promote cooperation and sharing have a better chance to survive.

c. 1800 BC   Egypt's "Eloquent peasant" story has been said to have the earliest known GR saying: "Do to the doer to cause that he do." But the translation is disputed and it takes much stretching to see this as GR. (See my §3.2e.)

c. 1450 BC–450 BC   The Jewish Bible has GR-like passages, including: "Don't oppress a foreigner, for you well know how it feels to be a foreigner, since you were foreigners yourselves in the land of Egypt" (Exodus 23:9) and "Love your neighbor as yourself" (Leviticus 19:18).

c. 700 BC   In Homer's Odyssey, goddess Calypso tells Odysseus: "I'll be as careful for you as I'd be for myself in like need. I know what is fair and right."

c. 624–546 BC   First philosopher Thales, when asked how to live virtuously, reportedly replies (according to the unreliable Diogenes Laertius c. 225 AD): "By never doing ourselves what we blame in others." A similar saying is attributed to Thales's contemporary, Pittacus of Mytilene.

c. 563–483 BC   Buddha in India teaches compassion and shunning unhealthy desires. His GR says: "There is nothing dearer to man than himself; therefore, as it is the same thing that is dear to you and to others, hurt not others with what pains yourself" (Dhammapada, Northern Canon, 5:18).

c. 551–479 BC   Confucius sums up his teaching as: "Don't do to others what you don't want them to do to you": 己所不欲勿施於人. (Analects 15:23)

c. 522 BC   Maeandrius of Samos (in Greece), taking over from an evil tyrant, says (according to the historian Herodotus c. 440 BC, in his Histories 3.142): "What I condemn in another I will, if I may, avoid myself." Xerxes of Persia c. 485 BC said something similar (Histories 7.136).

c. 500 BC   Jainism, a religion of India that promotes non-violence, compassion, and the sacredness of life, teaches GR: "A monk should treat all beings as he himself would be treated." (Jaina Sutras, Sutrakritanga, bk. 1, 10:1–3)

c. 500 BC   Taoist Laozi says: "To those who are good to me, I am good; and to those who are not good to me, I am also good; and thus all get to receive good." (Tao Te Ching 49) A later work says: "Regard your neighbor's gain as your gain and your neighbor's loss as your loss." (T'ai-Shang Kan-Ying P'ien)

c. 500 BC   Zoroaster in Persia teaches GR: "That character is best that doesn't do to another what isn't good for itself" and "Don't do to others what isn't good for you."

c. 479–438 BC   Mo Tzu in China teaches GR: "Universal love is to regard another's state as one's own. A person of universal love will take care of his friend as he does of himself, and take care of his friend's parents as his own. So when he finds his friend hungry he will feed him, and when he finds him cold he will clothe him." (Book of Mozi, ch. 4)

c. 440 BC   Socrates (c. 470–399 BC) and later Plato (c. 428–347 BC) begin the classical era of Greek philosophy. GR, while not prominent in their thinking, sometimes leaves a trace. As Socrates considers whether to escape from jail, he imagines himself in the place of the state, who would be harmed (Crito). And Plato says: "I'd have no one touch my property, if I can help it, or disturb it without consent on my part; if I'm a man of reason, I must treat the property of others the same way" (Laws). (Wattles 1996: 32–6)

c. 436–338 BC   Isocrates in Greece teaches GR as promoting self-interest (you do unto others so that they'll do unto you). He says: "Don't do to others what angers you when you experience it from others." GR then becomes common, in positive and negative forms, in Greco-Roman culture, in Sextus, Demosthenes, Xenophon, Cassius Dio, Diogenes Laertius, Ovid, and others. GR has less impact on Socrates, Plato, Aristotle, and early Stoics. (Meier 2009: 553f)

c. 400 BC   Hinduism has positive and negative GRs: "One who regards all creatures as his own self, and behaves towards them as towards his own self attains happiness. One should never do to another what one regards as hurtful to one's own self. This, in brief, is the rule of righteousness. In happiness and misery, in the agreeable and the disagreeable, one should judge effects as if they came to one's own self." (Mahabharata bk. 13: Anusasana Parva, §113)

384–322 BC Aristotle says: "As the virtuous man is to himself, he is to his friend also, for his friend is another self" (Nicomachean Ethics 9:9). Diogenes Laertius (c. 225 AD) reports Aristotle as saying that we should behave to our friends as we wish our friends to behave to us.

c. 372–289 BC Mencius, Confucius's follower, says (Works bk. 7, A:4): "Try your best to treat others as you would wish to be treated yourself, and you will find that this is the shortest way to benevolence."

c. 300 BC Sextus the Pythagorean in his Sentences expresses GR positively and negatively: "As you wish your neighbors to treat you, so treat them. What you censure, do not do." (Meier 2009: 554 & 628)

c. 150 BC Various Jewish sources have GR sayings. Tobit 4:16 says "See that you never do to another what you'd hate to have done to yourself." Sirach 31:15 says "Judge the needs of your guest by your own." And the Letter of Aristeas (see Meier 2009: 553f) says "Insofar as you [the king] do not wish evils to come to you, but to partake of every blessing, [it would be wise] if you did this with your subjects."

c. 30 BC–10 AD Rabbi Hillel, asked to explain the Torah while a Gentile stood on one foot, uses GR: "What is hateful to yourself, don't do to another. That is the whole Torah. The rest is commentary. Go and learn." The Aramaic has דעלך סני לחברך לא תעביד. (Sanhedrin of the Babylonian Talmud 56a)

c. 20 BC–50 AD Jewish thinker Philo of Alexandria, in speaking of unwritten customs and ordinances, mentions first "Don't do to another what you'd be unwilling to have done to you." (Hypothetica 7:6)

c. 4 BC–27 AD Jesus proclaims love (of God and neighbor) and GR to be the basis of how to live. Luke 6:31 gives GR in the context of loving your enemies, later illustrated by the Good Samaritan parable. Matthew 7:12 says: "Treat others as you want to be treated, for this sums up the Law and the prophets"; the Greek has πάντα οὖν ὅσα ἐὰν θέλητε ἵνα ποιῶσιν ὑμῖν οἱ ἄνθρωποι, οὕτως καὶ ὑμεῖς ποιεῖτε αὐτοῖς· οὗτος γάρ ἐστιν ὁ νόμος καὶ οἱ προφῆται.

c. 4 BC–65 AD Roman Stoic Seneca teaches GR: "Let us put ourselves in the place of the man with whom we are angry; we are often unwilling to bear what we would have been willing to inflict," "Let us give in the way we would like to receive – willingly, quickly, and without hesitation," and "Treat your inferiors as you would be treated by your betters." GR fits well the ethics of the Stoics, who propose a natural moral law, accessible to everyone's reason, that directs us to be just and considerate toward everyone. (Wattles 1996: 39f)

c. 56 AD Paul's letter to the Romans 2:1–3 expresses a GR-like idea: "We condemn ourselves when we condemn another for doing what we do."

c. 65 AD The western text of the Acts of the Apostles 15:20 & 29 has a negative GR: "What you don't want done to yourself, don't do to others."

c. 70 AD "The Two Ways," a Dead Sea Scroll discovered in the 1940s, says: "The way of life is this: First, you shall love the Lord your maker, and second-ly, your neighbor as yourself. And whatever you don't want to be done to you, don't do to anyone else." (Wattles 1996: 47)

c. 80 AD The Didache, summarizing early Christian teachings, begins: "There are two paths, one of life and one of death, and a great difference between them. The way of life is this. First, you shall love the God who made you. Second, you shall love your neighbor as yourself. And whatever you wouldn't have done to you, don't do to another."

c. 90 AD The ex-slave Stoic Epictetus writes: "What you shun enduring your-self, don't impose on others. You shun slavery – beware of enslaving others!"

c. 90 AD The apocryphal gospel of Thomas attributes a negative GR to Jesus (verse 6): "Don't do what you hate."

c. 120 AD Rabbi Akiba says: "This is the fundamental principle of the Law: Don't treat your neighbor how you hate to be treated yourself." (G. King 1928: 268) His students support GR: Rabbi Eleazar ("Let another's honor be as dear to you as your own") and Rabbi Jose ("Let another's property be as dear to you as your own"). (Wattles 1996: 202)

c. 130 AD Aristides defends his fellow Christians, who "never do to others what they would not wish to happen to themselves," against persecution.

c. 150 AD The Ethiopian version of the apocryphal Book of Thekla ascribes a negative GR to Paul: "What you will not that men should do to you, you also shall not do to another."

c. 150–1600 Many Christians, seeing GR's wide acceptance across religions and cultures, view GR as the core of the natural moral law that Paul saw as written on everyone's heart (Romans 2:14f). GR is proclaimed as the central norm of the natural moral law by Justin Martyr, Origen, Basil, Augustine, Gratian, Anselm of Canterbury, William of Champeaux, Peter Lombard, Hugh of St. Victor, John of Salisbury, Bonaventure, Duns Scotus, Luther, Calvin, and Erasmus. (Reiner 1983 and du Roy 2008)

222–235   Roman Emperor Alexander Severus adopts GR as his motto (in Latin, *Quod tibi non vis fieri, alteri ne feceris*), displays it on public buildings, and promotes peace among religions. Some say GR is called *golden* because Severus wrote it on his wall in gold.

c. 263–339   Eusebius of Caesarea's GR prayer begins: "May I be an enemy to no one and the friend of what abides eternally. May I never quarrel with those nearest me, and be reconciled quickly if I should. May I never plot evil against others, and if anyone plot evil against me, may I escape unharmed and without the need to hurt anyone else."

349–407   John Chrysostom teaches GR: "Whatever you would that men should do to you, do to them. Let your own will be the law. Do you wish to receive kindness? Be kind to another. And again: Don't do to another what you hate. Do you hate to be insulted? Don't insult another. If we hold fast to these two precepts, we won't need any other instruction." (du Roy 2008: 91)

354–430   Augustine says that GR is part of every nation's wisdom and leads us to love God and neighbor (since we want both to love us). He gives perhaps the first GR objection: if we want bad things done to us (e.g., we want others to get us drunk), by GR we'd have a duty to do these things to others. He in effect suggests taking GR to mean "Whatever *good things* you want done to yourself, do to others." [Actually, he thought that *willing*, as opposed to *desiring*, is always for the good; so he formulated GR in terms of *willing*.]

610   Muhammad receives the Qur'an, which instructs us to do good to all (4:36) and includes the GR-like saying: "Woe to those who cheat: they demand a fair measure from others but they do not give it themselves" (83:1–3). Several Hadiths (Bukhari 1:2:12, Muslim 1:72f, and An-Nawawi 13) attribute this GR to Muhammad: "None of you is a true believer unless he wishes for his brother what he wishes for himself."

c. 650   Imam Ali, Muhammad's relative, says: "What you prefer for yourself, prefer for others; what you find objectionable for yourself, treat as such for others. Don't wrong anyone, just as you would not like to be wronged; do good to others just as you would like others to do good to you; that which you consider immoral for others, consider immoral for yourself."

c. 700   Shintoism in Japan expresses GR: "Be charitable to all beings, love is

God's representative. Don't forget that the world is one great family. The heart of the person before you is a mirror; see there your own form."

c. 810   The Book of Kells, a gospel book lavishly illustrated by Irish monks, illustrates GR as a dog extending a paw of friendship to a rabbit.

c. 890   King Arthur's Laws emphasizes GR: "What you will that others not do to you, don't do to others. From this one law we can judge rightly."

c. 1060   Confucian philosopher Zhang Zai writes: "If one loves others just as one is disposed to love oneself, one realizes benevolence completely. This is illustrated by the words 'If something is done to you and you don't want it, then for your part don't do it to others.'" (Nivison 1996: 67)

c. 1093   Muslim Abu Hamid al-Ghazali in his Disciplining the Soul (the section on discovering faults) uses GR: "Were all people only to renounce the things they dislike in others, they would not need anyone to discipline them."

1140   Gratian, the father of canon law, identifies natural law with GR: "By natural law, each person is commanded to do to others what he wants done to himself and is prohibited from inflicting on others what he does not want done to himself. Natural law is common to all nations because it exists everywhere by natural instinct. It began with the appearance of rational creatures and does not change over time, but remains immutable." (Pennington 2008)

c. 1170   Moses Maimonides's Sefer Hamitzvoth (positive commandment 208) says: "Whatever I wish for myself, I am to wish for another; and whatever I do not wish for myself or for my friends, I am not to wish for another. This injunction is contained in His words: 'Love your neighbor as yourself.'"

c. 1200   Inca leader Manco Cápac in Peru teaches: "Each one should do unto others as he would have others do unto him." (Wattles 1996: 192)

c. 1200   The Tales of Sendebar, a popular romance in many languages, ends with words from the sage Sendebar to a king of India: "'My request is that you don't do to your neighbor what is hateful to you and that you love your neighbor as yourself.' The King did as Sendebar counseled him and was wiser than all the sages of India." (Epstein 1967: 297–9)

c. 1220   Francis of Assisi, who often invokes GR, at least four times formulates it using a same-situation clause (the earliest such use that I'm aware of), as in "Blessed is the person who supports his neighbor in his weakness as he would want to be supported were he in a similar situation."

c. 1230   Muslim Sufi thinker Ibn Arabi sees GR as applying to all creatures: "All the commandments are summed up in this, that whatever you would like the True One to do to you, that do to His creatures." (See my §3.1c.)

1259   *Gulistan*, by the Persian poet Sa'di, has these verses, which are now displayed at the entrance of the United Nations Hall of Nations: "Human beings are members of a whole, In creation of one essence and soul. If one member is afflicted with pain, Other members uneasy will remain. If you have no sympathy for human pain, The name of human you cannot retain."

1265–74   Thomas Aquinas's *Summa Theologica* (I-II, q. 94, a. 4) says GR is common to the gospels and to human reason. He adds (I-II, q. 99, a. 1) that "when it is said, 'All things whatsoever you would that men should do to you, do you also to them,' this is an explanation of the rule of neighborly love contained implicitly in the words, 'You shall love your neighbor as yourself.'"

c. 1400   Hindu Songs of Kabir (65) teach GR: "One who is kind and who practices righteousness, who considers all creatures on earth as his own self, attains the Immortal Being; the true God is ever with him."

c. 1400   Sikhism from India teaches: "Conquer your egotism. As you regard yourself, regard others as well." (Shri Guru Granth Sahib, Raag Aasaa 8:134)

1477   Earl Rivers's *Dictes and Sayings of the Philosophers*, the first book printed in England, has (p. 70): "Do to other as thou wouldst they should do to thee. And do to noon other but as thou wouldst be doon to."[1]

c. 1532   Martin Luther's commentary on the Sermon on the Mount says of GR: "With these words Jesus now concludes his teaching, as if he said: 'Would you like to know what I have preached, and what Moses and all the prophets teach you? Then I will tell you in a very few words.' There is surely no one who would like to be robbed. Why don't you then conclude that you shouldn't rob another? See, there is your heart that tells you truly how you would like to be treated, and your conscience that concludes that you should also do thus to others." (Raunio 2001 is a whole book on GR in Luther.)

1553   The Anglican Book of Common Prayer's catechism says: "What is your duty towards your neighbor? Answer: My duty towards my neighbor is, to love him as myself. And to do to all men as I would they should do unto me."

1558   John Calvin's commentary on Matthew, Mark, and Luke says: "Where our own advantage is concerned, there is not one of us who cannot explain

---

[1] Http://eebo.chadwyck.com has Rivers's book and almost every book published in English from 1477 to 1700, including the British books mentioned here.

minutely and ingeniously what ought to be done. Christ therefore shows that every man may be a rule of acting properly and justly towards his neighbors, if he do to others what he requires to be done to him."

1568   Humfrey Baker uses the term "golden rule" of the mathematical *rule of three*: if a/b = c/x then x = (b × c)/a. At this time, "golden rule" isn't yet applied to "Do unto others" but rather is used for key principles of any field. Many British writers of this time speak of "Do unto others" but don't call it the "golden rule" (these writers include John Ponet in 1554, Giovanni Battista Gelli in 1558, William Painter in 1567, Laurence Vaux in 1568, John Calvin in 1574, Everard Digby in 1590, and Olivier de La Marcha in 1592).

1568   Laurence Vaux's Catechism says that the last seven commandments are summed up in "Do unto others, as we would be done to ourselves."

1599   Edward Topsell writes that "Do unto others" serves well instead of other things that have been called *golden rules*.

1604   Charles Gibbon is perhaps the first author to explicitly call "Do unto others" the *golden rule*. At least 10 additional British authors before 1650 use *golden rule* to refer to "Do unto others": William Perkins in 1606, Thomas Taylor in 1612 & 1631, Robert Sanderson in 1627, John Mayo in 1630, Thomas Nash in 1633, John Clark in 1634, Simeon Ashe in 1643, John Ball in 1644, John Vicars in 1646, and Richard Farrar in 1648.

1616   Richard Eburne's *The Royal Law* discusses GR. Several other writers called GR *the royal law* (after James 2:8), but this usage didn't catch on.

1644   Rembrandt's *Good Samaritan* drawing depicts a GR example.

1651   Thomas Hobbes sees humans as naturally egoistic and amoral. Morality comes from a social contract that humans, to further their interests and prevent social chaos, agree to. GR sums up morality: "When you doubt the rightness of your action toward another, suppose yourself in the other's place. Then, when your self-love that weighs down one side of the scale be taken to the other side, it will be easy to see which way the balance turns." (*Leviathan*, ch. 15)

1660   Robert Sharrock attacks Hobbes and raises GR objections, including the criminal example. (*De Officiis secundum Naturae Jus*, ch. 2, §11)

1671   Benjamin Camfield publishes a GR book (*A Profitable Enquiry Into That Comprehensive Rule of Righteousness, Do As You Would Be Done By*) and uses a same-situation clause (p. 61): "We must suppose other men in our condition, rank, and place, and ourselves in theirs." Later GR books by

Boraston, Goodman, and Clarke use similar clauses.

1672   Samuel Pufendorf's *On the Law of Nature and Nations* (bk. 2, 3:13) sees GR as implanted into our reason by God, answers Sharrock's objections, defends GR by the idea that we ought to hold everyone equal to ourselves, and gives GR quotes from various sources (including Hobbes, Aristotle, Seneca, Confucius, and the Peruvian Manco Cápac).

1677   Baruch Spinoza's *Ethics* (pt. 4, prop. 37) states: "The good which a virtuous person aims at for himself he will also desire for the rest of mankind."

1684   George Boraston publishes a short GR book: *The Royal Law, or the Golden Rule of Justice and Charity*. He says (p. 4): "Our own regular and well-governed desires, what we are willing that other men should do, or not do to us, are a sufficient direction and admonition, what we in the like cases, ought to do or not to do to them."

1688   John Goodman publishes a GR book: *The Golden Rule, Or The Royal Law of Equity Explained*. He sees GR as universal across the globe, deals with objections, and puts GR in a Christian context. GR requires "That I both do, or refrain from doing (respectively) toward him, all that which (turning the tables and then consulting my own heart and conscience) I should think that neighbor of mine bound to do, or to refrain from doing toward me in the like case."

1688   Four Pennsylvania Quakers sign the first public protest against slavery in the American colonies, basing this on GR: "There is a saying, that we shall do unto others as we would have them do unto us – making no difference in generation, descent, or color. What in the world would be worse to do to us, than to have men steal us away and sell us for slaves to strange countries, separating us from our wives and children? This is not doing to others as we would be done by; therefore we are against this slave traffic."

1690   John Locke's *An Essay Concerning Human Understanding* contends that the human mind started as a blank slate and thus GR can't be innate or self-evident (bk. 1, ch. 2, §4): "Should that most unshaken rule of morality, 'That one should do as he would be done unto,' be proposed to one who never heard of it, might he not without absurdity ask why? And then aren't we bound to give a reason? This plainly shows it not to be innate." (We *can* give a why for GR – see my §§1.8 & 2.1d and ch. 12–13. But what is Locke's "No belief that can be questioned is innate or self-evident" premise based on? Is it innate or self-evident, or how is it proved?)

1693   Quaker George Keith, in an influential pamphlet, gives the first anti-slavery publication in the American colonies. He writes: "Christ commanded,

All things whatsoever you would that men should do unto you, do you even so to them. Therefore as we and our children would not be kept in perpetual bondage and slavery against our consent, neither should we keep others in perpetual bondage and slavery against their consent."

1698 Quaker Robert Piles writes: "Some time ago, I was inclined to buy Negroes to help my family (which includes some small children). But there arose a question in me about the lawfulness of this under the gospel command of Christ Jesus: *Do unto all men as you would have all men do unto you.* We ourselves would not willingly be lifelong slaves."

1704 Gottfried Leibniz raises objection 8 (in my §14.3d), that GR assumes antecedent moral norms: "The rule that we should do to others only what we are willing that they do to us requires not only proof but also elucidation. We would wish for more than our share if we had our way; so do we also owe to others more than their share? I will be told that the rule applies only to a just will. But then the rule, far from serving as a standard, will need a standard."

1706 Samuel Clarke's *Discourse Concerning the Unchangeable Obligations of Natural Religion* proposes: "Whatever I judge reasonable or unreasonable, for another to do for me, that, by the same judgment, I declare reasonable or unreasonable that I in the like case should do for him. And to deny this either in word or action, is as if a man should contend, that though two and three are equal to five, yet three and two are not so."

1715 John Hepburn's *American Defense of the Golden Rule* says: "Doing to others as we would not be done by is unlawful. But making slaves of Negroes is doing to others as we would not be done by. Therefore, making slaves of Negroes is unlawful."

1725 Jabez Fitch's "Sermon on the golden rule" defends GR against objections and bases it on Christ's authority, abstract justice, and self-interest.

1739 David Hume's *A Treatise of Human Nature,* disputing those who see humans as essentially egoistic, argues that sympathy is the powerful source of morality (bk. 3, pt. 2, §1): "There is no human whose happiness or misery does not affect us when brought near to us and represented in lively colors."

1741 Isaac Watts's *Improvement of the Mind,* in discussing key principles in various fields, says: "Such is that golden principle of morality, which our blessed Lord has given us, Do that to others, which you think just and reasonable that others should do to you, which is almost sufficient in itself to solve all cases of conscience which relate to our neighbor."

1747 Methodism founder John Wesley says that GR "commends itself, as soon as heard, to every man's conscience and understanding; no man can knowingly offend against it without carrying his condemnation in his own breast." (Sermon 30, on Mathew 7:1–12)

1754 John Wollman protests slavery on the basis of GR: "Jesus has laid down the best criterion by which mankind ought to judge of their own conduct: *Whatsoever you would that men should do unto you, do you even so to them.* One man ought not to look upon another man, or society of men, as so far beneath him, but he should put himself in their place, in all his actions towards them, and bring all to this test: How should I approve of this conduct, were I in their circumstance and they in mine?"

1762 Jean-Jacques Rousseau's *Émile* (bk. 4) says: "The precept of doing unto others as we would have them do unto us has no foundation other than conscience and sentiment. When an expansive soul makes me identify myself with my fellow, and I feel that I am, so to speak, in him, it is in order not to suffer that I do not want him to suffer. I am interested in him for love of myself, and nature leads me to desire my well-being wherever I feel my existence."

1763 Voltaire, inspired by Confucian writings that Jesuits brought from China, says: "The single fundamental and immutable law for men is the following: 'Treat others as you would be treated.' This law is from nature itself: it cannot be torn from the heart of man." (du Roy 2008: 94)

1774 Caesar Sarter, a black ex-slave, writes: "Let that excellent rule given by our Savior, *to do to others, as you would that they should do to you,* have its due weight. Suppose that you were ensnared away – the husband from the dear wife of his bosom – or children from their fond parents. Suppose you were thus ravished from such a blissful situation, and plunged into miserable slavery, in a distant land. Now, are you willing that all this should befall you?"

1776 Humphrey Primatt's *On the Duty of Mercy and Sin of Cruelty to Brute Animals* uses GR: "Do you that are a man so treat your horse, as you would be willing to be treated by your master, in case you were a horse."

1776 Thomas Jefferson writes the Declaration of Independence: "We hold these truths to be self-evident; that all men are created equal; that they are endowed by their creator with certain unalienable rights, that among these are life, liberty, and the pursuit of happiness." But he owns hundreds of slaves. The poet Phillis Wheatley, a black ex-slave, complains about the inconsistency between American words and actions about freedom.

1777 *New England Primer* for children has this poem: "Be you to others kind and true, As you'd have others be to you; And neither do nor say to men, Whate'er you would not take again." Some added a retaliatory second verse: "But if men do and say to you, That which is neither kind nor true, Take a good stick, and say to men, 'Don't say or do that same again.'"

1785 Immanuel Kant's *Groundwork of the Metaphysic of Morals* has a footnote objecting to the "trivial" GR, that it doesn't cover duties to oneself or benevolence to others (since many would agree not to be helped by others if they could be excused from helping others) and would force a judge not to punish a criminal. Kant's objections (which I answer in §14.3c) lowered GR's credibility for many. Yet Kant's larger ethical framework is GR-like. His "I ought never to act except in such a way that I can also will that my maxim should become a universal law" resembles Gold 7 of my §2.3. And his "Treat others as ends in themselves and not just as means" is perhaps well analyzed as "Treat others only as you're willing to be treated in the same situation."

1788 John Newton's *Thoughts upon the African Slave Trade* begins with GR and condemns the trade. A former slave trader, Newton during a storm at sea converted to Christianity. He wrote the *Amazing Grace* hymn, which begins "Amazing grace, how sweet the sound, that saved a wretch like me!"

1791–1855 Liu Pao-nan's *Textual Exegesis of Confucius's Analects* says: "Don't do to others what you don't want them to do to you. Then by necessity we must do to others what we want them to do to us." (W. Chan 1955: 300)

1800s The Underground Railroad is a secret network of Americans who help black slaves escape into Canada. To raise funds, they sell anti-slavery tokens, imprinted with things like GR or a crouching slave with the words "Am I not a man and a brother."

1812 The Grimm Brothers' "The old man and his grandson" tells how a grandson reminds his parents to follow GR toward Grandpa (§§1.1 & 6.3).

1817–92 Bahá'u'lláh in Persia establishes the Bahá'í faith, which believes in one God and ultimately just one religion. God revealed himself through prophets that include Abraham, Moses, Krishna, Buddha, Zoroaster, Christ, Muhammad, and Bahá'u'lláh. Humanity is one family and needs to live together in love and fellowship. The Bahá'í GR says: "One should wish for one's brother that which one wishes for oneself."

1818 Sir Walter Scott's *Rob Roy* novel says: "'Francis understands the principle of all moral accounting, the great ethic rule of three. Let A do to B, as he would have B do to him; the product will give the conduct required.' My father smiled at this reduction of the golden rule to arithmetical form."

1818   The Presbyterian General Assembly uses GR to condemn slavery.

1826   Joseph Butler, in a sermon on self-deceit, says: "Substitute another for yourself, consider yourself as the person affected by such a behavior, or toward whom such an action is done: and then you would not only see, but likewise feel, the reasonableness or unreasonableness of such an action."

1827   Joseph Smith receives the *Book of Mormon*, which has GR: "Therefore, all things whatsoever ye would that men should do to you, do ye even so to them, for this is the law and the prophets" (3 Nephi 14:12).

1828   The Methodist *Christian Advocate* uses GR to protest America's treatment of Indians.

1836   Angelina Grimké's *Appeal to the Christian Women of the South* asks: "Are you willing to enslave your children? You start back with horror at such a question. But why, if slavery is no wrong to those upon whom it is imposed? Why if, as has often been said, slaves are happier than their masters, free from the cares of providing for themselves? Do you not perceive that as soon as this golden rule of action is applied to *yourselves* that you shrink from the test?"

1840   Arthur Schopenhauer's *On the Basis of Morality* puts compassion at the center: an action has moral worth just if its ultimate motive is the happiness or misery of another (and not our own). Here I directly desire the happiness (or misery-avoidance) of another as if it were my one.

1841   Sarah Griffin's *Familiar Tales for Children* has a poem: "To do to others as I would, That they should do to me, Will make me gentle, kind, and good, As children ought to be." Some add: "The golden rule, the golden rule, Ah, that's the rule for me, To do to others as I wish, That they should do to me."

1850   Rev. James Thornwell criticizes anti-slavery arguments by attacking GR, using Kant's 1785 criminal example.

1850   President Millard Fillmore, in his State of the Union Address, says: "The great law of morality ought to have a national as well as a personal and individual application. We should act toward other nations as we wish them to act toward us, and justice and conscience should form the rule of conduct."

1851   Mormon Brigham Young, asked about law in Utah, says: "We have a *common law* which is written upon the tablets of the heart; one of its golden precepts is 'Do unto others as you would they should do unto you.'"

1852   Harriet Beecher Stowe's *Uncle Tom's Cabin* explains slave life and gets people to imagine themselves in slave shoes. One episode features two ministers. One quotes "Cursed be Canaan" from the Bible and explains that God intends Africans to be kept in low condition as servants. A second repeats GR. As a slave "John, aged thirty" is separated from his wife and dragged off the boat with much sorrow, the second minister tells a slave trader: "How dare you carry on a trade like this? Look at these poor creatures!" Stowe's novel became, after the Bible, the best-selling book of the 19th century.

1853   Abraham Lincoln appeals to consistency: "You say A is white and B black, and so A can enslave B. It is color, then, the lighter having the right to enslave the darker? By this rule, you are to be slave to the first man you meet with a fairer skin than yours. You do not mean color exactly? You mean whites are intellectually superior to blacks, and therefore have the right to enslave them? By this rule, you are to be slave to the first man you meet with an intellect superior to yours."

1854   Charles Dickens's *Hard Times* novel protests poverty caused by greed. Sissy Jupe, asked to give political economy's first principle, is scolded for her answer, "To do unto others as I would that they should do unto me."

1854   Abraham Lincoln quips: "Although volume upon volume is written to prove slavery a very good thing, we never hear of the man who wishes to take the good of it, by being a slave himself."

1855   Frederick Douglass, a black ex-slave, writes: "I love the religion of our blessed Savior. I love that religion that is based upon the glorious principle, of love to God and love to man; which makes its followers do unto others as they themselves would be done by. If you demand liberty to yourself, it says, grant it to your neighbors. If you claim a right to think for yourself, allow your neighbors the same right. It is because I love this religion that I hate the slaveholding, the woman-whipping, the mind-darkening, the soul-destroying religion that exists in the southern states of America."

1858   Abraham Lincoln gives this GR evaluation of slavery: "As I would not be a *slave*, so I would not be a *master*." The next year, he says: "He who would *be* no slave, must consent to *have* no slave."

1860   Rev. John Dagg defends slavery. He says blacks are incapable of exercising civil liberty (so being freed would hurt them), masters ought to care for their slaves (but their occasional cruelty doesn't show that slavery is wrong), the Bible by not condemning slavery implicitly teaches that it's permissible, and the abolitionist GR is flawed (using Kant's 1785 criminal example). (My §8.5 has a rebuttal.)

1861   John Stuart Mill's *Utilitarianism* argues that our duty is to do whatever maximizes the sum-total of everyone's good (measured by pleasure and pain). He states: "In the golden rule of Jesus, we read the complete spirit of the ethics of utility. To do as you would be done by, and to love your neighbor as yourself, constitute the ideal perfection of utilitarian morality."

1865   Abraham Lincoln quips: "I have always thought that all men should be free; but if any should be slaves, it should be first those who desire it for themselves, and secondly, those who desire it for others. When I hear anyone arguing for slavery, I feel a strong impulse to see it tried on him personally."

1867   Matilda Mackarness's *The Golden Rule: Stories Illustrative of the Ten Commandments* helps British children learn right from wrong. This was published by Routledge, as is this present book.

1867   Rev. Robert Dabney uses Kant's 1785 criminal example to ridicule the abolitionist use of GR to condemn slavery.

1870   Felix Adler's "The freedom of ethical fellowship" says GR "may be defended on various grounds. The egoist may advise us so to act on grounds of enlightened self-interest. The universalist may exhort us to carry out the rule in the interest of the general happiness. The evolutionist may recommend it as the indispensable condition of social order and progress. The Kantian may enforce it because it bears the test of universality and necessity. The follower of Schopenhauer may concur on grounds of sympathy. Is it not evident that the rule itself is more certain than any of the principles from which it may be deduced? With respect to them, men have differed and will differ. With respect to the rule itself, there is practical unanimity."

1871   Charles Darwin's *Descent of Man* talks about ethics and evolution. He argues that animals with social instincts naturally develop a moral sense as their intellectual powers develop. Human morality evolves from a limited tribal concern to a higher, universal concern that's summed up in GR.

1874   David Swing's *Truths for Today* says: "The golden rule underlies our public and private justice, our society, our charity, our education, our religion; and the sorrows of bad government, of famine, of war, of caste, of slavery, have come from contempt of this principle."

1874   Henry Sidgwick's *Methods of Ethics* says: "The golden rule, 'Do to others as you would have them do to you,' is imprecise in statement; for one might wish for another's co-operation in sin. Nor is it true to say that we ought to do to others only what we think it right for them to do to us; for there may be differences in circumstances which make it wrong for A to treat B in the way it is right for B to treat A. The rule strictly stated must take some form as this: 'It cannot be right for A to treat B in a manner in which it would be wrong for B to treat A, unless we can find reasonable ground for difference of treatment.' Such a principle does not give complete guidance; but its truth is self-evident and common sense has recognized its practical importance." (My §2.1b sees this proposed rule as impartiality, not as GR.)

1879 *McGuffey's Fourth Eclectic Reader* has a story about a little girl Susan who learns GR from her mother and then returns money she was given by mistake. McGuffey Readers were widely used in American grade schools, had a high GR moral content, and sold 120 million copies between 1836 and 1960.

1885 Mary Baker Eddy's *Science and Health* puts GR as one of six tenets of Christian Science, which she founded: "We promise to watch and pray for that mind to be in us which was also in Christ Jesus; to do unto others as we would have them do unto us; and to be merciful, just, and pure."

1886 Josiah Royce's *Religious Aspects of Philosophy* suggests (my paraphrase): Treat others as if you were both yourself and the other, with the experiences of both included in one life.[1]

1886 Friedrich Nietzsche's *Beyond Good and Evil* despises "Love your neighbor" as suited only for slaves; he praises the will to power and domination. Exploiting others and dominating the weak is part of our nature; compassion frustrates how we're built. (Nietzsche is the philosopher whose ideas most oppose GR; ch. 7 on egoism discusses his objections.)

1893 The first Parliament of the World's Religions, which meets with the Chicago World's Fair, is the first formal, global meeting of the religions of the world. GR is prominent. (Wattles 1996: 91f)

1897 Edward Bellamy's *Equality* novel describes the utopian 21st-century Republic of the Golden Rule, characterized by love toward all.

1897–1904 Samuel "Golden Rule" Jones is mayor of Toledo, Ohio and tries to run the city on GR terms. He had run an oil company on GR. His workers were paid fairly, worked hard, and felt like they shared a common enterprise. When he had trouble with workers, he'd try to understand their situation, imagine himself in their place, and then decide what to do using GR. Jones put GR as: "Do unto others as if you were the others."

1898 Mark Twain, a critic of discrimination, in "Concerning the Jews" writes:

---

[1] I here begin to paraphrase central ideas of several moral thinkers in GR-like ways. I thus emphasize a common theme, but without denying wide disagreements on other points.

"What has become of the golden rule? It exists, it continues to sparkle, and is well taken care of. It is Exhibit A in the Church's assets, and we pull it out every Sunday and give it an airing. It has never intruded into business; and Jewish persecution is not a religious passion, it is a business passion."

1899 American poet Edwin Markham in "The Man With the Hoe" describes a poor man who was crushed by the greed of others. When asked how to deal with this problem, he answers: "I have but one solution – that is the application of the golden rule. We have committed the golden rule to heart; now let us commit it to life." (Jones 1899: 194, 397)

c. 1900? From the Yoruba people in Nigeria comes this GR: "One who is going to take a pointed stick to pinch a baby bird should first try it on himself to feel how it hurts."

1900 Wu Ting-Fang, a diplomat from China to the U.S., writes an open letter about how both countries need to be fair and honest in cooperating for mutual economic advantage. He appeals to GR, which he sees as part of his Confucian tradition and as the basis for morality.

1902 J.C. Penney in Kemmerer, Wyoming opens the Golden Rule Store, so called (http://www.jcpenney.net/about-us.aspx) because he founded his company on the idea of treating customers the way he wanted to be treated. In 1950, he published a book called *Fifty Years with the Golden Rule*.

1903 Jack London's *People of the Abyss* novel denounces urban poverty: "The golden rule determines that East London is an unfit place to live. Where you would not have your own babe live is not a fit place for the babes of other men. It is a simple thing, this golden rule. What is not good enough for you is not good enough for other men."

1903 George Bernard Shaw quips against the literal GR: "Do not do unto others as you would that they should do unto you. Their tastes may not be the same." He adds: "The golden rule is that there are no golden rules."

1905 Helen Thompson's "Ethics in private practice" applies GR to nursing: "Would you be in sympathy with your patient? Would you win her confidence? Then regard this poor sufferer in the light of someone dear to you; put her in that other's stead. Someone has said, 'In ethics, you cannot better the golden rule.' Suppose you render it, 'Do unto others as you would they should do unto yours.' This is *your* mother; this *your* sister; this *your* child."

1906 Edward Westermarck's *Origin and Development of the Moral Ideas* emphasizes moral diversity but claims that all nations agree on GR.

1907   The *School Days* song mentions GR in the curriculum: "School days, school days, Dear old golden rule days, Readin' and 'ritin' and 'rithmetic, Taught to the tune of the hickory stick."

1908   John Dewey's *Ethics* suggests (my paraphrase): Treat others in a way that considers their needs on the same basis as your own.

1911   The first *Boy Scout Handbook* has this quote from Theodore Roosevelt: "No man is a good citizen unless he so acts as to show that he actually uses the Ten Commandments and translates the golden rule into his life conduct."

1912   Arthur Cadoux's "The implications of the golden rule," besides defending GR from Kant's criticisms, argues that GR seeks the fullness of individual and communal life through harmonizing desires.

1914   Mason leader Joseph Newton ends *The Builders* by saying: "High above all dogmas that divide, all bigotries that blind, will be written the simple words of the one eternal religion – the Fatherhood of God, the brotherhood of man, the moral law, the golden rule, and the hope of a life everlasting!"

1915–8   *The Golden Rule Books*, based on a U.S. series with the same name, are published to help teach morality to public-school students in Ontario.

1916   C.D. Broad's "False hypotheses in ethics" says: "Suppose Smith were in my circumstances and did the action I propose to do, what should I think of that? If we strongly condemn it, we may be fairly sure that our proposed action is wrong and that our tendency to approve it is due to personal prejudice."

1920   Francis Walters's *Principles of Health Control* suggests: "As we want others to protect us from their germs, so we should protect them from ours."

1920   W.E.B. du Bois's *Darkwater* protests America's treatment of blacks: "How could America condemn in Germany that which she commits within her own borders? A true and worthy ideal frees and uplifts a people; a false ideal imprisons and lowers. Say to men, earnestly and repeatedly: 'Honesty is best, knowledge is power; do unto others as you would be done by.' Say this and act it and the nation must move toward it. But say to a people: 'The one virtue is to be white,' and the people rush to the conclusion, 'Kill the n*****!'"

1921   President Warren Harding's inauguration speech says: "I would rejoice to acclaim the era of the golden rule and crown it with the autocracy of service." But scandals plague his administration.

1922   Hazrat Khan's "Ten Sufi Thoughts" says "Although different religions, in teaching man to act harmoniously and peacefully, have different laws, they all meet in one truth: do unto others as you would they should do unto you."

1923   Charles Vickrey creates Golden Rule Sunday, celebrated in the U.S. on the first Sunday of December. Families eat a modest dinner and give the money saved to hunger relief. This later becomes International Golden Rule Sunday.

1923   Arthur Nash's *Golden Rule in Business* explains how applying GR in his clothing business, besides being right, leads to contented employees who work hard and to contented customers who return.

1923   Annette Fiske's "Psychology" applies GR to nursing: "Some people say every nurse should herself have had a serious illness in order that she may get the patient's point of view. There are few people, however, who do not know the meaning of pain and who do not have sufficient imagination, if they care to exert it, to realize what it means to lie in bed helpless. What is needed is that they should stop to consider these facts, that they should give thought to their patients' feelings as well as to their symptoms and the means to relieve them."

1925   The Coca Cola Company distributes gold-colored GR rulers to school children in the U.S. and Canada.

1929   Leonidas Philippidis writes a German dissertation on GR in world religions: *Die "Goldene Regel" religionswissenschaftlich Untersucht.*

1930   Sigmund Freud's *Civilization and Its Discontents* gives a psychological approach unfriendly to GR: "What decides the purpose of life is the pleasure principle. It aims at absence of pain and experiencing of pleasure. There is no golden rule which applies to everyone. 'Love your neighbor as yourself' is an excellent example of the unpsychological proceedings of the cultural super-ego. The commandment is impossible to fulfill." (See my ch. 7.)

c. 1930s   Henry Ford, suggesting the role of GR in business, says: "If there is any one secret of success, it lies in the ability to get the other person's point of view and see things from that person's angle as well as from your own."

1932   Leonard Nelson's *System of Ethics* suggests (my paraphrase): Treat others as if a natural law would turn your way of acting on you.

1934   Joyce Hertzler's "On golden rules" discusses GR from a sociological perspective: GR exists in almost all societies and is a simple and effective means of social control that works from within instead of imposing external rules.

1935   Edwin Embree's "Rebirth of religion in Russia" states: "The central teachings of Jesus were brotherly love without regard to race or caste, the golden rule of doing to others what we would have them do to us, peace, humility, communal sharing of goods and services, the abrogation of worldly treasure. These are directly opposed to just those things which the Christian nations have built their power upon: capitalism, armaments, individualism, disregard of a neighbor of a different race, material wealth."

1936   Dale Carnegie's *How to Win Friends and Influence People*, a self-help book that sold 15 million copies, is based on GR: "Philosophers have been speculating on the rules of human relationships for thousands of years, and there has evolved only one important precept. Zoroaster taught it to his followers in Persia twenty-five hundred years ago. Confucius preached it in China. Lao-tse, the founder of Taoism, taught it to his disciples. Buddha preached it on the bank of the Ganges. The sacred books of Hinduism taught it a thousand years before that. Jesus summed it up in one thought – probably the most important rule in the world: 'Do unto others as you would have others do unto you.' You want a feeling that you are important in your little world. You don't want to listen to cheap, insincere flattery, but you do crave sincere appreciation. All of us want that. So let's obey the golden rule, and give unto others what we would have others give unto us."

1936   George Herbert Mead's "The problem of society" asks: "If you are going to have a society in which everyone is going to recognize the interests of everybody else – for example, in which the golden rule is to be the rule of conduct – how can that goal be reached?"

1939–45   Nazi genocide kills six million Jews, in one of the greatest moral atrocities ever. What has led to the deterioration of GR thinking?

1940   Michael Rooney founds the Golden Rule Insurance Company. If you search the Web for "golden rule," you'll find GR restaurants, travel agencies, contractors, and tattoo parlors. And you'll find many groups with GR in their motto or mission.

1941   Paul Weiss's "The golden rule" argues that GR works only if we know what we want, what we want is what we ought to desire, and what is good for us is also good for others. He thinks these conditions are usually satisfied.

1942   Ralph Perry suggests (my paraphrase): Treat others in a way that an impartial observer would see as best satisfying all claims.

1943   C.S. Lewis's *Mere Christianity* (p. 82) says: "The golden rule sums up of what everyone had always known to be right. Really great moral teachers never introduce new moralities: it is quacks and cranks who do that."

1944 A young Martin Luther King wins a high-school speech contest about civil rights. He says "We cannot be truly Christian people so long as we flaunt the central teachings of Jesus: brotherly love and the golden rule."

1946 Jean-Paul Sartre's *Existentialism and Human Emotions* suggests (my paraphrase): Treat others as if everyone were going to follow your example (and so treat you the same way).

1948 Jean Piaget's *Moral Judgment of the Child* explains how interacting children move to a higher morality. Young children think revenge is fair: if someone hits you, it's right to hit back. Older children, seeing that this leads to endless revenge, value forgiveness over revenge. Mutual respect grows and expresses itself in GR.

1948 The United Nations Declaration of Human Rights, supported by most nations of the world, begins with a GR-like idea: "All human beings are born free and equal in dignity and rights. They are endowed with reason and conscience and should act towards one another in a spirit of brotherhood."

1948 Hans Reiner's "Die Goldene Regel" revives a German discussion on GR that had stalled since Kant's objection (1785). Reiner distinguishes various GR interpretations and tries to answer the objections of Kant and Leibniz.

1948 A high-school teacher in Los Angeles conducts an experiment. Seniors agree to follow GR with their families, without telling them, for 10 days. The results are dramatic. Students find that they get along much better with their families and like living this way, even though their families are perplexed. Many vow to live this way forever. (See my §6.3.)

1950 C.D. Broad's "Imperatives, Categorical and Hypothetical" says "A person ought never to treat others in a way he would not be willing to be treated by others."

1950 Albert Tucker creates the prisoner's dilemma, a game-theory story where two prisoners can do better for themselves if they cooperate instead of following their individual interests. Many discuss how this relates to GR.

1955 C.I. Lewis's *Ground and Nature of the Right* gives the basic rational imperative as "Be consistent in thought and action." This involves the idea that no way of thinking or acting is valid for anyone unless it's be valid for everyone else in the same circumstances. He gives GR-like norms: "Act toward others as if the effects of your actions were to be realized with the poignancy of the immediate – hence, in your own person" and "Act as if you were to live out in sequence your life and the lives of those affected by your actions."

1956 Ullin Leavell introduces the *Golden Rule Series* of books for moral teaching in public grade schools.

1956 Erich Fromm's *Art of Loving* says we distort GR if we see it as having us respect the rights of others while caring little about their interests. Instead, GR calls us to oneness and brotherly love.

1957 Leon Festinger's theory of *cognitive dissonance* explains that we're distressed when we find that we're inconsistent, and so we try to rearrange our beliefs, desires, and actions so that they all fit together. This can be applied to GR consistency: we're distressed when our action (toward another) clashes with our desire about how we'd be treated in a similar situation.

1957 Damon Knight's novel *Rule Golden* describes a reversed GR enforced by aliens, whereby we receive the same treatment that we give to others. This makes it in our interest to follow GR.

1957 Chuck Berry's *School Days* song mentions GR in the curriculum: "Up in the mornin' and out to school, The teacher is teachin' the golden rule, American history and practical math, You study 'em hard and hopin' to pass."

1958 The *Golden Rule* ship travels into the Pacific to disrupt and protest the American nuclear atmospheric testing program (which was later stopped).

1958 Kurt Baier's *Moral Point of View* suggests (my paraphrase): Treat others only as you find acceptable whether you're on the "giving" or the "receiving" end.

1959 Dagobert Runes's *Pictorial History of Philosophy* begins with a sidebar listing GR sayings in nine world religions. Many similar lists would follow.

1960 Alan Gewirth's "Ethics and normative science" says: "There is good evidence that ideals like the golden rule have seemed no less cogent ethically than non-contradiction and experimentalism have seemed in science."

1961 Monk Thomas Merton's *New Seeds of Contemplation* (p. 71) explains God's will as requiring that we unite with one another in love: "You can call this the basic tenet of the Natural Law, which is that we should treat others as we would like them to treat us, that we should not do to another what we would not want another to do to us."

1961 Norman Rockwell's *Golden Rule* painting (showing GR and people from many religions, races, and nations) appears on the cover of the popular *Saturday Evening Post* magazine. The United Nations wasn't interested when

Rockwell wanted to paint it for them as a large mural. But the UN in 1985 put up a mosaic version and today you can buy several other versions of it at http://www.un.org/en (which has hundreds of GR references).

1962   Albrecht Dihle's *Die goldene Regel* studies GR in ancient Greece and sees it as about self-interest (you do for me and I'll do for you) and retaliation.

1963   Marcus Singer writes that GR has had little philosophical discussion, despite its importance and almost universal acceptance. He discusses absurdities that the usual formulas lead to (e.g., "If I love to hear tom-toms in the middle of the night, does GR tell me to inflict this on others?"). He suggests that we apply GR only to *general* actions (like treating someone with kindness) and not *specific* ones (like playing tom-toms). (But we still get absurdities like "If you want people to hate you (as you might do), then hate them.")

1963   R.M. Hare's *Freedom and Reason* argues that the logic of "ought" supports GR: You're inconsistent if you think you ought to do A to X but don't desire that A be done to you in an imagined reversed situation. Rational moral thinking requires understanding the facts, imagining ourselves in a vivid and accurate way in the other person's place, and seeing if we can hold our moral beliefs consistently (which involves GR). (My book builds on Hare.)

1963   Aldous Huxley writes: "In light of what we know about the relationships of living things to one another and to their inorganic environment – and what we know about overpopulation, ruinous farming, senseless forestry, water pollution, and air pollution – it has become clear that the golden rule applies not only to the dealings of human individuals and societies with one another, but also to their dealings with other living creatures and the planet."

1963   President John Kennedy appeals to GR in calling for an end to racism and segregation. He is assassinated later that year. In 1965, the U.S. government passes a Civil Rights Act; Senator Hubert Humphrey, in the act's closing defense, began by quoting GR.

1964   William Hamilton's "The genetic evolution of social behavior" looks at evolution as the survival of the fittest genes; this leads to sociobiology and discussions about *kin altruism, reciprocal altruism,* and GR's genetic basis.

1964   Erik Erikson's "The golden rule in the light of new insight" suggests (my paraphrase): Treat others in ways that strengthen and develop you and also strengthen and develop them.

1966   Bruce Alton at Stanford writes one of only two philosophy doctoral dissertations ever written on GR. He proposes this GR: "If A is rational about rule R, then if there are reasons for A to think R applies to others' conduct toward A, and A is similar to those others in relevant respects, then there are reasons for A to think R applies to A's conduct toward others."

1966 C.I. Lewis's *Values and Imperatives* says: "Suppose there are three persons involved in the situation: A, B, and C. Then nothing can be, for you, the right thing to do unless it should still be acceptable to you whether you should stand in the place of A, B, or C."

1966 Senator Robert Kennedy, in a speech in South Africa against racism, appeals to GR: "The golden rule is not sentimentality but practical wisdom. Cruelty is contagious. Where men can be deprived because their skin is black, others will be deprived because their skin is white. If men can suffer because they hold one belief, others may suffer for holding other beliefs. Our liberty can grow only when the liberties of all are secure."

1968 On December 6, R.M. Hare gives a GR talk at Wayne State University in Detroit. On this day, I (Gensler) become a GR junkie, with a love-hate relationship to Hare's GR approach.

1970 Thomas Nagel's *Possibility of Altruism* says (p. 82): "The rational altruism which I defend can be intuitively represented by the familiar argument, 'How would you like it if someone did that to you?' It is an argument to which we are all in some degree susceptible; but how it works, how it can be persuasive, is a matter of controversy."

1971 John Rawls's *A Theory of Justice* suggests (my paraphrase): Treat others only in ways that you'd support if you were informed and clear-headed but didn't know your place in the situation.

1971 Robert Trivers's "The evolution of reciprocal altruism" argues that organisms that mutually benefit each other will tend to develop an altruistic concern for each other. This is important for GR's genetic basis.

1977 Harry Gensler at Michigan writes one of only two philosophy doctoral dissertations ever written on GR. He proposes this (like Gold 1): "Don't act to treat another in a given way without consenting to yourself being treated that way in the reversed situation."

1978 Alan Gewirth's "The golden rule rationalized" points out absurdities that common GR sayings lead to and suggests instead (my paraphrase): Treat others only as it's rational for you to want others to treat you – and hence in a way that respects the right to freedom and well-being.

1979   Dr. Bernard Nathanson, who had fought to legalize abortion and later directed the world's largest abortion clinic, now appeals to GR against abortion. His *Aborting America* (p. 227) rejects his former view as falling "so short of the most profound tenet of human morality: 'Do unto others as you would have them do unto you.'"

1979   Milton Bennett attacks (the literal) GR as wrongly assuming that people have the same likes and dislikes. He proposes instead the platinum rule: "Treat others as *they* want to be treated." (See my §14.1.)

1981   Scientology founder L. Ron Hubbard publishes *The Path to Happiness*. Two chapters discuss easier-to-follow GRs: "Try not to do things to others that you would not like them to do to you" and "Try to treat others as you would want them to treat you."

1981–4   Lawrence Kohlberg's *Essays on Moral Development*, based on empirical data, claims that people of all cultures develop moral thinking through six stages. GR appears at every stage, but with higher clarity and motivation at higher stages. We treat others as we want to be treated because this helps us escape punishment (stage 1), encourages others to treat us better (2), wins Mommy's and Daddy's approval (3), is socially approved (4), is a socially useful practice (5), or treats others with dignity and respect (6). We can best teach children GR by discussing moral dilemmas with them and appealing to a stage just higher than what they use in their own thinking.

1983   Germain Grisez's *Christian Moral Principles* (q. 7-G) sees GR as about how to promote good and respect integral human fulfillment in an impartial way that doesn't unduly favor one person over another.

1983   Hans Reiner's "The golden rule and the natural law" sees GR as about autonomy. GR takes the standards I use in evaluating others and applies them to myself. GR, which all cultures recognize, is the basis for natural law. This suggests (my paraphrase): Treat others following the norms you use to evaluate their actions toward you.

1983   Jürgen Habermas's *Moral Consciousness and Communicative Action* suggests (my paraphrase): Treat others following norms that all affected parties could ideally accept.

1984   Robert Axelrod has game-theory experts propose strategies for playing matches made up of many prisoner-dilemma episodes. Strategies play against each other on a computer. The winner is TIT FOR TAT, which cooperates on the first move and then mimics what the other party did on the previous move (following "Treat others as they treat you").

1986   H.T.D. Rost, a Bahá'í, publishes *The Golden Rule: A Universal Ethic,* about GR in world religions.

1986   Pope John Paul II, speaking to world-religion leaders, says: "Jesus Christ reminded us of the golden rule: 'Treat others as you would like them to treat you.' Your various religious creeds may have a similar injunction. The observance of this golden rule is an excellent foundation of peace."

1987   Jeff Wattles's "Levels of meaning in the golden rule" proposes six levels, starting with sensual self-interest ("Do to others as you want them to gratify you") and ending with taking God's love for us as the model of how to love others ("Do to others as God wants you to do to them").

1990   Paul Ricoeur's *Oneself as Another* connects our self-identity with our narratives about ourselves, where we see ourselves as if we were another. The GR heart of morality is the opposite, to see another as ourself, to feel the pain of another is if it were our own, to act from love.

1990   Paul Ricoeur's "The golden rule," in talking about GR in Luke's gospel, argues that the context rules out a self-interested interpretation (we treat others well just so they'll treat us well), that "Love your enemies" is more demanding than GR but less useful as a general guide, and that the proper motivation for these norms is gratitude for God's love.

1992   Armand Volkas, a drama therapist whose parents were Holocaust survivors, conducts workshops that bring together children of Nazis and children of Holocaust victims. The participants role play, taking the other side's place. Volkas says: "If you can stand in somebody's shoes, you cannot dehumanize that person." (Wattles 1996: 117f)

1992   Harry Handlin's "The company built upon the golden rule: Lincoln Electric" says: "If, as managers, we treat our employees the way that we would like to be treated, we are rewarded with a dedicated, talented, and loyal work force that will consistently meet the needs of the marketplace."

1992   Donald Evans's *Spirituality and Human Nature* (p. 36) warns against a prideful misuse of GR: I follow GR toward others but don't let others help me.

1993   Mark Johnson's *Moral Imagination* says (p. 199): "Unless we can put ourselves in the place of another, enlarge our perspective through an imaginative encounter with others, and let our values be called into question from various points of view, we cannot be morally sensitive."

1993   The second Parliament of the World's Religions, led by theologian Hans

Küng, overwhelmingly supports a "Declaration for a global ethic" that calls GR "the irrevocable, unconditional norm for all areas of life." For the first time, representatives of the world's religions formally agree on a global ethic.

1993   The *Catechism of the Catholic Church* says three rules always apply in conscience formation: "One may never do evil so that good may result; the golden rule; and charity always respects one's neighbor and his conscience."

1993   Stephen Holoviak's *Golden Rule Management: Give Respect, Get Results* explains how to use GR in business.

1994   Neil Cooper's "The intellectual virtues" says: "The readiness to cooperate critically in humility and honesty for the advancement of knowledge is an intellectual virtue required by our goals. We should treat others in argument as we would have them treat us. This is the golden rule of the ethic of inquiry."

1994   Nicholas Rescher's *American Philosophy Today* proposes this GR (p. 72): "In interpreting the discussions of a philosopher, do all you reasonably can to render them coherent and systematic. The operative principle is charity: do unto another as you would ideally do for yourself."

1995   Dan Bruce's *Thru-Hiker's Handbook* for the AT (Appalachian Trail, a 2000-mile Georgia-to-Maine footpath that I completed in 1979) commends GR as "a good standard to live by on the AT (as in the rest of life), and the relatively few problems that develop among hikers could be eliminated if this simple rule were observed by everyone. It requires that you value and respect your fellow hikers in the same way you expect them to value and respect you."

1996   Jeff Wattles's *The Golden Rule*, the first scholarly book in English on GR since the 17th century, gives an historical, religious, psychological, and philosophical analysis of GR.

1996   Harry Gensler's *Formal Ethics* studies moral consistency principles, emphasizing GR.

1996   Confucian scholar David Nivison calls GR "the ground of community, without which no morality could develop: it is the attitude that the other person is not just a physical object, that I might use or manipulate, but a person like myself, whom I should treat accordingly."

1996   Tony Alessandra and Michael O'Connor's *The Platinum Rule* proposes that, instead of treating others as *we* want to be treated, we treat others as *they* want to be treated. (See my §14.1.)

1996 Amitai Etzioni's *The New Golden Rule* dismisses GR in two brief sentences and gives as the "new golden rule" a norm to balance shared values with individual freedoms: "Respect and uphold society's moral order as you would have society respect and uphold your autonomy." (See my §11.1 Q14.)

1997 Nancy Ammerman's "Golden rule Christians" gives a sociological analysis of liberal Christians who emphasize doing good more than orthodoxy.

2000 Paul McKenna, an interfaith GR activist with Scarboro Missions in Toronto, creates a poster that teaches GR's global importance and presence in the world's religions. The poster has sold 100,000 copies across the globe, with copies in different languages and many prominent places.

2000 Richard Kinnier's "A short list of universal moral values" summarizes research into which values are common to nearly all societies. GR is seen as the clearest and most impressive universal value.

2000s DUO ("Do unto others" – connecting GR with volunteer work to help the larger community) and TEAM ("Treat everyone as me" – emphasizing people helping each other within a given school, sports team, company, or military unit) become popular models for implementing GR.

2001 Tom Carson's "Deception and withholding information in sales" uses GR to determine the duties of salespeople. Carson has us look at proposed practices from the standpoint of the salesperson (who must earn a living), the customer (who wants a good product for a reasonable price), and the employer (who needs to sell products). Any action we propose as permissible must be something we'd consent to in the place of any of the three parties.

2001–9 Republican President George W. Bush in at least eighteen speeches uses some variation of this distinctive GR phrasing: "Love your neighbor just like you'd like to be loved yourself."

2001 Terrorists on 11 September crash hijacked planes into the World Trade Center and the Pentagon, killing 3,000 people. A key challenge of the 21st century arises: How can diverse religions live together in peace? This same day, Leslie Mezei is to interview Paul McKenna about his interfaith GR poster (see http://www.interfaithunity.ca/essays/goldenruleposter.htm).

2002 Pam Evans, a world-religions teacher in Wales, is distressed at the bullying of her Muslim students. She designs a *Peace Mala* interfaith-GR bracelet (http://www.peacemala.org.uk), as a symbol of GR commitment.

2002 Don Eberly, at the end of his *Soul of Civil Society*, describes how societies suffer from moral decay and confusion about values. He proposes that we turn to GR, which appeals to people, is rooted in diverse cultures and religions, and gives a solid practical guide for moral living.

2002   Richard Toenjes's "Why be moral in business?" says: "The widespread appeal of the golden rule can be seen as an expression of the desire to justify our actions to others in terms they could not reasonably reject."

2003   John Maxwell's *There's No Such Thing as "Business" Ethics* claims that the same GR covers both personal life and business.

2004   Howard (Q.C.) Terry's *Golden Rules and Silver Rules of Humanity* in seeking a universal wisdom uncovers a great variety of GR-like formulas.

2005   A British television station surveys 44,000 people to create a new "ten commandments." GR was by far the most popular commandment: "Treat others as you want to be treated." (Spier 2005)

2005   Izzy Kalman's *Bullies to Buddies* describes a GR anti-bullying program. He suggests that victims be calm and treat bullies not as enemies (treating them as they treat you) but as friends (treating them as you want to be treated).

2005   Ken Binmore and others explore GR's role in our hunter-and-gatherer phase. Small, genetically similar clans that use GR to promote cooperative hunting and sharing have a better chance to survive.

2005   Singer Helen Reddy's *The Woman I Am* (p. 112) recalls her daughter asking, "Mummy, when you're not with me, how can I tell if something is right or wrong?" Reddy answered, "Ask yourself, is this what I'd want someone to do to me? Think about how you'd feel if you were the other person."

2006   Responding to a negative comment from Pope Benedict, 38 Muslim leaders write a letter to correct misconceptions, point out Muslim-Christian similarities, and call for dialogue. By 2009, this becomes a book, *A Common Word*, signed by 300 Muslim leaders and 460 organizations, stressing the Islamic GR ("None of you has faith until you love for your neighbor what you love for yourself") and the ideals of loving God and neighbor that both faiths share. Christians, including the pope, respond positively.

2006   Mussie Hailu, an interfaith GR activist from Ethiopia, translates McKenna's interfaith GR poster into African languages and starts distributing fifty thousand copies, including one to every African head of state. He sees GR as a path to peace, justice, and interfaith harmony.

2007   World climate experts, at the Intergovernmental Panel on Climate Change, say global warming is likely caused by humans and may lead to massive food shortages. A key 21st-century challenge arises: Will we treat future generations as we ourselves want to be treated?

2007   Donald Pfaff's *Neuroscience of Fair Play: Why We (Usually) Follow the Golden Rule* explains the physical basis for GR thinking. The brain blurs the difference between ourselves and the other person: "It is *decreased* social recognition that leads someone to obey the golden rule. A person momentarily forgets the difference between himself and the other." This suggests (my paraphrase): Treat others as if the difference between you and them were blurred.

2008   Jacob Neusner and Bruce Chilton sponsor, at Bard College in New York state, a three-day academic conference on GR in world religions. The papers were published in Neusner & Chilton (2008 & 2009).

2008   Pope Benedict XVI as he prepares to visit the United States proclaims: "Do to others as you would have them do to you, and avoid doing what you would not want them to do. This 'golden rule' is given in the Bible, but it is valid for all people, including non-believers. It is the law written on the human heart; on this we can all agree, so that when we come to address other matters we can do so in a positive and constructive manner."

2008   Abdullah An-Na'im's *Islam and the Secular State* (p. 24) argues "for a secular state, constitutionalism, human rights, and citizenship from an Islamic perspective because that approach is indispensable for protecting the freedom of each person to affirm, challenge, or transform his or her cultural or religious identity. My right to be myself requires me to accept and respect the right of others to be themselves too, on their own terms. The golden rule is the ultimate cross-cultural foundation of the universality of human rights."

2008   Christian Troll, a German Jesuit who does Christian-Muslim dialogue, suggests a GR for understanding other religions: "Try to understand the other's faith as you would like your own faith to be understood."

2008   Barack Obama highlights GR in a video at the Democratic Convention. He often appeals to GR in speeches as president.

2008   Deepak Chopra's *Third Jesus* begins by emphasizing how radical it is to try to treat everyone (even our enemies) as we want to be treated.

2008   Karen Armstrong, a world-religions expert who emphasizes GR and compassion, wins a TED award which she uses to launch the Charter for Compassion (http://charterforcompassion.org). Her acceptance speech urges:

"If we don't manage to implement the golden rule globally, so that we treat all peoples as though they were as important as ourselves, I doubt that we'll have a viable world to hand on to the next generation."

2009 C.K. Cole's "Math proves the golden rule" (in his *The Universe and the Teacup*) argues from game theory that cooperative strategies do best, even though they "sound a lot like old-fashioned homilies: think ahead, cooperate, don't covet your neighbor's success, and be prepared to forgive those who trespass against you." A cutthroat strategy at first may work but later will "destroy the very environment it needs for its own success."

2009 Paul McKenna helps develop interfaith GR retreats for high-school students in Toronto. His http://www.scarboromissions.ca/Golden_rule is the most extensive GR site on the Web, with materials on GR workshops, GR meditations, GR school curricula, and a GR movie (produced by Tina Petrova).

2009 Laurie Keller's *Do Unto Otters* is a children's book about how various animals learn to get along using GR.

2009 Ramona Moreno Winner's *The Wooden Bowl, El Bol de Madera* is a bilingual children's book telling how a grandson reminds his parents to follow GR toward Grandpa. (See my §§1.1 & 6.3.)

2009 Neil Duxbury's "Golden rule reasoning, moral judgment, and law" defends GR but raises questions about its meaning: "Does 'do unto' mean 'do good unto'? Does 'others' mean all others? Are we doing unto others as they would do unto us *if we were them*, or *if we were us in their shoes?*"

2009 Olivier du Roy's *La Règle d'Or: Le retour d'une maxime oubliée*, the first GR book in French, looks to the return of GR as the natural-law norm common to all peoples.

2010 At a GR conference in Edinburgh, Sohaib Saeed proposes an Islamic GR: "Treat others as you hope God will treat you, in this life or the next."

2010 Martin Bauschke's *Die Goldene Regel: Staunen, Verstehen, Handeln* marvels at GR's global universality, understands how GR functions to promote everyone's good, and promotes acting on GR to lead to a better world.

2010 Mussie Hailu has the United Nations adopt April 5 as international golden rule day. Hailu promotes GR with the UN, the United Religions Initiative (http://www.uri.org), and many other organizations.

2010 *The Berenstain Bears and the Golden Rule* is the first GR iPhone app for children, besides being a book. Sister Bear gets a GR locket and then learns to apply GR when a new bear comes to school and gets ignored.

2010   Tom Carson's "The golden rule and a theory of moral reasoning," in his *Lying and Deception*, builds on Hare and Gensler and argues for this GR: "Consistency requires that if I think it would be morally permissible for someone to do a certain act to another, then I must not object to someone doing the same act to me (or someone I love) in relevantly similar circumstances."

2011   John Finnis's *Natural Law and Human Rights*, second edition, says (p. 420): "To violate the golden rule is to allow emotional motivations for self-interested preference to override the rational rule of fair impartiality."

2011   Germain Grisez's "Health care technology and justice" suggests that we decide government's role in providing health care for poor people "by considering available resources and competing needs, and applying the golden rule."

2011   Richard Kinnier's "The main contributors to a future utopia" gives the results of an American survey about what has contributed most to a possible future utopia (described as a time when GR is universally lived). The top individuals were Gandhi, Martin Luther King, Buddha, Socrates, Lincoln, and Jesus – and the top events were the abolitionist movement, the bill of rights, the end of apartheid, the civil rights movement, and the feminist movement.

2011   NAIN (North American Interfaith Network) sponsors a three-day conference in Arizona on GR under Paul Eppinger's leadership. It ends with a spirited singing of a song by Zephryn Conte and Rene Morgan Brooks: "Living the golden rule, we are living the golden rule, with our brothers and sisters all over the world, we're living the golden rule."

2012   Alex Knapp of *Forbes* magazine suggests this customer service GR: "Do unto your customers as you want to be treated when you are a customer. That is the whole of customer service. The rest is commentary."

2012   Felipe Santos's "A very brief history of the universe, earth, and life" (in his *Humans on Earth*) states "The golden rule represents a very important ethical step forward and is present in the main religions. We may only conjecture as to how different the world would be if we did not have that rule, or at the other extreme, if it was actually followed and applied by everyone."

2012   Olivier du Roy's *Histoire de la règle d'or* is a monumental two-volume study on the history of the golden rule.

CHAPTER 6
Moral Education

Teaching morality (including GR) to the next generation is one of life's most important challenges. Here we'll first apply to moral education what we learned about GR reasoning in earlier chapters. Then we'll look at psychological theory, and then practical suggestions. Finally, we'll ask why GR hasn't made more impact on people's lives.

This chapter has many ideas, often idealistic, about how to teach morality. Parents and teachers need to reflect on which of these can most readily be applied to their often messy situations.

6.1   Content and method

On the "commonsense approach" to moral education, adults know the moral rules and teach these to children by personal example, verbal instruction, praise and blame, and reward and punishment. Personal example is most important. Children tend to follow what we *do*: morality is more *caught* than *taught*. We also give verbal rules. At first, the rules are simple, like "Don't hit your sister" and "Tell the truth." Later we add rules about homework, dating, driving, and drinking. Rule-followers are praised and rewarded; rule-breakers are scolded and punished. The process can be frustrating, because our "Don't hit your sister" may be broken immediately. And children are swayed by peer pressure to act against our teaching. But the process more or less works.

This approach is fine as far as it goes. But it doesn't go far enough, since it ignores method. It gives rules but doesn't say how to get the rules.

Morality needs to be taught more like how we teach science. Science involves *content* – for example, that a freely falling body (neglecting air resistance) in t seconds falls a distance d, as given by this formula:

$$d = \frac{1}{2}gt^2$$

Where: d = distance in meters, g = a gravitational constant of 9.8 m/s² (meters per second squared), and t = time in seconds

So in one second the object falls 4.9 meters, in two seconds it falls 19.6 meters, and so on. This is content. But science also teaches *method*, about how to get to the content. *Scientific method* is about observing, formulating hypotheses, testing them by experiment, and so on (Gensler 2010: 104–12). The content is based on the method. If you have doubts about the content, you could in principle check it out using the method.

The commonsense approach to moral education ignores method. We teach moral rules but don't say how to get the rules or why we should follow these instead of other rules. It seems arbitrary. This is a shame, especially since the world's religions have taught the idea that holds the rules together. Confucius, Hillel, and Jesus summed up the rules in a way that shows their point.

Neglecting method brings further problems. Children

- are less motivated to follow the rules, since they don't understand their point;
- won't know what to do in cases not covered by the rules;
- will be confused when they later have to decide whether to accept or reject the rules they were taught; and
- can learn bad values if their adults have bad values.

Regarding the last point, the commonsense approach can teach Nazi bigotry. Adult example and words can teach that Jews are to be hated. We can praise our children when they follow our racist example and punish them when they act kindly toward Jews. If such training succeeds, our children will internalize Nazi values. And we won't have taught them how to criticize bad values.

Besides *content*, we also need to teach *method*. I propose:

Six key commandments of rational moral thinking	1. Make informed decisions. 2. Be consistent in your beliefs and ends-means. 3. Make similar evaluations about similar actions. 4. Live in harmony with your moral beliefs. 5. Imagine yourself in the other's place. 6. Treat others as you want to be treated.

Teach these by your example and by encouraging related skills and attitudes.

(1) *Make informed decisions.* To teach this by example, follow it yourself, especially in actions that affect your children. Know your children (and how things affect them) before making decisions about them. This requires communication, and especially *listening*. To teach the corresponding skills and attitudes, talk with children about their decisions. Get them to ask questions like: "What consequences would this action have on myself and others?" – "What are my alternatives?" – "What are the pros and cons here?" Encourage children to get and reflect on data needed to make decisions; don't just make every decision for them. And at times, bring children into family decisions.

Teach children to respect truth, which gives the factual basis for decisions. Don't tolerate misinformation, especially lies or negative stereotypes.

(2) *Be consistent in your beliefs and ends-means.* To teach this by example,

be consistent in your own beliefs. Give consistent rules that have clear and acceptable implications. And have your means be in harmony with your ends; you give a poor example if you have a goal (perhaps to control your drinking) but don't carry out the means. To teach the corresponding skills and attitudes, encourage children to develop their logical skills, to reason things out, to raise objections to proposed rules, and to avoid inconsistent beliefs. And encourage them to be clear on their goals, to pick realistic and compatible goals, to decide on proper means, and to carry out the means.

(3) *Make similar evaluations about similar actions.* First follow this yourself. Apply the same standards to everyone and give reasons for differences in treatment. Respond carefully when asked things like, "Mom, why can Jimmy do this but not me?" Don't answer, "Just shut up and do what I say!" Also challenge children to think through their decisions and to propose principles or reasons (applicable to everyone alike) why actions are right or wrong. Encourage them to apply the same principles to themselves that they apply to others; confront them when they themselves do what they complain about in others.

(4) *Live in harmony with your moral beliefs.* Follow this yourself. Take your moral beliefs seriously and put them into practice. Don't teach children by your example to say, "Yes, it's wrong, but I don't care." Also encourage children to take their moral beliefs seriously and follow them conscientiously. Stress the importance of doing the right thing.

(5) *Imagine yourself in the other's place.* Follow this yourself, especially toward your children. Listen to them; try to imagine what their lives are like. This teaches by example how important it is to appreciate another's perspective. Also encourage children to share ideas and reactions, to listen to others, and to reflect on what an action looks like from another's perspective. Get them to ask questions like, "What would it be like if I were Suzy and this happened to me?" And have them read stories or watch movies that portray people's lives realistically and get us to envision ourselves in their situation.

(6) *Treat others as you want to be treated.* Follow GR yourself, especially toward your children. Reflect on how your actions affect them, imagine yourself in their place, and treat them only as you're willing to be treated by a parent in their place. Don't be seen treating them or others in inconsiderate ways. And encourage your children to follow GR. Challenge them, when they do something rude or vicious, by asking, "Do you want us to treat you that way?" Help them to think through moral problems using GR.

Your example can be more effective if you explain how you make decisions. You might explain how you're working hard to get the facts needed to make a certain decision and how you imagine how different possible actions would affect various parties. And you might ask your children if they can think of important factors that you missed.

For religious people, these elements can be integrated with religious beliefs and attitudes. Our attempt to grow wiser in our moral thinking can be seen as an attempt to draw closer to God's supreme wisdom.

Children should know a GR formula. And they should learn that GR is practically universal across the world; Paul McKenna's poster with GR in world religions (http://www.scarboromissions.ca/Golden_rule/poster_order.php) is a great tool for teaching this. A particularly good day to teach about GR is April 5, which is international GR day (§3.3).

Older children can learn the Kita procedure (Know-Imagine-Test-Act) and the story about the foolish and wise GR monkeys (§§1.2–3 & 2.1b). Still older children can learn the GR fallacies. And young adults can read this book.

As you teach GR, keep two things in mind. (1) Inside us there's something that responds to GR (§3.4 Q13) – but also opposing forces (like egoism, groupism, revenge, and laziness, §6.4). (2) GR is *scalable* (§2.4): it can be understood and applied in a way that's simple (for young children) or in a way that's more sophisticated (for adults, who may use GR to run a company in a way that respects everyone's rights and interests).[1]

6.2   Kohlberg's moral stages

Morality's *scalability* comes out in the work of the Harvard psychologist Lawrence Kohlberg (1927–87).

Kohlberg, unhappy with the relativism of many social scientists, sought empirical support for a more objective approach to morality. He found, on the basis of studies, that people of all cultures develop moral thinking through six stages (people do most thinking at one stage, but can go higher or lower):

Pre-conventional (Self-centered)

1. *Punishment/obedience*: "Good" is what is commanded and rewarded. "Bad" is what is forbidden and punished. We all begin with this approach.
2. *Self-interest*: "Good" is what brings what you want. "Bad" is what frustrates self-interest. Children, seeing that obedience needn't promote self-interest, become manipulative.

Conventional (Conformity)

3. *Parental approval*: "Good" is what makes Mommy and Daddy proud of you. "Bad" is what brings disapproval. Self-worth comes from parental approval.
4. *Group approval (cultural relativism)*: "Good" is what one's group approves of. "Bad" is what brings group disapproval. Teenagers turn to their peer group for support and values, and to define the *right* clothes and the *right* music. Beginning college students often struggle with this stage. Later, "good" and "bad" are defined by the larger society.

---

[1] For more on teaching GR to children, see Schulman & Mekler 1994 and Stilwell *et al.* 2000.

Post-conventional (Rational)

5. *Social contract or utilitarian*: Moral rules are evaluated more rationally, by whether they promote society's good.
6. *Principled conscience*: Moral beliefs are evaluated by consistency, justice, and concern for everyone's equal dignity. Kohlberg mentions "Act only as you'd be willing that everyone should act in the same situation" [like Gold 7] and calls the imagined switching of roles *moral musical chairs*. Our actions must be *reversible*: acceptable to us even if we're on the receiving end.

Later stages on the list are *higher* in that they appear later in time, are preferred by those who understand both stages, and are philosophically better. In moving between stages, children aren't absorbing values from the outside; instead, they're developing better ways to think about values.[1]

Children use GR at every stage, but with greater clarity and motivation at higher stages. They follow GR because this helps them escape punishment (stage 1), brings better treatment from others (2), wins Mommy's and Daddy's approval (3), is socially approved (4), is a socially useful practice (5), or treats others with dignity and respect (6). Lower stages tend to distort GR:

> My young son thought if Eskimos killed and ate seals, it was right to kill and eat Eskimos.... My son interpreted reciprocity not as reversibility (doing as you would wish to be done by) but as exchange (doing back what is done to you).... We have systematically asked children who "know" or can repeat the golden rule the question, "If someone comes up on the street and hits you, what would the golden rule say to do?" Children at the first and second moral stages say "Hit him back. Do unto others as they do unto you." (Kohlberg 1979: 265f)

According to Piaget, whom Kohlberg builds on, young children think revenge is fair. Older children see that revenge leads to further revenge: if we all follow "An eye for an eye and a tooth for a tooth," then we'll all end up blind and toothless (Gandhi). So older children value forgiveness over revenge. Mutual respect grows and expresses itself in GR.[2]

When dealing with children, we need to grasp how *they* think about values. Teach GR by appealing to the stage they're on, or one stage higher. So little Juanita at stage 2 or 3 might be told that it makes Mommy and Daddy proud of her when she follows GR. Juanita will understand and smile. If you tell her the same thing when she's 30, she'll feel insulted.

Kohlberg began his research by giving moral dilemmas to a group of 72

---

[1] The stage-sequence isn't programmed genetically. Instead, it comes from the child's moving to better ways of thinking and interacting with others. Still, the stage-sequence must connect with the evolutionary and neurological stories of §7.4; someone needs to develop these connections.
[2] Kohlberg 1973 & 1979, Kohlberg *et al.* 1983 & 1990, Piaget 1948, and Erikson 1964 all take higher GR forms to reflect psychologically advanced forms of moral thinking. Kohlberg thinks that everyone would reach stage 6 if developmental conditions were optimal.

boys. The Heinz dilemma, for example, asks whether it would be right to steal overpriced medicine that your wife needs. The reasons the boys gave for their answers were put into one stage or another. The original subjects were interviewed again every few years to gauge their progress. Similar studies done throughout the world revealed the same stages. Children with higher logical thinking or higher empathy tend to be more advanced.

Kohlberg contrasts three approaches to moral education, which rest on differing views about moral philosophy and moral psychology:

- *Commonsense*: Adults intuitively know the moral norms and teach these to children by example, words, praise/blame, and reward/punishment. Values are conveyed, but little is done to promote rational moral thinking.
- *Relativistic-emotional*: Moral rules are arbitrary cultural standards. Children internalize these standards, and adults need to help children adjust to them.
- *Cognitive-developmental*: Morality is based on principles of justice valid for every culture. Children develop moral thinking through stages. Adults need to help children grow toward higher stages.

Kohlberg supports the last approach (which resembles my previous section). Adults can help children improve their moral thinking by helping them to grow in logical skills, to expand their social experience (and thus their ability to empathize), and to discuss moral dilemmas (where the teacher helps students understand the moral reasoning of the stage just above theirs). Since those at higher stages tend more to act on their moral beliefs, promoting growth in moral thinking also promotes increased moral action.

Kohlberg's ideas, while influential, have faced criticism. Some think his stage sequence makes matters neater than they actually are. Others, including utilitarians (stage 5), are skeptical about stage 6, which Kohlberg admits is rarely achieved; stages 1–4 have a stronger empirical basis than stages 5–6. Others argue that, while Kohlberg has done good work on justice, other areas of morality need investigation too.

Carol Gilligan, a Harvard colleague of Kohlberg, objected that Kohlberg's stages, developed from interviews with boys, apply mainly to males. She thought women tend to think differently. Gilligan's *In a Different Voice* (1982) posits two mature ways to think about morality: justice and caring. Men tend to think of justice, principles, rights, and duties; women tend to think of caring, feelings, personal relationships, and responsibilities. Gilligan proposes that females typically go through three stages of moral thinking: self-centered, self-sacrificing, and a mature perspective that balances our needs with the needs of others. Gilligan's book led to a debate. Some developed a feminist *ethics of care*, while others questioned Gilligan's data and conclusions.

Kohlberg, while adjusting his system, claimed that empirical research continues to show that females go through the same stages of moral thinking as males. So little girls also have a "what makes Mommy and Daddy proud of me" stage 3 and then move toward a "all my friends are doing it" stage 4. But he admitted that the tension between caring for oneself and caring for others has a special importance for many females.

Is the golden rule *gendered* – typical more of one gender than the other?[1] It seems not. My students shake their heads no when I ask them this, and my experience of teaching GR over many decades confirms the no. But perhaps the "rule" and "impartiality" side of GR is more male – while the "empathy" and "care" side of GR is more female? Or perhaps not.[2]

While there are controversies here, Kohlberg's influential approach may further explain why GR is so universal: it's part of a natural stage-sequence of thinking. And it makes suggestions about teaching GR: understand how the child thinks about morality, appeal to this or to a stage above, challenge children with moral dilemmas, and develop their empathy and logical thinking.

6.3   Practical hints

I'll now gather from various sources some practical hints about teaching GR to children. We'll start with toddlers.

Suppose your two-year-old son Todd hits his little sister Susan. You think to yourself, "What a wonderful opportunity to teach Todd the golden rule!" No, you probably don't think this; but maybe you should.

You've got to make clear to Todd that *hitting Susan is bad* because *it hurts her*.[3] Both things together are important. Make it clear in various ways: words, tone of voice, shake your finger, and so on. Say things like, "Bad to hit Susan – it makes Susan feel bad!" or "Poor Susan is crying – never hit her!" or "No, no – this hurts Susan!" or "Mommy is sad when you make Susan cry!" Say and show it in different ways. Make clear that *hitting is wrong* and *why it's wrong*.

Todd is new at human interaction. He needs your help. Even if you do everything right, don't expect immediate miracles in how he acts. Even adults may need several lessons before they get the point.

Here are ways *not* to respond to Todd: just sit back and do nothing, just

---

[1] The meager empirical evidence that I found on this is mixed. Schminke & Ambrose 1997 did a study where slightly more women than men (74% to 58%) favor GR over other approaches. C. Perry & McIntire 1994 mention a study where fairness+GR+principles is slightly more popular among men; but combining GR with other ideas muddies whether GR itself is gendered. Tsalikis & Ortiz-Buonafina 1990 did a study where men and women made very similar ethical judgments; some previous studies showed significant gender difference while others didn't. Das 2005 mentions empirical studies that suggest that GR is a very common way to make moral decisions.

[2] Pfaff 2007 argues that GR brain functions first evolved to promote the care of mothers toward their babies (§7.4). This would give GR a female origin. But Pfaff doesn't mention any difference in GR brain functions between males and females.

[3] These suggestions are based on a study by Zahn-Waxler *et al.* 1979 about how different ways of treating toddlers tend to help or hinder pro-social behavior.

move him away from Susan, scold him for hitting without letting him know why it's wrong, slap him without explanation, or sometimes punish him for hitting and sometimes not (depending on your mood). Such responses teach poorly. Hey, imagine yourself in Todd's place, knowing little about how to treat others and being responded to in these ways. You'd be confused.

Children at a young age begin to say things like "I'm sorry I made Susan cry" or "This isn't fair." They're beginning to know right from wrong. This needs to be nourished and developed.

Children love to have stories read to them. Most children's books can provide GR lessons. Parents can ask questions like "Was such and such a good thing to do?" or "How would you feel if such and such were done to you?" Here are some children's books with a GR slant:

- *The Wooden Bowl, El Bol de Madera*, by Ramona Moreno Winner (a bilingual children's version of the Grimm 1812 story in §1.1).
- *The Berenstain Bears and the Golden Rule*, by Mike, Stan, and Jan Berenstain (Sister Bear gets a GR locket and then learns to apply GR when a new bear comes to school and gets ignored). This is also an iPad/iPhone app; I've used this with three little ones, and they loved it.
- Two books about how animal characters learn to get along using GR: *Do Unto Otters*, by Laurie Keller, and *Adventures at Walnut Grove*, by Dana Lehman.
- *The Golden Rule*, by Ilene Cooper (grandfather explains interfaith GR).
- *Confucius: The Golden Rule*, by Russell Freedman (for older children).
- Three books about manners as expressing GR: *Manners Matter*, by Hermine Hartley, *A Little Book of Manners* (for young ladies), by Emilie Barnes, and *A Little Book of Manners for Boys*, by Bob and Emilie Barnes.

I also recommend the Smothers Brothers' *Aesop's Fables*, which is an instructive but hilarious CD or set of mp3 music files.

And of course it's important that a child grow up in a nurturing and loving family, preferably with two parents who love each other and their children. This provides the best soil for the GR seed to grow.

A teacher interacts with students in many ways: as setting the tone for the class, as discussion leader and lecturer, as grader, as disciplinarian, as social organizer, as one who listens and gives guidance, as one who fosters mutual respect and opposes meanness, and so on. So teachers have many opportunities to teach GR. Personal example is crucial. You'll give excellent GR example if you get to know your students, imagine yourself in their place, and treat them only as you're willing to be treated in their place. You'll then also be more effective as a teacher, since you'll better know how to connect with your students.[1]

---

[1] For more on these aspects, see Frymier 1969, Glad 1962, Glenn 1998, Gordon 1967, Horowitz 1987, Keck 1939, and Schnoor 1953. See also Dyck & Padilla 2009.

Most of this is true also of coaches. Sports teach life skills and should teach GR, applied toward teammates and even opponents (§14.3a).

Teachers can also display GR in the classroom, explain the formula, talk about its presence in many cultures and religions, apply it to classroom rules, and have students give examples of its use. Most students will respond. Those who reject GR and endorse egoism can be challenged: "Zoe, so you don't want us to follow GR toward you? Listen everyone, Zoe doesn't want us to follow GR toward her. Are you sure about this Zoe?" or "Which would you rather live in: a place where they follow GR or a place of selfishness? And in which direction do you want to nudge your group?"

Some students resent rules imposed on them. Explain how rules protect us from an egoistic chaos. And explain how GR doesn't *impose* a rule on us from the outside but rather takes *our own rule* (e.g., "Don't steal from me!") and pushes us to apply it consistently to how we treat others.

Here are three further suggestions. Suggestion 1 has two parts. (1) Have students write down a couple ways in which they want to be (or not to be) treated. Have them read their answers or put them on slips of paper. Write them on the board. If an answer is specific (like "I want people to congratulate me when I pitch a no hitter"), then write a general version (like "I want people to congratulate me when I do well"). (2) Introduce GR, which transforms these into ways that we ought to treat others. So if we want others to congratulate us when we do well, then we should do the same to them.

Suggestion 2 (from E. Russell 1943) also has two parts. (1) Have students write out and drop in a box descriptions of some difficult choices that they might face. For example, "I saw a friend stealing a candy bar from the store; what should I do?" or "If I go to a football game and find someone in my seat, what should I do?" (2) Later open the box and have the class discuss some of the problems together. As they discuss, have students imagine themselves in the place of the various parties. Feature the GR question: *"Am I now willing that if I were in the same situation then this be done to me?"*

Suggestion 3 has you, the teacher, tell a story from the perspective of one character. Then have a student tell the same story, maybe elaborating on details, from the perspective of another character. The story might involve one person being cruel to another (for example, in picking sides for a game, one child is excluded or made fun of); but it needn't involve this. This exercise teaches putting yourself in another's place. Or you might have a group of students act out the story, and then afterwards talk about what they felt from the perspective of their individual characters.

Literature is useful, both in teaching about GR moral struggles and in helping us to imagine ourselves in another's place. Shapiro 1952 talks about using Shakespeare's *Merchant of Venice* to raise issues about racism (the treatment of the Jew Shylock). Hoskisson & Biskin 1979 talk about using the Grimm 1812 story, "The old man and his grandson":

There was once a very old man ... when he sat at table he could hardly hold the spoon, and spilt the broth upon the table-cloth or let it run out of his mouth. His son and his son's wife were disgusted at this, so the old grandfather at last had to sit in the corner behind the stove.... Once, too, his trembling hands could not hold the bowl, and it fell to the ground and broke. The young wife scolded him.... Then they brought him a wooden bowl for a few half-pence, out of which he had to eat....

The little grandson of four years old began to gather together some bits of wood upon the ground. "What are you doing there?" asked the father. "I am making a little bowl," answered the child, "for father and mother to eat out of when I am big." The man and his wife looked at each other for a while, and presently began to cry. Then they took the old grandfather to the table, and henceforth always let him eat with them, and likewise said nothing if he did spill a little of anything.

Most literature deals with people mistreating each other; ask students whether ways of acting are right or wrong, and refer often to GR. Also useful for teaching GR are stories involving *poetic justice*, whereby your action later turns on yourself, or *role reversal*, whereby, for example, a mother and her daughter mysteriously switch places.

Carleton 1950 writes about literature and imagination:

The person who doesn't develop his imagination so that he can see himself in another's position can't be a good member of organized society. He can't possibly understand, much less obey, the golden rule. Wide reading of plays, novels, and short stories develops insight into the basic feelings and desires of human beings which can be obtained in no other way.

Doris 1978, on the other hand, states:

English teachers are not the only ones that teach a subject area rich with moral conflict and/or role-taking opportunities. The film instructor can lead discussions from such films as *Requiem for a Heavy Weight, On the Waterfront,* and *Jules and Jim.* The art or humanities instructor can discuss Picasso's *Guernica* or Van Gogh's *Self Portrait.* The history teacher can lead a class to consider Lincoln's decision to sign the Emancipation Proclamation or Truman's decision to drop atomic bombs. And social studies teachers have opportunity to discuss moral conflict situations and to encourage role-taking with such topics as American slave trade, civil rights, the equal rights amendment, or Watergate.

Many subjects can help to teach GR.

When I wrote this chapter, I decided to mention some movies that connect with GR. The next movie I saw was *Avatar* (2009), which clearly connected. Here most humans on the mission to the planet Pandora think nothing of destroying the culture, happiness, and lives of the natives. But a few GR humans object and try to protect the natives, who, even though not human, have beliefs, desires, hopes, fears, distresses, and loves just as we do.[1] Then I saw *My Fair Lady* (1964) yet again. Here Professor Henry Higgins (Rex Harrison) teaches the poor, dirty Eliza Doolittle (Audrey Hepburn) to speak and act like a refined lady. Higgins is so insensitive to Eliza's feelings that he congratulates himself, and not her, at her success; he desperately needs more GR in his life. I then reflected that so many movies show how we bring misery to ourselves and others through lies, cheating, infidelity, and other GR violations. I concluded that almost every movie connects with GR.

My student Amy Gunderman wrote a fine paper about the Disney movie *Pocahontas* (1995) and GR. Most of the British and the Indians think of the other side in negative stereotypes, making little effort to know them or treat them fairly. But Pocahontas, the Indian chief's daughter, tries to understand others and treat them as she wants to be treated. After much conflict, Pocahontas helps the others to stop killing each other and to grow in GR. Also striking is *The Boy in the Striped Pajamas* (2008). Bruno is the eight-year-old son of a Nazi in charge of a concentration camp. Bruno is told lies about the wonderful life that Jews enjoy in the camp. He sneaks off, gets to know a Jewish boy (in prison pajamas) in the camp, and in the end is killed by mistake with the Jews. Bruno's family has unbearable grief about their child being killed, even though they care little about Jewish children being killed. Also striking was the TV mini-series *Roots* (1977), which portrayed several generations of black slaves and helped white Americans imagine themselves in their place.

Art teachers will be happy that GR has a presence in their area. The *Book of Kells*, an illustrated gospels book created by Irish monks around 810, represents GR by a dog extending a paw of friendship to a rabbit. The cover of Wattles's GR book (1996) shows Rembrandt's *Good Samaritan* (1644). Norman Rockwell's *Golden Rule* (1961) has "Do unto others" and people from many religions, races, and nations; it was on the cover of the popular *Saturday Evening Post* magazine and became a mosaic at the United Nations. Gloria Cigolini-DePietro's *Golden Rule* (recent) shows an angel writing GR on a script in Hebrew. Michelle Leavitt-Djonlic's *Golden Rule* (recent) shows a sad little girl holding a shamrock that says "Kiss me." Searching the Web also uncovered GR drawings by an unnamed grade-school student (with GR quotations from world religions arranged to form a heart) and the six-year-old Koen (with GR words against the backdrop of golden suns, animals, clouds, etc.). The two winners of a Scarboro Missions GR art contest in 2007 were Andriy Lykhovoy (grade 11, Toronto, showing a globe supported by a tree and symbols for the world's religions) and A.J.M. Sharala (grade 6, Sri Lanka, showing people from different nations holding hands across the globe). Art teachers can have students do their own artistic versions of GR.

[1] Science fiction stories like *Avatar* and *Dark Angel* (2000), in showing how we can be cruel or kind to weird inhabitants of other planets or transgenic combinations of humans and other creatures, can teach how we need to apply GR to those different from us.

Religion teachers have great resources (ch. 3). Christian teachers, for example, have biblical resources (including the sayings, parables, and life of Jesus), the saints, and the commandments to love God and neighbor. Other faiths have other resources. And *all* religion teachers should talk about GR's presence in the world's religions and the need to apply GR to those of other religions.

There are also non-classroom ways for schools to teach GR, for example:

- INTERFAITH RETREATS: Scarboro Missions in Toronto has one-day interfaith GR retreats for high-school students. The students pray, sketch, sing, dance, and do skits about GR in different religions – emphasizing mutual understanding and respect for people who are different. I've been to a retreat and I recommend them. See http://www.scarboromissions.ca/Golden_rule – which also has a GR movie (produced and directed by Tina Petrova) and GR school curricula (by Gregory McKenna and by Brant Abrahamson and Fred Smith).
- DUO ("Do unto others"): A model that connects GR with volunteer work for the larger community. DUO started in Vermont but spread to other places.
- TEAM ("Treat everyone as me"): A model that emphasizes helping each other within a given a school, sports team, company, military unit, or whatever.
- SENIOR EXPERIMENT: A high-school teacher in Los Angeles (Phi Delta Kappan 1948) had seniors agree to follow GR with their families for 10 days without telling them. The results were dramatic. Students found they got along much better with their families and liked living this way, even though their families were perplexed. Many vowed to live this way forever.
- FASHION ACCESSORIES: Pam Evans, a world-religions teacher in Wales, was distressed at the bullying of her Muslim students. She designed a *Peace Mala* interfaith-GR bracelet (http://www.peacemala.org.uk) in response; I'm wearing one as I write this. For students, wearing such a physical symbol can express a GR commitment. I've also heard of schools with a gay-bashing problem using GR buttons in a similar way. And there are even GR shirts and mugs (see http://www.harryhiker.com/gr).
- BULLYING: This is a big problem in schools. Beane *et al.* 2008 (http://www .bullyfree.com) and Kalman 2005 (http://bullies2buddies.com) have contrasting GR approaches to bullying. Izzy Kalman focuses on how victims should respond. I attended his GR anger-management workshop and was part of a role-playing exercise. My task was to insult Kalman and compare two ways he responded: (1) by getting angry and treating me as an enemy (as I was treating him) or (2) by being calm and treating me as a friend (as he wanted to be treated); the second approach worked better and quickly stopped my insults.

For more information, search the Web (for example, for "bullying golden rule"). Many other non-classroom GR programs are possible. These six can jump-start your thinking about further programs.

Stories can teach GR. I really like the Grimm 1812 "The old man and his grandson" story, also called "The wooden bowl." Fansler 1921 tells how this story exists in many countries, including India, Mexico, the Philippines, and across Europe. In these stories, Father is about to mistreat the aging Grandpa in some way (e.g., Grandpa will be made to eat alone or sent off to the woods to die). Then Grandson shows his intention to treat Father the same way (and he does this using a wooden bowl, cloth, rope, or hole). Finally Father, seeing that he'd hate to be treated as he treats the old man, has a change of heart.[1]

A GR story should have an easily expressed moral. Chapter 1 uses the story about the old man to introduce GR; the moral of the story is that we need to imagine our actions being done to us (*switching places*). Or maybe the moral is how different generations can respect and learn from each other, or how we can unthinkingly hurt those we love. When you tell a GR story, you might ask people what they think the moral is.

My first chapter is mostly stories. The monkeys teach that people differ and GR needs to respect this; so ask: "Am I now willing that <u>if I were in the same situation</u> then this be done to me?" The squirrels teach about tough love; GR lets us discipline baby squirrel as long as we're willing that we be disciplined in a like situation. Frazzled Frannie teaches that GR lets us say no to others, so long as we're willing that others say no to us in a like situation. Pre-law Lucy teaches that GR needs to be applied to third parties too. Electra teaches that GR can be applied foolishly if we get our facts wrong. And Rich teaches how to apply GR to a complex coal-mine business.

The rest of the book also has many pedagogically useful stories. For example, Hillel teaches that life's complexities shouldn't blind us to what's most important. The Good Samaritan teaches us to apply GR even to those we've been taught to hate. And Queen Mallika (Buddhist) teaches that another's suffering is as important to that person as our own suffering is to us.

Since stories can teach GR so well, I'm developing on my Web site a collection of GR stories, as a help to teachers. Here are four more examples of GR stories. The first is in many places on the Web (search for: "golden rule" Li-li) and teaches how GR can help us to love our enemies:

> A Chinese girl named Li-li got married and lived with her mother-in-law. Since the mother-in-law was obnoxious, Li-li decided to kill her. Li-li went to her doctor to get slow-acting poison. The doctor said, "Just so that people don't suspect you, treat your mother-in-law very nice, as you'd like to be treated." So Li-li was nice to her mother-in-law as she slipped a little poison into her food each day. Now a funny thing happened: the two started getting along much better and became best friends. So Li-li went back to the doctor and said, "I now love my mother-in-law and don't want to kill her; please give me something to counteract the poison." The doctor replied, "I gave you ordinary vitamins; the only poison was in your attitude."

[1] To see the story's power, do a Web search for: "golden rule" "wooden bowl" (both together, using quotes). An ancient Buddhist story (http://www.sacred-texts.com/bud/j4/j4010.htm) has Father about to kill and bury Grandpa; but Grandson digs a second hole for when, following family custom, he has to kill Father.

So gold can transform relationships.

This next one really happened (search for: "Kent Nerburn" "cab ride"):

> A taxi driver picked up an elderly lady in the middle of the night. He loaded her baggage and held her hand as she limped into the taxi. "Why are you so kind?" she asked. He replied, "It's nothing; I just try to treat my passengers as I'd want my mother to be treated." The lady was alone, sick, and going to a hospice to spend her last days; but she had great memories of where she used to live with her husband and where she used to work. The driver offered to take her by these places on the way to the hospice, which made her very happy. As they arrived at the hospice, the lady tried to pay; but the driver said, "No charge – it was my pleasure." The driver always remembered that day, which was a high point of his life.

So gold can deepen our lives.

This next one may be familiar (search for: "Benjamin Franklin" "spoons to eat the stew"):

> A woman died and was taken to heaven. The angel wanted her to see hell, so they stopped there first. Hell had a lake of nutritious stew, but the people had only 12-foot spoons and so were frustrated when they tried to feed themselves. So the people were miserable and hungry. Then the woman was taken to heaven. Amazingly, heaven was exactly the same, with the same stew and 12-foot spoons; but here the people were happy and well-fed. The woman asked, "Why are these people so different?" The angel replied, "They feed each other; these people have learned the way of love."

So gold can transform society. Narayan 1989 says that stories that are similar, but may instead have long chopsticks or locked elbows, exist among Hindus, Chinese, Japanese, Jews, and others.

I made up this last story (but the "I cut, you choose" strategy has been around for a long time):

> Ryan and Tyler were twins. When the family had pie for desert, each boy complained that the other got a bigger piece. So Mom decided on this policy. She would first cut a double-size piece; then one boy would cut this into two equal pieces and the other boy would choose one of the pieces. The twins appreciated the fairness of this policy.

> Later the boys asked, "Mom, is there any way to bring such fairness to other choices?" Mom answered: "There are bound to be disputes; but we can minimize these by applying the golden rule: 'Treat another only in ways that you're willing that you'd be treated in the same situation.' If people followed this, there'd be few complaints about unfair treatment."

So gold can minimize complaints about unfair treatment. For more stories, go to my http://www.harryhiker.com/stories page.

Public schools in the U.S. and Canada used to be run as Protestant schools. In Ontario, "Every Public School shall be opened with the reading of the Scriptures and the repeating of the Lord's Prayer" (*Biblical World* 1917). Jews and Catholics were unhappy and often set up their own schools.

Textbooks in public grade schools taught GR and the Ten Commandments in a Christian context. *McGuffey Readers* were widely used, had high moral content, and sold 120 million copies between 1836 and 1960. They taught by stories, poems, and songs. For example, a story called "The golden rule" in McGuffey (1879: 139–43) tells about a little girl Susan who learns GR (in the King James Bible translation and exemplified by the Good Samaritan) from her mother and then struggles to return money she was given by mistake. British children had *The Golden Rule: Stories Illustrative of the Ten Commandments* (Mackarness 1867). Canadian children had *The Golden Rule Books* (Ontario 1915–8), based on a U.S. series with the same name. Ullin Leavell 1956 later introduced *The Golden Rule Series* as an updated McGuffey. As the titles suggest, GR was a central theme of public-school moral education.

While these books have many stories for teaching a GR-based morality, their explicit Christianity (except Leavell) made them unsuited for public schools in a pluralistic society. Public schools changed from Protestant, to Judeo-Christian, to secular (avoiding any religious stance). In 1980, the U.S. Supreme Court (Stone v. Graham, http://laws.findlaw.com/us/449/39.html) declared unconstitutional a Kentucky law requiring the posting of the Ten Commandments in public schools. Since then, there's been much debate about the teaching of morality in public schools. Many say morality is controversial and better left to family and church. Others say the core of morality is widely agreed on and needs to be taught to promote good citizenship.

GR is almost universal among the religions and peoples of the world and is important for children to learn. But the Ten Commandments are Judeo-Christian and alien to other traditions. A good compromise is to teach GR and the three most agreed-upon commandments – against physical harm, stealing, and lying – but avoid Judeo-Christian wording. So we'd have "Don't lie" or "Be truthful" instead of "You shall not bear false witness."

6.4 Why not more successful

In August 2009, I e-mailed 41 people with a special interest in GR (including philosophers, religious thinkers, educators, and activists) asking them to feed me GR objections. The psychologist Burke Brown suggested also asking "Why is GR not succeeding?" I got sixty responses in all.[1]

---

[1] I especially thank Lee Beaumont at http://www.emotionalcompetency.com for many ideas (see http://www.emotionalcompetency.com/ga).

This section refines Brown's question to "Why isn't the golden rule *more successful?*" To some extent, GR has been successful. Many people usually follow it, and almost everyone sometimes follows it. Without GR, life would be horrifyingly worse – "solitary, poor, nasty, brutish, and short" in Hobbes's words (§7.2). But still, there's a problem. For many centuries, practically all of the world's religions and cultures have taught GR. But these same centuries have seen much war, hatred, and evil action. How can this be? Why don't people follow GR better? Why don't we all live in the utopia that would result if GR (with knowledge and imagination) prevailed?

There are *many* reasons why people (including you and me) don't follow GR better. I'll divide these reasons into three groups. (1) Flawed *thinking*:

- We misunderstand GR. We're confused on how to apply it or think it's too vague to help with life's problems (ch. 1, 2, & 14).
- We misunderstand our religion, which we think tells us to hate those of other religions (ch. 3).
- We're at a low stage of moral thinking (§6.2).
- We don't understand how GR promotes our self-interest (e.g., that if we treat others better, they'll generally treat us better) (ch. 7).
- We don't understand how GR promotes our group's interest (e.g., that if we treat other groups better, they'll generally treat our group better) (ch. 8).
- We want to follow GR but don't know concretely what to do. For example, we want to preserve the environment for future generations and avoid cruelty to animals, but we don't know how to make a difference in these areas (ch. 9).

(2) Flawed *choosing*:

- We must decide how to live – to follow GR or not. Many choose against GR.
- We have motivations that pull against GR. We're attracted by immediate gains for ourselves (instead of remote gains for everyone that also benefit us) – we act out of revenge, habit, laziness, or conformity – or we feel we're too *special* to be bound by GR.
- We need to *care more* about getting the facts, developing imagination, and following GR.
- We need to be *more attentive* to how our actions affect others. We often hurt others because we don't think of what we're doing.
- We need to be *more honest* about ourselves. We often think that only other people violate GR. Growth requires that we recognize our shortcomings.
- We need to be *more aggressive* in demanding better treatment. We need to let others know if they're hurting us.
- We need to take GR to the *next level*. GR has us do good and not harm to others (ch. 10); maybe we're doing fine on *not harming* but less well on *doing good*. Or maybe we're fine at applying GR to our own group, but poor at applying GR to other groups (ch. 8).
- We need *genuine religion* to purify our motives and move us higher.

(3) Flawed *socializing*:

- Moral education is often poor (ch. 6). And family life is deteriorating; many children are abused or taught to care only about themselves (L. Thomas 1996).
- Society can hinder us in applying GR. Imagine how difficult it would be to apply GR in a dog-eat-dog society or in Nazi Germany.
- Society needs to change the reward/penalty system so that decisions that are individually sensible don't hurt society (§§7.2 & 14.3f, and Platt 1973).
- We need to cooperate better. In politics, for example, partisanship often trumps concern for people (§9.4).

Why we don't follow GR is a complex problem – involving flawed thinking, choosing, and socializing. There's much room for individuals to help with some aspect of the problem, to light a candle rather than curse the darkness.[1]

While many forces can hinder us from living GR, none of these is a good excuse. To think otherwise is to surrender to what existentialists call "bad faith." It's our decision whether to live in a golden manner. And there are *many* reasons to live this way (§11.1 Q16).

What can we as individuals do to promote GR in a world where GR has so many obstacles? Often the best approach is to become a *GR role model*: live it yourself. Yes, GR does exist in each person's heart – but sometimes as a small, fragile seed covered by rocks. GR seeds grow by encountering a strong GR-presence. My sister Carol gave me this example: maybe I notice that someone really listens to me, and I say, "Hey, I could do that for others." GR is contagious. When we experience GR from others, we feel its attraction and yearn for a world of golden relationships.

Sometimes a big goal is best achieved by small steps. The Kita procedure gives a way to grow toward a golden life by 4 steps: Know-Imagine-Test-Act. If our conversion to GR is big change, we might spend a week on each step. We'd first consider how our actions affect others, writing this down. We'd then spend time imagining ourselves in the place of our victims. Then we'd work to uncover the GR consistencies in our lives. Last would come action.

Will our world ever completely achieve GR? Probably not. But at least GR gives us a goal, a direction. While we can't do everything, we can at least move a little toward a golden ideal.

---

[1] J. Maxwell 2003: 71–90 gives five p-factors that can "tarnish" GR: *pressure* (we're pushed to succeed at whatever cost), *pleasure* (we pursue possessions and lack discipline), *power* (we abuse it and become self-centered), *pride* (in being better than others), and *priorities* (we sacrifice what matters most for the sake of what matters least).

CHAPTER 7
Egoism, Hobbes, Darwin

Some object to the golden rule from self-interest. They say GR is *foolish* (since we often can do better for ourselves by breaking GR) or *impossible* (since we're built to pursue only self-interest). In answering these objections, I'll talk about Hobbes (social contract) and Darwin (evolution).

7.1 Foolish or impossible

Philosophers distinguish two kinds of egoism; each provides an objection to GR. First, *ethical egoism* says we *ought* to do whatever maximizes good consequences for ourselves, regardless of how this affects others. So GR is foolish:

Objection 4: ethical egoism	We ought to have concern, ultimately, only for our own good. Thus it's foolish to follow GR, since we can often do better for ourselves by cheating.

Imagine Old Joe at the bar, bragging about how he just sold his car for more money by lying about its condition. Joe says, "Hey, why not? Everyone does it. Honesty hurts my wallet." His friends object, "Would you want someone to cheat you?" He responds, "No, I'd complain if someone cheated me! But so what?" They ask, "Don't you believe in the golden rule?" Joe responds, "Hell no! I believe in doing what you can get away with!" He continues in verse:

> "Any who follow the golden rule
> shall surely be treated like a fool"
> says Old Joe on the barstool.

GR is for naïve fools. Smart folks can do better for themselves by being amoral and not caring about GR.

A scene from the classic movie *On the Waterfront* (1954) makes a similar point. Terry (Marlon Brando) is an egoistic tough guy. He's developing a crush on Edie (Eve Marie Saint). Terry rambles to Edie about his prizefighting, and then there's this dialogue (at 38:45):

Terry: … What do you really care, am I right?

Edie: Shouldn't everybody care about everybody else?

Terry: Oh, what a fruitcake you are!

Edie: I mean, isn't everybody a part of everybody else?

Terry: And you really believe that drool.

Edie: Yes, I do….

Terry: You wanna hear my philosophy of life? (And he holds out his fist.) Do it to him before he does it to you.

Edie: I've never met anyone like you. There's not a spark of sentiment, romance, or human kindness in your whole body.

Terry: What good does it do you besides get you in trouble?

So we can choose to care about others or care only about ourselves.

Psychological egoism goes further; it says everyone by nature is motivated only by self-interest. So even Edie ultimately cares only about herself. When she acts to help someone else, she's thinking, perhaps unconsciously, that this will in some way help *her*, and that's why she does it.

We're products of evolution, which is about survival of the fittest. We survive by caring about our own good, not by caring about another's good. Since GR goes against our nature, following it is *impossible*:

Objection 5: psychological egoism	We're so built (as products of evolution) that by nature we have concern ultimately only for our own good. Thus following GR is impossible and trying to follow it leads to frustration.

GR is unrealistic and impractical; it just won't work.

Woody Allen's *Whatever Works* (2009) movie begins:

The basic teachings of Jesus are quite wonderful. So, by the way, is the original intention of Karl Marx. Hey, what could be bad? Everybody should share equally. Do unto others. Democracy…. These are all great ideas, but they all suffer from one fatal flaw. They're all based on the fallacious notion that people are fundamentally decent. Give them a chance to do right and they'll take it. They're not stupid, selfish, greedy, cowardly, short-sighted worms…. I'm sorry to say, we're a failed species.

Psychological egoism speaks a purer cynicism: "Egoism inescapably rules our nature." Because of how we're built, we ultimately care only about ourselves and can't do otherwise. Evolution hardwired an egoistic psychology into us.

So GR is seen as foolish (ethical egoism) or impossible (psychological egoism). I see both forms of egoism as false. But it's interesting that we can defend GR fairly well even if we assume both kinds of egoism.

7.2   Hobbes and social contracts

Thomas Hobbes (1588–1679) accepted both kinds of egoism: self-interest *ought to* and *does* govern us completely. But enlightened self-interest moves us to create a social contract based on the golden rule.

Hobbes has us imagine, either as an early human condition or as a thought experiment, a *state of nature* without moral or social rules. Without rules, egoistic humans would lie, steal, or kill whenever it was in their interest. No one could farm, since others would just steal their crops. We'd fight for resources and fear attack; since we're roughly equal, we couldn't protect themselves from others. The resulting social chaos would make life miserable for everybody and promote nobody's interests. Life, in Hobbes's words, would be "solitary, poor, nasty, brutish, and short."

So rational egoists in a state of nature would agree to social rules to protect their interests. Wanting their own property to be respected, they'd agree to respect the property of others. Wanting their own lives to be respected, they'd agree to respect the lives of others. They'd set up social rules with a GR pattern: "We want others to treat us in such and such a way, and so we agree to treat them likewise." Egoists would agree to a GR-society because this serves their self-interest. Morality is born. Morality (as summed up in GR) is a social contract that egoistic humans, to further their interests and prevent a harmful social chaos, would agree to in the state of nature (Hobbes 1651: 84–105).[1]

After agreeing to a social contract, egoists wouldn't actually follow it unless they thought this was in their self-interest. So Hobbes has his egoists set up an absolute monarch to punish rule-breakers. Recent Hobbesians dislike monarchy and propose other sanctions. Richard Brandt 1972 suggests that society needs to make rule-breakers suffer penalties both external (alienation, social disapproval, legal penalties) and internal (guilt, anxiety, loss of self-respect); and rule-followers would be praised and made to feel good about themselves. These ensure that it's in our interest to follow the rules. In short, it's in everyone's interest to bring about a situation where anti-GR behavior serves no one's interest – and such an situation by and large exists.[2]

Game theory (a mathematical analysis of the interacting choices of multiple agents, §14.3f) is another way to view Hobbes's problem. I'll use my own story instead of the usual *prisoner's dilemma*.

In the *farmer's dilemma*, two rival farming families, the Hatfields and the McCoys, can do better for themselves if both cooperate instead of pursuing their individual interests. Each family wants only to gain the most money, and

---

[1] On Devil's Island, a penal colony for the worst French criminals, life became so bad that the prisoners were similarly moved to adopt GR rules of conduct (Aull 1950).
[2] People sometimes say that GR promotes self-interest only in small groups, where people know each other. But large groups may just require more structures (like Web reviews).

each must choose between stealing and being honest. If both sides are honest, each earns $6000 from crops. If one steals and the other is honest, then the one who steals gets $8000 and the honest one gets only $1000. (Stealing and guarding crops take time away from growing crops.) If both steal, both get only $2000 worth of crops. This chart shows choices and outcomes.

Hatfields		McCoys	
honest	$6000	honest	$6000
steal	$8000	honest	$1000
honest	$1000	steal	$8000
steal	$2000	steal	$2000

You're the Hatfields. What should you do? If the McCoys are honest, you gain more by stealing ($8000 instead of $6000). If the McCoys steal, you again gain more by stealing ($2000 instead of $1000). Either way you gain more by stealing. So you steal. The McCoys reason the same way; so they steal too. So both, following the egoist strategy, steal and thus gain a poor $2000.

Each side wants to be treated honestly and not be stolen from. So GR would say to be honest. If both sides had been honest, then each would have gained $6000. So it's better for each if both follow GR rather than both being egoistic. *GR communities outperform egoistic communities.* But in Hobbes's state of nature, each side is egoistic, and so gains only $2000.

You're still the Hatfields. There are four possible financial outcomes for you, here ranked from best to worst:

1. You steal and the McCoys are honest: you gain $8000.
2. You and the McCoys are both honest: you gain $6000.
3. You and the McCoys both steal: you gain $2000.
4. You're honest and the McCoys steal: you gain $1000.

While outcome 1 is the best for you, there's no practical way to achieve it in the Hobbesean state of nature (since the McCoys won't let themselves be taken advantage of). Since both sides choose on an egoistic basis, both sides choose to steal (since, regardless of whether the other side is honest or steals, stealing gains more money than honesty). This gives outcome 3: you gain a poor $2000. So egoism hurts both sides.

Both sides need to agree, in Hobbesian fashion, to set up a government structure to penalize stealing. Let's say, for example, that the structure gives a $3000 penalty for stealing and costs everyone $500 to maintain. This changes the outcomes and gives a new ranking:

1. You and the McCoys are both honest: you gain $5500 ($6000-$500).
2. You steal and the McCoys are honest: you gain $4500 ($8000-$3500).
3. You're honest and the McCoys steal: you gain $500 ($1000-$500).
4. You and the McCoys both steal: you *lose* $1500 ($2000-$3500).

Given the penalty for stealing, rational egoists will be honest and gain $5500.

A better solution, if we could make it work, is for everyone to just *choose* to follow GR in the state of nature. The payoff would be better: we'd all gain $6000 and avoid the $500 government overhead. But Hobbseans say this won't work, since egoism is part of our nature. If we're all going to follow GR, then society must make GR be in our self-interest.

Hobbes's ideas created quite a stir. John Locke, Joseph Butler, and Jean-Jacques Rousseau disputed many points, claiming that:

- Humans by nature aren't completely amoral and egoistic. Instead, we naturally have some GR sense of right and wrong, and some concern for others.
- In the state of nature, we'd agree to set up a democracy (not an absolute monarchy) to protect natural rights that we already have or ought to have.
- Punishments are a low motive to act morally.

Hobbes's contribution was to defend GR using unfriendly assumptions: that humans by nature are egoistic and have no sense of right and wrong.[1]

7.3 GR promotes self-interest

Old Joe gave us a poem about how GR is foolish (§7.1). If we versify to Joe as he's done to us, we can say:

> If you shun the golden rule,
> you'll be treated oh so cruel,
> you will be the biggest fool.

But *how* is Old Joe foolish (in terms of self-interest) to shun GR? And *how* does following GR promote self-interest?

GR promotes our self-interest in many ways:

- People mostly treat us as we treat them. So it pays to treat others well.
- Following GR promotes cooperation (which benefits everyone), self-respect, and respect and admiration from others.
- Selfishness brings conflict (which hurts everyone), guilt, alienation, disapproval, and legal penalties.

Some of these factors may be part of human nature. Others may have a social, Hobbsean explanation. In a society where people are even moderately egoistic, it's in everyone's interest to promote a "social karma," whereby those who harm others will receive harm (internal guilt and lowered self-respect – and

---

[1] Hobbes defends GR to a large degree but may limit its scope (§9.5). A social contract to promote contractors' interests may poorly protect the weak (like the disabled and animals).

disapproval, alienation, and punishment from others).

What about Old Joe? He may fear or suffer legal penalties for cheating. His reputation will be harmed. Would you trust someone who brags about his lies? He hurts relationships essential to his well-being. If his friends aren't jerks themselves (perhaps a greater curse), they'll see him as an inconsiderate jerk. And Old Joe will likely feel guilt, anxiety, and lowered self-respect. We try to socialize people so they feel bad when they violate GR – regardless of whether others find out. So yes, Old Joe gained a few extra dollars; but he loses much. If he thinks the dollars matter more to his well-being, he's fooling himself.

Further factors include *cognitive dissonance* and *self-worth*. First, humans tend to be distressed when they find they're inconsistent. Psychologists call this *cognitive dissonance*. So when students discover that the first sentence in their paragraph is inconsistent with their last sentence – or that their goal to become a doctor is inconsistent with their actions – they feel not joy but distress; and they scramble to rearrange their beliefs, desires, and actions so they all fit together. Festinger 1957: 3 claims that avoiding inconsistency is a basic motivation (see also Aronson 1969):

> Dissonance ... is a motivating factor in its own right.... Cognitive dissonance ... leads to activity oriented toward dissonance reduction just as hunger leads to activity oriented toward hunger reduction. It is a very different motivation from what psychologists are used to dealing with but, as we shall see, nonetheless powerful.

Since consistency promotes survival, cognitive dissonance likely comes from how we evolved and are socialized. GR violations are inconsistencies: our action (toward another) clashes with our desire about how we'd be treated in a similar situation. When we recognize our GR-inconsistency, we feel that something is wrong inside us – we feel a distressing cognitive dissonance.

Second, an essential ingredient in happiness is a sense of *self-worth*. We won't be happy if we lack this, even if we have great possessions. Our sense of self-worth depends on GR. If we violate GR, we treat others as having no worth. But then how can we see ourselves as having worth? Since you and I are cut from the same cloth, if I see you as having (or lacking) worth, I similarly see myself as having (or lacking) worth. So following GR ennobles us. I see myself as having worth because that's the way I see everyone. Having a sense of self-worth is more significant than getting a higher price for our used car. Foolish Old Joe doesn't understand this.

How we treat others has a major impact on our happiness. Ask people who do volunteer work; they'll report that they "receive from others" much more than they "give unto others." Helping others helps to make us happy. Rimland 1982 came up with a simple classroom experiment to test this idea. Have students list up to 10 names of people they know well. Have them put H/N (happy/not happy) after the names – and then S/U (selfish/unselfish). Have them cross out names where they can't assign H/N or S/U with confidence. Then count and add up the combinations. Strikingly, almost all H (happy) people are U (unselfish) – and most U people are H.[1]

If you want to make yourself miserable, focus your life on promoting your self-interest. Others will likely despise you, and you may end up despising yourself. Much of our good is social, and selfishness poisons relationships. You promote your own interest better if you respect the good of others the same way that you respect your own good.[2]

GR is an important element in life. Without it, nothing works very well. If we don't live it, then our lives lack something of central importance.

Some may say, "Yes, this is true in general, but there are exceptions. Intelligent crooks might better promote their interests by not following GR. To avoid guilt, they become callous inside. To avoid external sanctions, they fool others into thinking they're honest." But this life involves heavy costs – the fear of being caught, a shallow and unsatisfying existence, much cognitive dissonance, and low self-worth. This strategy rarely succeeds in the end.

A clearer counterexample is the rare case where GR requires great heroism (§11.1 Q10). Suppose you're a prison guard in a Nazi concentration camp. If you follow GR toward prisoners, you may suffer greatly. GR may require sacrificing self-interest, unless we bring in religious considerations (like afterlife rewards/punishments, karma, or reincarnation). Without religion, we can at most claim that GR promotes self-interest in the great majority of cases. With religion, GR may promote self-interest in *all* cases.

GR has been accused (§14.4 Obj. 30–31) of requiring *selfish motivation* (we treat others well so they'll treat us well) or of requiring *pure benevolence* (alleged to be uncommon and unrealistic). But GR just says "Treat others as you want to be treated"; it doesn't mention motivation and can appeal to widely different motivations (§11.1 Q16). While some feel that GR requires a self-interest justification, others are disgusted that anyone needs this.

7.4   Darwin and evolution

Do humans have any *genuine concern* for others for their own sake? If they do, then is this concern *learned* or *innate*? Here are three views:

- We have *no concern* for others for their own sake. If we care about others, this is only because we somehow think this benefits us. (Thomas Hobbes)

---

[1] Post 2007 gives further empirical data that we benefit by living GR.

[2] Betty 2001: 71, in defending William James's claim that ideas that produce good are more likely to be true, uses GR as an example: "If people who strive to live by the golden rule are happier on the whole and over the long run than those who dismiss it as so much romantic rubbish, then the golden rule would be a truer moral law than one based on ethical egoism."

- We have some *socially taught concern* for others for their own sake, but this isn't innate. (John Stuart Mill)
- We have some *innate concern* for others. (David Hume and Charles Darwin)

Evolution tends to support the *innate concern* view.

Charles Darwin (1809–82) proposed the theory of evolution. His *Origin of Species* (1859) claims that our present biological species evolved from earlier ones through *mutation* and *selection*. *Mutation* means that a species randomly produces organisms with slight differences; so some are bigger and some can move faster. *Selection* means that those with some features are more likely to survive and produce offspring with these same features.[1] Repeating the mutation-selection process many millions of times produces radically new life forms. Evolution explains many facts about organisms: comparative structure, embryology, geographical distribution, and fossil records.

Darwin's *Descent of Man* (1871) focuses on human evolution. Darwin claims that the moral sense (conscience), which is rightfully supreme over human action, is the most important difference between humans and lower animals. Analogues of morality exist in other social animals, such as dogs, wolves, ants, and bees. Wolves work together in packs and help each other. Dogs sympathize with another's distress or danger, and can show fidelity and obedience. Baboons follow a leader and enjoy being with each other; this promotes their survival. Many social animals have concern for the welfare of their offspring or comrades, even risking their own safety. With social animals, evolution encourages instincts and behaviors that benefit the group's survival.

Humans are social animals, living in families or groups. Like other such animals, we evolved social instincts. We enjoy helping others and are distressed by another's misery. We often show concern for others, especially offspring and members of our group. We value the approval of others, internalize group values, and follow the leader. Opposing our social instincts are impulses that can be anti-social, like lust, greed, and vengeance.

According to Darwin, primitive morality had arbitrary taboos, little discipline, and little concern for those outside one's clan or tribe. But humans gradually developed their intellectual powers through observation, language, inductive reasoning, and abstract thinking. So morality became more rational, disciplined, and concerned with consequences. As human groups expanded, so did our circle of concern. Religion purified our social feelings and moral instincts. We struggled toward a higher morality, supported by reason and directed to the good of everyone, even the weak and animals. Our noblest attribute became a disinterested love for all living creatures. GR sums up this higher morality: "Treat others as you want to be treated."

---

[1] Darwin was vague about how these features get passed on to offspring. Gregor Mendel (1822–84), an Augustinian monk, developed genetics, which helps us understand how this works. The recent Genome Project, which mapped human genes, was another step forward.

So what is Darwin's natural-history explanation of why we think morally? Evolution gave us two great gifts to promote our survival: *social instincts* and *reason*. Any animal with strong social instincts would develop a moral sense when its reason becomes well developed. And so humans over many centuries developed from a narrow, instinctive concern for offspring and fellow tribal members toward a higher, rational GR morality of concern for everyone.[1]

Social Darwinism (which differs from what Darwin held) was popular in the 19th century. On this view, evolution is a dog-eat-dog struggle where the strong survive and overcome the weak. Human life follows and ought to follow this same pattern. So it accords with nature and is right that strong individuals, businesses, social classes, and nations rise to power and overcome the weak. Evolution built into us egoism and domination, not concern for others; benevolent organisms have lower survival chances and would die off. Friedrich Nietzsche (1886) had similar ideas; he thought benevolence goes against our nature and leads to frustration. Social Darwinism (the opposite of what Darwin held) opposes GR.

This dispute raises a question: "What is the unit of evolutionary selection: the individual or the group?" Darwin picked the group: *altruistic groups* survive better. Social Darwinists picked the individual: *altruistic individuals* die off. Which side is right? According to many recent sociobiologists, like William Hamilton, Robert Trivers, and Edward Wilson, both sides are wrong. The gene is the unit of selection.[2] Well-adapted genes tend to be transmitted to future organisms. Evolution promotes the survival of the fittest genes.

Consider bees. The only female with offspring is the queen. But female worker bees share the same genes as the queen. By promoting the bee society, these workers insure that their genes go into future organisms. Something similar holds for human society. We're biologically oriented to pass our genes into the future. We can do this by having offspring ourselves or by helping those who have similar genes to have offspring. We tend to give greater help to close relatives since we share more genes with them.

Besides such *kin altruism*, there's also *reciprocal altruism*, often between different species. For example, some small fish act as "cleaners," eating food from a larger fish's gills. Each side benefits and develops an instinctive concern for the other side, since this promotes the survival of its genes. Other animals with connected interests, like humans, similarly evolve an innate tendency to cooperate with and show concern for each other.

So evolution built a tendency to altruism into us, especially toward close relatives or cooperation partners. The explanation is genetic: such altruism promotes the survival of our genes. Some talk about "selfish genes"; evolution works as if genes promoted their survival by using organisms. But this is just a

---

[1] Section 8.1 talks more about the forces that move us from groupism to a higher morality.

[2] Hamilton 1964; Trivers 1971, 1985, 2002; D. Wilson 2003; and E. Wilson 2000. Vogel 2004 nicely sketches GR's evolutionary roots. Gensler 2009b has more on Darwin's ethics.

metaphor to explain how instinctive concern for others evolved.

Several thinkers (like Shermer 2004, Binmore 2005, and Boehm 2009) discuss GR's role in our hunter-and-gatherer phase, which is how we humans lived for most of our existence. Cooperative hunting works better. Small, genetically similar clans that used GR to promote cooperation and sharing had a greater chance to survive. This example supports *group selection*.

Donald Pfaff works in the neuroscience of morality (Pfaff 2007 and Pfaff *et al.* 2008). He claims that our forebrain mechanisms dispose us toward following GR. He breaks GR brain activity into four steps (I'll skip the technical details):

1.   You consider an action (e.g., knifing someone in the stomach).
2.   You envision the target of this action.
3.   You *blur the difference* between the other person and yourself.
4.   You decide what to do.

Step 3 is crucial, where the brain *blurs the difference* between yourself and the other person – so you see the action as being done to you. Pfaff says this is easy for the brain to do and doesn't involve complex abilities.

Pfaff's four steps remind me of Kita (Know, Imagine, Test, Act). Pfaff's first two steps correspond to my Know, his third step is my Imagine, and his fourth step leads to my Act. My Test-for-consistency step has you ask, "Am I now willing that if I were in the same situation then this be done to me?" Its neurological analogue may be the cognitive dissonance that comes from a GR violation and motivates us to change our action (or our desire). Perhaps cognitive dissonance could be incorporated into the neurological approach. And perhaps a similar mechanism helps us to envision future consequences on ourselves as if they were present (§2.3).

Pfaff thinks the GR brain mechanism began so a mother could have concern for her baby. Unlike most animals, humans are born defenseless and need years of care. For society to exist, people (usually the mother) must have concern for infants. So Hobbes's state of nature, where everyone is entirely egoistic, couldn't have evolved: someone needs to care for babies!

These biological discussions get complicated as they try to explain how we developed a mix of benevolence and egoism. There's much controversy about details and about the relative contributions of genetics and socialization.

To sum up, evolutionary theory gives evidence that humans have an innate, inherent concern for others (which would make psychological egoism false). It gives a plausible story about how this concern for others, combined with reason and/or brain mechanisms, leads to a GR-based morality. And so it supports GR and helps us understand why GR is so widespread across the globe. In short, GR is hardwired into our genes and brain mechanisms.

There are other scientific explanations of human altruism. Some explain it by classical conditioning. Pavlov's dogs associated a bell with food, and later salivated when the bell rang without food. So too we associate pain behavior (such as crying) with our inner distress, and later experience the same distress from seeing another's pain behavior. So we develop a motivation to prevent in another what would cause pain if done to us. Some say this begins very early; babies are distressed when they hear other babies cry.

Other approaches talk about the advantages of altruistic socialization for group survival (sociology), how adults teach altruism by example and other methods (social learning theory), and how reason moves us to construct altruistic rules for mutual benefit (developmental psychology). All of these are compatible with the evolutionary approach.[1]

The bottom line here is that science supports the belief that people can care about others.

[1] See Brandt 1976, Erikson 1964, Hoffman 1981, Kohlberg 1979, Kohlberg et al. 1983 & 1990, Krebs 1982, Piaget 1948, and Rushton & Sorrentino 1981. Rushton 1982 gives a good overview of altruism from a scientific perspective. Anyone skeptical of genuine altruism should read Monroe et al. 1990, which is a psychological study of thirteen people who risked their lives to help Jews escape from the Nazis.

CHAPTER 8
Racism and Other Groupisms

*R*acism is *having concern only for members of your race.* So if you're a white racist, then you have concern only for whites; you don't care what happens to others, except as this affects whites. *Groupism,* a broader notion, is *having concern only for members of your group;* you might define "your group" by race, religion, ethnicity, gender, sexual orientation, or whatever.

We'll first consider groupist objections to GR. Then we'll talk about how to criticize groupism by appealing to consistency and GR. Finally, we'll look at the historic slavery debate in the U.S., which featured GR.

8.1   Groupist GR objections

Groupism is a plural egoism. Groupism is having concern just for your group, while egoism is having concern just for yourself. Our groupism discussion in this section mirrors the egoism discussion in Chapter 7.

Two forms of groupism give GR objections. First, *ethical groupism* says we ought to do whatever promotes good and prevents harm for our group, regardless of how this affects others. So applying GR to others is disloyal and wrong:

Objection 6: ethical groupism	We ought to have concern only for our own group. Thus it's disloyal to our group and wrong to apply GR to those outside of our group.

So we as whites (or blacks, Jews, Palestinians, Tutsis, Hutus, Catholics, Protestants, or whatever) ought to have concern only for "our own kind." GR is fine, but it's to be applied only to our own group – not to outsiders.

Thomas Hobbes argued that *enlightened egoism* leads to GR (§7.2), since individuals live better when GR prevails between individuals. *Enlightened groupism* likewise leads to GR, since groups live better when GR prevails between groups. Imagine a world where each group cares only for itself and accepts no duties toward other groups. Each group lies, steals, or kills when this serves its interest. Every group would suffer from the war between groups.

A wise group leader might say: "This constant war hurts our group. It's in our group's interest that there be peace and justice between groups. We must act justly toward other groups and get other groups to act justly toward us. Wanting our property to be respected, we'll agree to respect their property. Wanting our lives to be respected, we'll agree to respect their lives. All groups need to enforce GR rules that consider everyone's interests. We need to insure that those who treat other groups badly will suffer alienation, social disapproval, and legal penalties (external sanctions) – and guilt, anxiety, and low self-respect (internal sanctions); and we need to praise those who treat other groups well. All groups need to do this. If this happens, our group (and others) will prosper and won't suffer from this war between groups."

For a group to compromise, it must be unhappy with its current situation. It may be unhappy because it suffers from violence (harm to people or property) or non-violent resistance (demonstrations, strikes, economic boycotts, or sit-ins). Even a small oppressed group, when organized, can make it in the oppressor's interest to end the oppression and follow GR toward other groups.

As groups mix over time, groupism faces the further problem of *fuzzy group identity*. There may be intermarriage, as between blacks and whites, or Jews and Muslims. Cultures may mix, as when whites learn to do rap music. And groups may combine in endless ways, which shake up our prejudices; imagine a gay-bashing Republican who gets to know a firm Republican who is gay. In complex societies, where groups mix and combine in different ways, it becomes less clear what "my group" is and what people I'm supposed to be against.

Psychological groupism says people by nature are motivated to have concern only for their own group. GR is a social trait we evolved to promote cooperation within our own clan. Since we're genetically programmed to apply GR just to our group, a universal GR goes against human nature:

Objection 7: psychological groupism	We're built (as products of evolution) to have concern only for our own group. Thus applying GR outside our group goes against nature, is unrealistic, and leads to frustration.

Applying GR to everyone won't work, since it goes against how we're built.

We're certainly inclined toward in-groups and out-groups (just as we're inclined toward egoism). There's "us" and there's "them." But the "us" and "them" can, in complex societies, vary from moment to moment. We're playing football against a rival team; "us" is my team, and we try to defeat the other team. I'm at a company meeting; "us" is my company, and we try to outsell the other company. I'm with my family (another "us"). I'm with my class or church group (each forming another "us"). In each case, I focus on serving a specific group; but I may still treat other groups fairly, by GR.

Consider evolution (§7.4). According to Darwin, our *social instincts* evolved to promote the good of our group. So a purely instinctual ethics would be groupist. But *social evolution* (including religion and reason) moves us to a higher morality of concern for everyone, even our enemies, as expressed in GR.[1] While Darwin was vague about what forces move us from groupism to a universal GR, I'd highlight four key factors:

- War between groups or individuals hurts everyone. So group-interest and self-interest move us to promote a universal GR.
- As groups mix over time, groupism faces the further problem of *fuzzy group identity*. This hurts groupism.
- Every major religion teaches a universal GR (ch. 3).
- Consistency pushes us to a universal GR (as we saw in ch. 1–2) and away from groupism (which we'll see is riddled with inconsistencies).

So social, religious, and rational forces support a universal GR. The "rational forces" here include consistency and rational self- and group-interest.

Darwin saw groupism as a *lower morality* and a universal GR as a *higher morality*. Those who spread division (racial, ethnic, religious, or whatever) are promoting a groupism that's a relic from our evolutionary past, when small clans with similar genes competed for survival against other such clans. A universal GR better promotes the good of groups and individuals.

Gold, besides being a *metal*, is a *color*. Let's name five *natural forces* inside us after the colors of autumn leaves:

- Golden rule: Do unto others as you'd have them do unto you.
- Yellow rule (self-interest): Do unto yourself.
- Brown rule (group-interest): Do unto your group.
- Red rule (repayment/retaliation): Treat others as they treat you.
- Purple rule (consistency): Be consistent in thought and action.

Which should we follow? GR, of course! But the others can lead to GR. Enlightened self-interest (yellow) can push us to promote a society where individuals follow GR (§7.2). Enlightened group-interest (brown) can push us to promote a world where groups follow GR toward other groups. Repayment/retaliation (red), if practiced by others, makes it in our interest to follow GR, since then the treatment we give is the treatment we get (§§11.2 Q8 & 14.3f). Consistency (purple) has us shun GR inconsistencies. So these five primal forces, if we understand them, can all point us in the same golden direction.

---

[1] Darwin (1871 ch. 4) wrote: "To do good in return for evil, to love your enemy, is a height of morality to which it may be doubted whether the social instincts would, by themselves, have ever led us. It is necessary that these instincts, together with sympathy, should have been highly cultivated and extended by the aid of reason, instruction, and the love or fear of God, before any such golden rule would ever be thought of and obeyed."

8.2 Extreme groupist principles

Conscientiousness (§§1.8 & 2.1c) is the requirement that we *keep our life (including our actions, intentions, etc.) in harmony with our moral beliefs.* This gives a way to criticize groupist principles. Let's call "All short people ought to be beat up, just because they're short" *shortism.* If I hold shortism then I must, to be consistent, *desire* that if I were short then I be beat up. And this I likely can't do. But then my thinking would be inconsistent.

Here are some extreme groupist principles:

- Jews ought to be put into concentration camps and killed, just because they're Jews.
- Blacks ought to be enslaved, just because they're black.
- Women ought to be denied educational and voting opportunities, just because they're women.
- Gay people ought to be beaten up, just because they're gay.

If you accept such principles consistently, then you must *desire* that if you were Jewish (black, female, gay, or whatever) then you'd be treated in an awful way. So such principles are difficult to hold consistently.

Instead of appealing to consistency against groupism, we might be tempted to counter with our own principle, like "People of all races ought to be treated with respect." While this is a fine principle, a groupist will just reject it. And so we'll have a stalemate, where the groupist has his principle and we have ours, and neither can convince the other. A consistency appeal is more effective, since it turns the groupist's own principle against himself.

In rare cases, groupists might pass the consistency test; then we need to appeal to other factors, like knowledge and imagination. Perhaps the Nazi genuinely desires that if he were a Jew then he be put into a concentration camp and killed. There's an allegedly true story about a Nazi who reacted this way when he discovered his Jewish ancestry. Since he hated Jews so much, he came to hate himself and his family. So he had himself and his family put into concentration camps and killed. This Nazi was consistent.

Such hateful anti-Jewish desires may come from:

- current false beliefs. The Nazi may think Aryans are superior to Jews and racially pure. We can criticize this on factual grounds.
- previous false beliefs. The Nazi may hate Jews because of previous false beliefs about Jews. He's given up these beliefs, but his hatred of Jews remains.
- social conditioning. The Nazi may have been taught to hate Jews. Maybe his family and friends hated Jews, called them names, and promoted stereotypes about them. And maybe he met only a few atypically nasty Jews. Then the Nazi's hateful desires would diminish if he understood the origin of his hatred and broadened his experience of Jews in an open way.

The Nazi's anti-Jewish desires came from false beliefs and social conditioning. Such flawed desires would diminish with greater knowledge and experience.

We also can have the Nazi consider other socially taught prejudices. All over the world, people in one group are taught to dislike those of another group. We teach young children: "Be suspicious of *those other people*. They're of a different race (religion, ethnic background, sexual orientation, or caste). They aren't our kind. They have strange customs and do strange things. They're evil and inferior." When we broaden our knowledge and experience, we conclude, "They're people too, much like us, with many of the same virtues and vices."

Hatreds programmed into us from our youth may never completely disappear; but a wider knowledge and experience will reduce them. That's all that our consistency arguments need. Only a very strong hatred of Jews can make us desire that if we were Jews then we be put into a concentration camp and killed. And we can criticize such desires on rational grounds.

While this example was about Nazis, the same idea applies to one who desires that he be mistreated if he were black, female, or gay. In each case, the desire is likely flawed (since it's based on a social conditioning that uses false beliefs and stereotypes) and would be given up if we expanded our knowledge and experience of the group in an open way.

8.3 Groupist arguments

Many racists present arguments. For example, a white racist may argue that blacks should be treated as second-class citizens because they're inferior. This is an argument, with a *premise* ("Blacks are inferior") and *conclusion* ("Blacks ought to be treated as second-class citizens"). How should we respond? Should we dispute the racist's premise, and say "All races are genetically equal"? Or should we counter with "People of all races ought to be treated equally"? Either strategy will likely bring a stalemate, where the racist has his beliefs and we have ours, and neither side can convince the other.

I suggest instead that we express the racist's argument clearly and then watch it explode in his face. His conclusion, presumably, is about how *all* blacks ought to be treated. Since the conclusion has "all," the premises also must have "all." So he needs to claim that *all* blacks are inferior. And he needs to add that *all* inferior people ought to be treated as second-class citizens (denied voting, better education, better jobs, etc.). His argument then goes this way:

> All blacks are inferior.
> All who are inferior ought to be treated as second-class citizens.
> ∴ All blacks ought to be treated as second-class citizens.

To clarify this further, we can ask what the racist means by "inferior." What exactly puts someone into the "inferior" group? Is it IQ, education, wealth, physical strength, or what? Let's suppose the racist decides on an IQ criterion: "inferior" = "of IQ below 80." Then his argument goes:

> All blacks have an IQ below 80.
> All who have an IQ below 80 ought to be treated as second-class citizens.
> ∴ All blacks ought to be treated as second-class citizens.

The first premise is clearly false, since every race has some IQs below 80 and some above 80. And the second premise also applies to whites:

> All of IQ below 80 ought to be treated as second-class citizens.
> ∴ All *whites* of IQ below 80 ought to be treated as second-class citizens.

To be consistent, the racist must believe that he ought to treat low-IQ whites as second-class citizens (as he treats blacks). And he must treat these whites this way himself, and desire that others do so. The racist won't be consistent.

Racist arguments also need to define the oppressed group. What makes a person "black" or "Jewish"? One might be *black* by skin color, racial features, culture, or descent. One might be *Jewish* by religion, racial features, culture, or descent. These factors can exist in many combinations, degrees, and mixtures; racism requires giving precise boundaries to something that by nature is vague. The Nazis in 1935 used arbitrary stipulations: you were Jewish (and perse-cuted) if *one* of your grandparents was a clear case of being a Jew (Haas 1988: 62–5 & 133–5). Traditional American racism stipulated that *any* black ancestor makes you *black* – even if you're 99% white by descent, culture, and appear-ance (Zack 1993); so "All blacks have an IQ below 80" means "All who have at least one black ancestor have an IQ below 80." Racist arguments get even crazier when we try to clarify them.[1]

Our strategy for criticizing racist arguments has three steps:

1. Formulate the argument. The premises must be clearly stated, and the conclu-sion must clearly follow from the premises.
2. Criticize the factual premises, if necessary.
3. See if the racist applies his moral premise consistently to his own race.

If the racist's conclusion is about how *all* blacks (or Jews, or whatever) are to be treated, then he needs a criterion to separate the groups cleanly, so all blacks

---

[1] It's unwise to spend much time debating the *average* genetic IQ of various groups. First, there are issues about the value and cultural neutrality of the IQ test. Second, it's difficult to separate genetic from environmental factors; oppressed groups can be expected to perform poorer (Silber-man 1964). Third, the moral relevance of average IQ is unclear. Suppose we prove a group to have a lower *average* genetic IQ; why should we conclude that *all* members of the group ought to be treated as second-class citizens – even those with a high IQ? If we proved that blondes have a lower *average* genetic IQ, why should we exclude an unusually bright blonde (like the heroine in the 2001 movie *Legally Blonde*) from law school on the basis of being blonde? If you don't think this would be crazy, imagine that you're kept out of law school on this basis.

will be on one side and all whites on the other. An IQ number doesn't do this – and neither does any other plausible criterion. These considerations of logic and consistency will destroy most racist arguments.

Consider a racist who argues that blacks should be treated as second-class citizens because they have dark skin:

> All blacks have dark skin.
> All who have dark skin ought to be treated as second-class citizens.
> ∴ All blacks ought to be treated as second-class citizens.

The first premise is false, since many albino blacks have light skin; but the racist wants to treat them as second-class citizens too. And many whites have dark tans; the racist must treat them as second-class citizens. And if a *Skin So Pale* cosmetic were invented that turned black skin permanently white, the racist must discriminate only against blacks who didn't use it.

The racist also must desire that if he and his family had dark skin then they'd be treated as second-class citizens. To dramatize the idea, we could tell him R.M. Hare's 1963: 218 story about the color-changing germ that's about to infect the world. The germ turns originally light skin permanently dark and originally dark skin permanently light. Does the racist really desire that if this happened then the newly light-skinned people be treated well, and the newly dark-skinned people (including himself and his family) be treated as second-class citizens? With questions like these, we can show him that his moral thinking is inconsistent and thus flawed.

Abraham Lincoln (1850s-65: 2:223f) similarly used consistency to criticize pro-slavery views. Suppose, Lincoln asks, you think that having a lighter skin (or greater intelligence) gives you the right to enslave another. Then you must accept that you are to be slave to the first person you meet with a lighter skin (or greater intelligence).

Sexism is another groupism. In the U.S. before 1920, men could vote but not women. And women were long denied equal education and employment. Women were thought to be intellectually inferior – less logical and more emotional. Here's the argument:

> Men are more intelligent than women.
> All who are more intelligent, and only those, ought to be allowed to vote, participate in higher education, and assume leadership roles in government and business.
> ∴ Men, but not women, ought to be allowed to vote, participate in higher education, and assume leadership roles in government and business.

The premise about men being more intelligent has been criticized in two ways. Many say that, if we compare men and women with the same education and background, both groups have equal intellectual abilities. Experiments with college students, for example, show no difference in logical skills between men and women.[1] Another response contends that, while the intellectual skills of both groups differ, both are equally valuable. Logical skills are only part of intelligence. Woman have other qualities, such as emotional sensitivity and a more holistic intuition, that are just as important.

What does the first premise, "Men are more intelligent than women," mean? We might take this as "Every man is more intelligent than any woman" (there's some intelligence level that every man is above and every woman is below); this claim is entirely implausible but needed to derive the conclusion that "*Every* man ought to be allowed to vote (and so on) but *no* woman ought to be allowed to do this." Or we might take the first premise as "The average intelligence level of men is higher than the average level of women." But even this doubtful claim wouldn't justify banning *every* woman from voting, higher education, or leadership roles in government and business. Clearly many women have greater intelligence than most men who participate in these activities. One who holds the second premise ("All who are more intelligent, and only those, ought to be allowed to vote...") must, to be consistent, allow the vote to women of greater intelligence but not to men of lesser intelligence.

This section analyzed old-fashioned racist and sexist arguments that used to be influential. It's important to understand *why* such arguments are wrong and *how* to criticize them. Other groupist arguments have similar patterns: we ought to treat members of a group (Tutsis, Muslims, gays, etc.) in an unfavorable way because they have such and such a defect. But do they *all* have this defect? And what about people in *your* group who have this defect?

8.4   Groupist actions

Applying GR to groupist actions is straightforward. Let's consider a white racist who mistreats blacks. Kita suggests four steps.

(K) Get the racist to *know* the facts, especially about race (including the capabilities of different races) and about how his actions affect others. When President Kennedy applied GR to racism (§§1.3 & 2.2), he first tried to get whites to understand what segregation was doing to black people. Blacks were treated as second-class citizens because of skin color. They couldn't vote, go to the best public schools, eat at most public restaurants, or sit in the front of the bus. These practices brought further poverty and frustration, and a low sense of self-worth. We can learn about another's situation by observation and testimony. So we might have the racist *observe* blacks – how they live and how segregation affects them. And we might have him listen to the *testimony* of

---

[1] In my forty years of teaching logic, I've started with a pretest, on which males and females do equally well (http://www.harryhiker.com/logic.htm).

blacks about how they're treated.

(I) Try to get the racist to *imagine* himself, vividly and accurately, in his victim's place, on the receiving end of the action. So he might read a novel or watch a movie that portrays their lives. Or he might act out the role of someone discriminated against. Or he might relive, in his imagination, cases where he himself was treated poorly because of his background. Or he might just explore in his imagination what it would be like to receive such treatment.

(T) Have the racist *test* his consistency by asking, "Am I now willing that if I were in the same situation then this be done to me?" Most racists will answer no. If the racist answers yes, then he's consistent but likely has flawed desires based on social conditioning. Then we need to have him understand the origin of his desires and expand his knowledge and experience of blacks.

(A) The racist needs to *act* toward others only as he's willing to be treated in the same situation. This will lead him away from his flawed racism.

If racism is flawed, why did so many otherwise normal people embrace it? Haas 1988 explains the rise of Nazism. He talks about ancient racial animosities; about nationalism, charismatic leaders, powerful organizations, and social pressures; about fear, greed, hatred, and blind obedience; about lies, stereotypes, ignorance, and uncriticalness; and about how people get used to killing when their friends find it acceptable. Also, the Nazis compartmentalized their thinking. They applied empathy and GR to their own families but not to Jews. They were rational in choosing means to ends but not in appraising ends. These powerful forces overcame the weak voice of reason.

Something similar explains American racism toward blacks. The story begins with a racist world that tolerates slavery. It continues with the greed of the slave traders and slave owners, America's ignoring of its founding principle ("All men are created equal"), inherited racial stereotypes and animosities, compartmentalized thinking (empathy and GR are applied to whites but not blacks), fear of change, group pressures, and so on. There are many reasons why we don't apply GR (§6.4).

8.5   History, slavery, and GR

GR was prominent in the historic American debate on slavery. Before getting into this, let's note that GR led to one of the few condemnations of slavery in the ancient world. Epictetus (90: 33, ch. 41), who was born a slave in 55 AD but became an important Stoic philosopher after being freed, wrote: "What you shun enduring yourself, attempt not to impose on others. You shun slavery – beware of enslaving others! If you can endure to do that, one would think you had been once upon a time a slave yourself."

In the American colonies, slavery was permitted everywhere. The first public protest against slavery was signed by four Pennsylvania Quakers in 1688 on the basis of GR (Bruns 1977: 3f):[1]

> There is a saying, that we shall do unto others as we would have them do unto us – making no difference in generation, descent, or color…. What in the world would be worse to do to us, than to have men steal us away and sell us for slaves to strange countries, separating us from our wives and children? This is not doing to others as we would be done by; therefore we are against this slave traffic.

This hand-written resolution went to a larger Quaker meeting in New Jersey, where it was tabled. Many northern Quakers owned slaves.

Colonial Quakers produced many publications denouncing slavery on the basis of GR. Here are some quotes (the last one is from a black ex-slave):

> To buy souls and bodies of men for money, to enslave them and their posterity to the end of the world, we judge is … cruelty and oppression, and theft and robbery of the highest nature … and transgresses that golden rule and law, To do to others what we would have others do to us. (George Keith 1693, in Bruns 1977: 5–8)

> Some time ago, I was inclined to buy Negroes … to help my family (which includes some small children). But there arose a question in me about the lawfulness of this under the gospel command of Christ Jesus: Do unto all men as you would have all men do unto you. We ourselves would not willingly be lifelong slaves. (Robert Piles 1698, in Bruns 1977: 9f)

> Doing to others as we would not be done by is unlawful. But making slaves of Negroes is doing to others as we would not be done by. Therefore, making slaves of Negroes is unlawful. (John Hepburn 1715, in Bruns 1977: 16–31)

> Jesus has laid down the best criterion by which mankind ought to judge of their own conduct …: Whatsoever you would that men should do unto you, do you even so to them…. One man ought not to look upon another man, or society of men, as so far beneath him, but he should put himself in their place, in all his actions towards them, and bring all to this test: How should I approve of this conduct, were I in their circumstance and they in mine? (John Wollman 1754, in Bruns 1977: 68–78)

> Let that excellent rule given by our Savior, to do to others, as you would that they should do to you, have its due weight…. Suppose that you were ensnared away – the husband from the dear wife of his bosom … – or children from their fond parents…. Suppose, that you were thus ravished from such a blissful situation, and plunged into miserable slavery, in a distant quarter of the globe…. Now, are you willing that all this should befall you? (Caesar Sarter 1774, in Bruns 1977: 337–40)

[1] I put the quotes from Bruns into modern English.

The philosopher Jonathan Edwards (1791) after American independence wrote the most rigorous piece; he starts with GR, talks about the slave trade, and criticizes pro-slavery arguments (appealing to consistency).[1]

American Revolutionary leaders were inconsistent about slavery. Patrick Henry declared, "Give me liberty or give me death!"; but he owned slaves. Henry had slaves because life without them would be "inconvenient"; but he admitted the strength of the anti-slavery arguments (Bruns 1977: 222). Thomas Jefferson penned the words that begin the Declaration of Independence: "We hold these truths to be self-evident; that all men are created equal; that they are endowed by their creator with certain unalienable rights, that among these are life, liberty, and the pursuit of happiness";[2] but he too owned slaves. George Washington complained that England had tried to enslave the colonies; but he too owned slaves.[3] The poet Phillis Wheatley, a black ex-slave, wrote in 1774 of the love of freedom that God implanted in everyone, including her people; she complained about the inconsistency between American words and actions about freedom (Bruns 1977: 307f).

Before the Revolution, both North and South had slaves; Boston in 1700 had 400 black slaves, bought and sold like other commodities (Greene 1928). But slavery disappeared in the North as anti-slavery forces grew. William Lloyd Garrison in 1832 established the New England Anti-Slavery Society, which called for the immediate end of slavery based on GR (Garrison 1833: 30). Slavery increasingly divided North and South, leading to the Civil War.

Since GR pushes us to look at both sides of an issue, we'll now consider arguments on the other side. Rev. John Dagg, president of Mercer University in Georgia, gave one of the fullest and most articulate defenses of slavery, which I'll summarize under four headings:

(1) *Capabilities of blacks*: Black slaves are incapable of exercising citizenship and civil liberty. So the state has the authority to institute a system of domestic slavery, whereby the master ought to care for and protect the slave, who in turn ought to work for and be faithful to the master. A master has duties to slaves and ought to treat them kindly. But, since blacks (like perpetual minors) are totally unqualified for citizenship and freedom, there's no duty to treat them as equals or give them freedom, which would hurt them. Abolishing slavery would bring social chaos. Blacks by nature are without enterprise, indolent and improvident. (Dagg 1860: 338–44, 361–5, 357–9)

(2) *Mistreatment of slaves*: A master ought to care for his slaves, even when

---

[1] For early GR opposition to slavery, see Aptheker 1940, Binder-Johnson 1941, Cantor 1963, Crothers 2005, Huston 2000, Rosenberg 2004, and Zeitz 2000. Bruns 1977 has primary sources.

[2] Many said GR and "All men are created equal" mean the same thing. The latter can't mean that we're all born *factually equal*; for some are born stronger, smarter, or richer. Rather it asserts a *moral equality*. We're all entitled to equal moral consideration: everyone has the right to be treated by others only as these others are willing to be treated themselves in the same situation.

[3] Twelve American presidents owned slaves at one time or other, including eight while in office (http://home.nas.com/lopresti/ps.htm). History buffs might try to identify these.

they're old and sick. Regrettably, some masters are cruel. This doesn't show that slavery is wrong (just as the cruelty of some husbands doesn't show that marriage is wrong). While a slave can't refuse slavery, neither can a poor laborer refuse work; some are born slaves as others are born poor. If having a laborer is just, then so is having a slave. Slavery benefits black slaves, and their being brought to America was part of God's benevolent plan. (351–9)

(3) *Biblical teaching*: The Bible often mentions slavery without condemning it and thus implicitly teaches that there's nothing inherently wrong with it. Genesis 9:25 records the origin of slavery: "Cursed be Canaan; a servant of servants shall he be unto his brethren." Noah pronounced this curse because of a crime by Canaan's father. Black slaves are Canaan's descendents, and the curse explains their degradation. God made humans unequal. (344–50)

(4) *The golden rule*: It's bad reasoning to argue that, since the master doesn't want to be held in bondage by the slave, therefore he shouldn't hold the slave in bondage. This same reasoning would forbid the jailor to imprison the criminal (since the jailor doesn't want to be imprisoned by the criminal). GR's intent isn't to forbid imprisonment or slavery, but rather to have us be kind toward prisoners and slaves. Society has a right to restrict freedom for the common good; it restricts the freedom of black slaves (who are incapable of exercising full freedom) and of criminals. The misguided reasoning that would lead to abolishing slavery would, if consistently applied, lead to abolishing prisons and thus destroying society. (354–7, 365–74)

What can be said against Dagg? My first criticism is that Dagg does little to get his facts straight. He believes that blacks are inherently stupid (like "perpetual minors") but gives no evidence for this. He doesn't say, for example, "Many have tried to teach black slave children to read, but with no success." Such an experiment would have proved him wrong.[1] Dagg takes it as true beyond question, and needing no evidence, that blacks by nature are stupid. And he, uncritically, never considers that black slaves might show less intelligence because they're kept uneducated.

At that time, there were two views about the capabilities of the blacks and about how blacks were treated:

- *Pro-slavery view*: Blacks by nature are dull-witted. Most slave owners treat slaves well, as if the slaves were their own retarded children. Slavery benefits both slaves (who'd do poorly on their own) and slave owners (who profit from the work of slaves).
- *Anti-slavery view*: Blacks by nature are fairly intelligent (although less than whites[2]) and can live well on their own. Slave owners often treat slaves cruelly, as when they separate slave families for financial gain. Slavery benefits slave owners at the expense of slaves.

[1] This experiment would have been illegal. The law, while allowing masters to chain and beat slaves, forbad them to teach slaves to read.
[2] Even the anti-slavery side held false racial stereotypes. Back then, it was commonly thought that various groups (including women and the Irish) were by nature less intelligent.

There was strong evidence against the pro-slavery view. (1) There was much testimony from European visitors to Africa that blacks were just as bright, just, and good natured as whites (Bruns 1977: 79–96 & 145–84). (2) Many blacks who escaped from slavery did well on their own, living as free people in the North and describing the horrors of slavery; especially impressive ex-slaves include authors Harriet Jacobs and Frederick Douglass, and activists Harriet Tubman and Sojourner Truth. Here's a quote from Douglass (1855: 151):

> I love the religion of our blessed Savior.... I love that religion that is based upon the glorious principle, of love to God and love to man; which makes its followers do unto others as they themselves would be done by. If you demand liberty to yourself, it says, grant it to your neighbors. If you claim a right to think for yourself, allow your neighbors the same right.... It is because I love this religion that I hate the slaveholding, the woman-whipping, the mind-darkening, the soul-destroying religion that exists in the southern states of America.

If Dagg had read Douglass (who was a popular writer), could he still believe that all blacks are stupid? The black ex-slave Douglass seems much brighter than Dagg; compare their critical thinking skills (see my previous comments about Dagg), their writing style (Douglass's prose sparkles with brilliance), and the obstacles that Douglass overcame (his learning to read as a slave was against the law). Douglass also better understood Christianity.[1]

Uncle Tom's Cabin, a novel written by Harriet Beecher Stowe, was a strong anti-slavery force; it described slave life and got people to imagine themselves in slave shoes. Stowe lived in Cincinnati, where she listened to slaves who crossed into freedom. This dialogue from Stowe (1852: 126f, somewhat edited) gives a debate between two women about slavery:

A: "The most dreadful part of slavery, to my mind, is its outrages on the feelings and affections – the separating of families, for example."

B: "That *is* a bad thing, certainly," said the other lady; "but then, I fancy, it doesn't occur often."

A: "Oh, it does," said the first lady; "I've lived many years in Kentucky and Virginia both, and I've seen enough to make one's heart sick. Suppose, ma'am, that your two children, there, be taken from you and sold?"

B: "We can't reason from our feelings to those of this class of persons," said the other lady.

A: "Indeed, ma'am, you can know nothing of them, if you say so," answered the first lady, warmly. "I was born and brought up among them. I know they *do* feel, just as keenly – even more so, perhaps – as we do."

So black slaves don't feel the pain that whites would feel? To rebut this idea, the novel described how a young slave woman, whose young son was taken

---

[1] Mieder 2001 calls Douglass "the most visible and influential African American of the 19th century" and a great champion of GR. Douglass deserves to be better known and appreciated.

from her and sold, was heartbroken and drowned herself.[1]

We talked earlier about "Kita." The first two letters stand for the "know" and "imagine" ingredients in moral thinking. Dagg was poor on the "know" part, on getting the facts right. He was also poor on the "imagine" part. In discussing slavery, he never imagines himself or his children in the place of the black slaves. He never considers what it would be like if *he* were stolen off from Africa, separated from family members, and sentenced to lifelong slavery. A slave state can't encourage its members to *know* the slaves accurately (including their capabilities and sufferings) or *imagine* themselves in their place.

Abraham Lincoln (1850s-65: 2:222, 2:532, 3:357) often appealed to switching places, using phrases like "As I would not be a *slave*, so I would not be a *master*" and "He who would *be* no slave, must consent to *have* no slave." And he suggested that slaveholders who describe the life of slaves in glowing terms take advantage of this life themselves by becoming slaves. Angelina Grimké's *Appeal to the Christian Women of the South* (1836: 13f) similarly states:

> Are you willing to enslave your children? You start back with horror … at such a question. But why, if slavery is no wrong to those upon whom it is imposed? Why, if as has often been said, slaves are happier than their masters, free from the cares and perplexities of providing for themselves and their families? … Do you not perceive that as soon as this golden rule of action is applied to *yourselves* that you involuntarily shrink from the test?

Grimké was born and raised in a slaveholding family in South Carolina, where her remarkable pamphlet was latter banned and publicly burned.

What about Dagg's challenge: "If racism is so clearly wrong, why wasn't it condemned in the Bible?"? The anti-slave people answer:[2]

- Slavery broke many biblical norms: about kidnapping people to make them slaves (Exodus 21:16, "Anyone who kidnaps another and either sells him or is found holding him captive, shall be put to death" – *by this law alone, all the slaves in America are held unlawfully*), stealing (labor or body or soul), dividing families, brutality, GR, etc. (John Hepburn in 1715, in Bruns 1977: 28f)
- The Old Testament said that every Hebrew slave must be offered freedom after seven years (Deuteronomy 15:12 and Jeremiah 34:14). Jesus, in telling us to view everyone as neighbors and brothers, extended this to all. He didn't tell people directly to free their slaves, because he didn't want to interfere with government. But many things Jesus said (about love, the Good Samaritan,

---

[1] Stowe's novel was, after the Bible, the best-selling book of the 19th century. Many southerners objected that Stowe was ignorant and that slavery was more humane than northern capitalism (which was bad too). Stowe's novel was banned in much of the South, and six pro-slavery novels were written in response. But many defended Stowe, and she eventually won out. Her book was translated into many languages and became perhaps the most influential novel of all time.

[2] Allen 1860, Bourne 1845, and *New Englander* 1857 argued that the Bible is against slavery. See also Shanks 1931 and Harrill 2000.

greed, etc.) give seeds for arguments against slavery. (Benjamin Rush in 1773, in Bruns 1977: 227)
- Slavery in biblical times was much different, not based just on race, and much more humane. Slaves in biblical times were more like servants and protected by biblical laws. The biblical languages themselves are unclear about the distinction between "slave" and "servant." (Grimké 1836: 4–15)

Black slaves appealed to the Bible in their own way against slavery. Their Negro Spirituals added African melodies to words about the exodus of the Jewish slaves from Egypt. *Go Down Moses* (c. 1853) says:

> When Israel was in Egypt's land, Let My people go!
> Oppressed so hard they could not stand, Let My people go!
>
> Go down, Moses, Way down in Egypt's land;
> Tell old Pharaoh, To let My people go!
>
> No more shall they in bondage toil, Let My people go!
> Let them come out with Egypt's spoil, Let My people go!
>
> Oh, let us all from bondage flee, Let My people go!
> And let us all in Christ be free, Let My people go!
>
> You need not always weep and mourn, Let My people go!
> And wear these slav'ry chains forlorn, Let My people go!

Such songs well captured the spirit of the Bible about slavery.

What about Genesis 9:25: "Cursed be Canaan; a servant of servants shall he be unto his brethren"? Dagg and others misinterpreted this when they applied it to black Africans. The Bible tells us:

> Canaan's descendents include Sidon, Hittites, Jebusites, Amorites, Girga-shites, Hivites, Arkites, Sinites, Arvadites, Zemarites, and Hamathites. The Canaanite land stretched from Sidon toward Sodom, Gomorrah, Admah and Zeboim, and as far as Lesha. (Genesis 10: 15–19)

The Canaanite land is roughly what is now Israel, Palestine, Lebanon, and part of Syria. The term "Canaan" and its cognates occur 160 times in my digital Bible, each time referring to people of the area around Israel. Nothing in the Bible relates Canaan to black Africa. Connecting Canaan with black Africans is a racist idea with no basis in the Bible.[1]

Harriet Beecher Stowe, a minister's daughter, has a section in *Uncle Tom's Cabin* about two ministers (1852: 127f). One quotes "Cursed be Canaan" and explains that God intends that Africans be kept in a low condition as servants. This brings joy to a slave seller who took up the trade to make money and intended to repent later; this verse saves him the trouble of repenting. But then a second minister breaks in and repeats GR, adding that it's scripture too. As a

---

[1] Edwards (1791: 13–5), Grimké (1836: 3f), and Bourne (1845: 24–6) answered similarly.

slave ("John, aged thirty") is separated from his wife and dragged off the boat with much sorrow, the second minister tells the slave trader: "How dare you carry on a trade like this? Look at these poor creatures!"

What about GR? The pro-slavery James Thornwell (1850: 42f), John Dagg (1860: 256), and Robert Dabney (1867: 196 or 124) all ridiculed GR using the criminal example from Immanuel Kant (1785: 97). We explained and answered this objection earlier, in §2.1c (see also §§1.4, 2.4, & 14.3c):

> You're a judge, about to sentence a dangerous criminal to jail. The criminal protests and appeals (incorrectly) to GR: "If you were in my place, you'd want not to be sent to jail; so by GR you can't send me to jail." You should respond: "I can send you to jail, because I'm now willing that if I were in your place (as a dangerous criminal) then I be sent to jail." You could add, "If I do such things, then please send me to jail too!"

The criminal objection commits the "soft GR fallacy," which assumes that GR prevents us from ever going against what the other person wants.

Once we understand GR reasoning more clearly (and avoid the criminal objection), know the facts (about the capabilities of blacks and the way they were treated), and exercise our imagination (picturing ourselves in their place), the GR case against slavery becomes crystal clear. It's a shame that the U.S. had to fight a bloody civil war to resolve the issue.

Dagg and friends suggest that we should apply GR, not to *whether* we should have slaves, but to *how* we should treat the slaves that we do have. So we should be *kind* slave masters. This reminds me of a thief who tries to rob people in a kind way – or a hired murderer who tries to kill people painlessly. This approach doesn't go far enough.

The debate about slavery brought out the best and the worst in Christianity. Chapter 3 noted that nearly all of the world's religions support GR. But some religious people put GR at the center, while others ignore it and instead teach stereotypes and divisiveness. Christianity isn't immune to this problem.

And so, for centuries slavery was accepted almost everywhere. But a few voices began to criticize slavery on the basis of GR. These voices grew louder and more powerful, eventually bringing social change.

CHAPTER 9
Applied Ethics

We'll begin by seeing how GR can contribute to courses in applied ethics. Then we'll talk about business ethics, medical ethics, and the ethics of discussion. Then we'll address issues about GR's scope (for example, whether GR applies to how we treat animals) and highlight other key issues to which GR can contribute.

9.1 Applied ethics courses

Applied ethics studies moral issues like lying and stealing, or moral questions in specific areas. The most developed branches are business ethics and medical ethics. Other branches deal with animals, computer ethics, disability ethics, environmental ethics, global ethics, moral education, professional ethics, sexual ethics, and so on. Applied ethics courses often first teach ethical theories (such as utilitarianism, egoism, and nonconsequentialism) and then discuss cases. How can GR contribute to such courses?

Students studying applied ethics, while searching for ideas to help them live better lives, are often relativistic. GR answers both concerns: GR is a practical and attractive tool for moral living that refines a procedure that they may be using already; it's also a global norm that's common to all major world religions and can be defended rationally. Teachers who add a GR component should begin with GR reasoning, GR fallacies, and the Kita procedure (ch. 1 or 2); they might also consider briefly GR's global presence across different religions and cultures and GR's non-religious justifications (ch. 3 & 12).

Kita suggests that, in applying GR, we must try to *know* the facts (especially about how our action affects others) and *imagine* ourselves in the other's place on the receiving end of the action. The GR question then *tests* a proposed action for consistency: "Am I now willing that if I were in the same situation then this be done to me?" Problems may arise:

- *Knowing* the facts may be difficult; for example, there often are controversies about how different people will be affected by a proposed action.
- *Imagining* ourselves in the place of the various parties (especially those different from us) may also be difficult.

- *Creativity* may be needed to find policies that we can approve of regardless of where we imagine ourselves in the situation.
- *Testing for consistency* may not bring agreement. Maybe you're willing that such and such be done to you, but someone else isn't.

GR narrows the range of acceptable views (so that not just anything goes) but doesn't always bring complete agreement. The goal of an applied ethics course isn't to bring complete agreement, but rather to improve the quality of our moral thinking. GR and Kita can help.

GR and Kita *supplement* other ethical theories by providing additional consistency tools for thinking about moral issues. GR and Kita don't replace the usual ethical theories. Teachers will still want to bring in approaches like utilitarianism, egoism, and nonconsequentialism.

9.2 Business ethics

Many *business people* are interested in GR.[1] Two company presidents wrote books about how to run a successful business using GR: Arthur Nash 1923, who ran a Cincinnati clothing company, and James Penney 1950, who started the JCPenney stores (originally called "Golden Rule Stores"). Both say GR works well in business, leading to happy employees who work hard and happy customers who return.[2]

If you're interested in GR in business, I suggest two readings. The first is John Maxwell's *There's No Such Thing as "Business" Ethics* (2003). The title means that the same GR covers both personal life and business. This book gives the big picture, and is motivational and easy to read. Maxwell argues that being ethical tends to enhance business success in the long run, that ethics is based on GR, and that GR can be used to create common ground with any reasonable person and thus bring mutually beneficial "win-win" outcomes. We all want to be valued, appreciated, trusted, respected, understood, and not be taken advantage of; employees treated that way will work harder, cooperate better, and be more committed to the company. Maxwell peppers his book with snappy quotations and stories.

I also suggest Tom Carson's "Deception and withholding information in sales" (2010: 169–81 or 2001). The article gets down to details; it's tightly argued and appeals to GR consistency (§13.2). Carson argues that salespeople have a duty, other things equal, to:

- warn customers of potential hazards (unless these are well-known, like the hazards of smoking);

---

[1] Other chapters refer to over a dozen articles in business-ethics journals discussing GR. And business examples have come up often, as in §§1.7, 2.1d, 2.2, 3.1a, 10.0, 10.5, 14.1, & 14.3a.
[2] For more on Nash and Penney, see Wattles 1996: 97–103.

- refrain from lying and deception (*deception* can involve saying something true to get someone to believe a falsehood – so when asked whether you set back the car's odometer, which you did, you answer in a shocked voice "That's illegal!");
- fully (if possible) and honestly answer questions about what you sell (but don't answer whether another store has the same item at a lower price); and
- not steer customers toward purchases you have reason to think will harm them (by being overly expensive, for example, or being something that they'd likely regret buying if they understood the facts).

Carson has us look at proposed practices from the standpoint of the salesperson (who must earn a living), the customer (who wants to buy a good product for a reasonable price), and the employer (who needs to sell products). Any action we propose as permissible must be something we'd consent to in the place of any of the three parties. Carson gives a good model of how to apply GR to the details of business.[1]

9.3 Medical ethics

Medical ethics started about 400 BC in ancient Greece, when Hippocrates wrote the *Hippocratic Oath* for doctors. This speaks of prescribing for the patients' good, not intentionally harming, not giving lethal drugs, not causing abortions, keeping matters confidential, and so on. Dr. Louis Lasagna wrote a modern version that's widely used today; here's an excerpt (Kligler & R. Lee 2004: 4):

> I will apply, for the benefit of the sick, all measures which are required, avoiding those twin traps of overtreatment and therapeutic nihilism. I will remember that there is art to medicine as well as science, and that warmth, sympathy, and understanding may outweigh the surgeon's knife or the chemist's drug. I will not be ashamed to say "I know not," nor will I fail to call in my colleagues when the skills of another are needed for a patient's recovery. I will respect the privacy of my patients, for their problems are not disclosed to me that the world may know…. I will remember that I do not treat a fever chart, a cancerous growth, but a sick human being.

Many professions have ethics codes. These give rules that experts draw up, we hope, on the basis of GR combined with wide knowledge and empathy. Ethics codes are especially useful for those new to a profession, who lack the experience needed for wise professional decisions. Graves 1924: 50 says that an ethics code should be "a kind of golden rule, expanded, and concretely and definitely applied to the particular conditions of a particular business."

---

[1] For more on GR in business, see Barach & Elstrott 1988, Bruton 2004, Burton & Goldsby 2005, Cunningham 1998, Dole 1895, Donaldson 1989, Holoviak 1993, Keirstead 1923, Melé 2009, Romar 2002, and Spinello 2002 & 2005. Tullberg 2011 criticizes the use of GR in business.

When I started researching this book, I searched databases for articles and book chapters on "golden rule" and "do unto others," and then I downloaded a thousand publications to my hard disk. I found that many professions have an interest in GR. But the group with the most interest was nurses. Again and again, publications by or about nurses appeared.

Years ago, my parents spent much time in hospitals; it made a big difference to their well-being whether they were cared for by considerate GR nurses. When you're sick and need help, nurses can be angels or demons. Here are some quotes about GR and nursing:

> Would you be in sympathy with your patient? Would you win her confidence? Then regard this poor sufferer in the light of someone dear to you; put her in that other's stead. Someone has said, "In Ethics, you cannot better the golden rule." Suppose you render it, "Do unto others as you would they should do unto yours." This is *your* mother; this *your* sister; this *your* child. (Thompson 1905: 164)

> The nurse who graduates from a hospital training school where every convenience is at hand must use her inventive faculty when caring for a patient in the home. The thought in the mind of the nurse should be, "How would I like to be cared for if in this patient's place?" It is the little things that count for so much when a person is ill. (*American Journal of Nursing* 1920)

> Some people say every nurse should herself have had a serious illness in order that she may get the patient's point of view. There are few people, however, who do not know the meaning of pain and who do not have sufficient imagination, if they care to exert it, to realize what it means to lie in bed helpless. What is needed is that they should stop to consider these facts, that they should give thought to their patients' feelings as well as to their symptoms and the means to relieve them. (Fiske 1923: 1013)

> What sort of physician, nurse, lawyer, do we desire where our own interests are in question? The answer will be precisely a description of that sort of nurse or physician which we ourselves, embarked on that career, should strive to become. This is the golden rule – to do unto others as we would that others should do unto us – and it is wonderfully clear, practical, and illuminating. We know so well what manner of nurse we should like to have … a nurse of the highest personal character and devotion to duty, kind, sympathetic, tactful, gentle, one who has greatly profited from experience and observations, one with all the good elements of character and none of the undesirable ones. That is therefore precisely the sort of nurse we should strive to become. (Garesché 1927: 903)

> Always remember the golden rule of doing unto others as you would have them do unto you. Keep in mind that we all will be patients ourselves one day. Imagine how you would like to be treated by the health care personnel looking after you. (Donald 2007: 717)

Much of this is good advice for other medical and non-medical personnel too.[1]

Especially important today is the issue of what role government should have in health care; GR can be of help here (Grisez 2011).

9.4 Ethics of discussion

GR applies nicely to the *ethics of discussion*: "Treat the views of others as you want your own views to be treated."[2] GR leads to norms like these:

- Understand a view before you criticize it. Never distort another's view to make your view look better.
- Be open to give or accept constructive criticisms. Evaluate your views by standards as strict as those you use to evaluate another's views. Challenge flawed ideas and actions, but hesitate to criticize people.
- Be clear and understandable. Aim to communicate more than impress, and to cooperate more than alienate.

GR can be applied to any discussion, whether in classrooms, academic journals, families, labor-management negotiations, international disputes, or politics. Too many discussions are ungolden. In politics, for example, it's common for partisan speeches or ads to use misleading language or downright falsehoods to influence voters. Governments would run much better without this. Journalists need to expose such violations of the ethics of discussion.[3]

9.5 GR's scope

When GR says "Do unto others," who are these "others"? The simple answer is "everyone." But does this "everyone" include mountains, the earth, plants, animals, Martians, ourselves, nations, the unborn, the dead, or God? How we answer has implications for applied ethics.

> (Q1) Which beings should the golden rule be applied to? Should we apply it just to human beings – or perhaps just to our tribe or group? Should we apply it to animals or things?

---

[1] See also *American Journal of Nursing* 1953, Dull *et al.* 1941, Dyck & Padilla 2009, and Fredriksson & Eriksson 2003.

[2] This is like Troll's interfaith GR: "Try to understand the other's faith as you would like your own faith to be understood" (§3.1).

[3] For more about applying GR to the ethics of discussion, see N. Cooper 1994, Giri 2004, Jackson 1970, and D. Johnson & R. Johnson 2009. See also Spahn 2011.

GR deals with how to treat *sentient beings* – those capable of experiences (past, present, or future). So GR applies to how to treat humans and animals. GR is vacuous when we apply it to non-sentient objects.

Chapters 1 and 2 derived GR from two consistency norms:

- *Impartiality* requires that we make similar evaluations about similar actions, regardless of the individuals involved.
- *Conscientiousness* requires that we keep our life (including our actions, intentions, etc.) in harmony with our moral beliefs.

If I'm consistent (in a broad sense that includes being impartial and conscientious), I'll necessarily follow GR.

Let's review how our GR derivation works. Let's derive this instance of Gold 1 (which leaves unspecified what kind of being X is):

| Don't step on X without consenting to the idea of your being stepped on in the same situation. | GR *instance about stepping on X* |

Suppose I'm consistent and step on X. Then (being conscientious) I wouldn't do this unless I believed my act was all right (permissible). And (being impartial) I wouldn't believe this unless I believed it would be all right for me to be stepped on in the same situation. And (being conscientious again), I wouldn't believe this unless I was willing that I be stepped on in the same situation. Hence if I'm consistent, then I won't step on X unless I'm willing that I be stepped on in the same situation (where I'm in X's place).

This argument works regardless of the kind of being that X is, human or not. We defined "impartial" and "conscientious" in general terms, not mentioning "human." So our GR instance about stepping on X, and other instances, aren't restricted to how to treat *humans* (nor to how to treat our *tribe* or *group*).

The GR instance about stepping on X works normally if X is a sentient being – like a friend, stranger, or dog. I care about whether I be stepped on if I were in the place of these, since then being stepped on would hurt me. The GR instance is vacuous if X is a rock or other non-sentient being, for two reasons:

- I don't care if I be stepped on if I were in the place of a rock. Rocks feel no pain.
- It makes little sense to imagine myself in the place of a rock (or another non-sentient object). Imagining myself in X's place involves imagining myself having X's experiences or potential experiences. I can do this if X is a sentient being, like a human or a dog. But rocks have no experiences or potential experiences. What could it mean to imagine myself in the place of *this* rock, having all and only its properties, instead of in the place of *that* rock?

So I step freely on rocks – but not on friends, strangers, or dogs.

So GR applies to how to treat, not just members of our tribe or group, and not just humans, but all sentient beings. Consider this GR instance about torturing your dog: "Don't torture your dog without consenting to the idea of your being tortured if you were in your dog's place." This works like GR as applied to humans. It's more difficult to imagine yourself in your dog's place; but this example doesn't demand a subtle knowledge of dogs. So I see no reason not to apply GR to animals (and not just to pets).[1]

Hinduism, Jainism, and Buddhism (§§3.2a–b) are clear about applying GR to animals. Western religions are less clear on this. But Jesus calls himself the good shepherd who cares for his sheep (John 10:1–18) and the Muslim thinker Ibn Arabi saw GR as applying to all God's creatures (§3.1c).

I'm reminded of an African proverb: "One who is going to take a pointed stick to pinch a baby bird should first try it on himself to feel how it hurts." This suggests that we apply GR to baby birds and all other sentient creatures.

(Q2) Would applying GR to animals lead to vegetarianism?

I see two defensible views here. Many *vegetarians* say that, since they aren't willing that they be killed for food in the place of animals, they won't kill animals for food. Many add that eating meat (1) harms our health (promoting obesity, cancer, and heart disease); (2) increases world hunger (more resources are needed to produce animal protein than vegetable protein); (3) harms the environment (the meat industry's heavy use of fossil fuels promotes global warming); and (4) harms animals (especially those raised in factory farms).

In contrast, *demi-vegetarians* eat a little meat, from animals raised humanely. They argue (with Hare 1993b) that this (1) is as healthy as eating no meat, (2) is better for world hunger than vegetarianism (since some hilly or arid land can be grazed but not farmed), (3) does little harm to the environment, and (4) serves the interest of farm animals who are raised in a happy manner (since otherwise they wouldn't exist). And yes, they're willing that if they were farm animals then they be raised humanely but later eaten.

GR would, however, clearly oppose the cruel treatment of animals on factory farms (see http://www.meat.org).

(Q3) Can we have GR duties to beings of other planets, if such exist?

Yes. In the movie *Avatar* (2009), humans travel to the planet Pandora. Most think nothing of destroying the happiness, culture, and lives of the natives who, even though not human, have beliefs, desires, hopes, fears, distresses, and loves just as we do. This is wrong and violates GR.

---

[1] Bono & De Mori 2005, Darnell 1967, Hopkins 1906, A. Huxley 1963, Montgomery 1978, Mulholland 1988, Panaman 2008, Smart 1981, and D. Thomas 2005 endorse applying GR to animals, as do many others (search http://www.peta.org for "golden rule"); M. Adler 1990 and Duxbury 2009 dissent. See also P. Singer 1975.

People sometimes emphasize humanity's common origin; some say we all came from a small group of humans who existed about 50,000 years ago. Such ideas make us feel more like a family. But we can still have GR duties to beings of a different biological ancestry.

(Q4) If we can't apply GR to non-sentient beings, then what about the *green rule*: "Do unto the earth as you would have it do unto you"?

This *green rule* makes no sense if taken literally. It has silly implications like "If you don't want the earth to send you hurricanes, then don't send it hurricanes." Nor does it make sense to ask how I'm willing that I be treated if I were in the exact place of the earth. I can't see how to express this rule more adequately, to fix the problems. But I guess this green rule is OK as a rough slogan, to supplement (but not replace) GR. To emphasize this, I favor expressing it as a more obvious metaphor: "Do unto Mother Earth as you'd have her do unto you." Better yet, use my *carbon rule* (§§1.6 & 2.3): "Keep the earth livable for future generations, as we want past generations to have done for us." This is GR applied to how to treat future generations.

GR can contribute much to environmental concern. *Sustainable living*, for example, requires living in a way that we satisfy GR toward future generations (and don't use up all the resources now). And GR can back up our duties toward animals. So GR makes a strong argument for treating the earth in a way that promotes the long-term interests of both humans and animals.

Some environmentalists go further. They say that plants, mountains, and canyons deserve to exist too – and not just for the long-term interests of humans and animals. Richard Routley 1973 argues for the *intrinsic value of the natural world*. He has us imagine that there's one person left on Earth who could arrange for the destruction of the natural world after he dies. We'd see this action as wrong, which assumes that the natural world has intrinsic value.

GR can defend the value of plants, mountains, and canyons – but for the sake of humans and animals. As I write this chapter, I'm planning my eighteenth trip to the Grand Canyon, where I've spent many months hiking or rafting. The Grand Canyon is awesomely beautiful and needs to be preserved for future generations. GR supports this. As we want those of previous generations to have preserved the Grand Canyon and other places of natural beauty for our generation, so too we need to preserve these for future generations.

Routley would go further: the Grand Canyon ought to be preserved for its own sake too, even if we were the last generation on the planet. I agree with Routley on this. GR provides no basis for this further step, no basis for *the intrinsic value of the natural world*. But that's OK by me.

GR needn't provide a basis for *all* my moral beliefs. GR has little to say about some ethical issues – for example, about whether pleasure is the only thing of intrinsic worth (§11.1 Q5). How do we answer questions about intrinsic worth, then, if not by GR? I suggest we appeal to what we'd favor insofar as we're rational, which includes being informed, imaginative, and consistent. And on this basis I'd defend Routley's view about the intrinsic value of the natural world. Insofar as we have a deep experience of the Grand Canyon, we'd want it preserved for its own sake, as a thing of beauty and value in its own right (besides contributing to further generations). People who don't appreciate the intrinsic value of the Grand Canyon need to expand their experience. They need to hike down the Hermit Trail, raft over Hance Rapids, listen to those who have done such things, or at least view the Grand Canyon pictures on my Web site. People who deeply experience the natural world tend to appreciate its intrinsic value.

(Q5) Can we apply the golden rule to how we treat the unborn?

Yes. Suppose Suzy is a heavy smoker and becomes pregnant. She knows that smoking can harm the baby. She asks "Am I willing that my mother would have smoked in similar conditions while pregnant with me?" After reflection, she answers no. So she decides to give up smoking while pregnant (and maybe after too). This use of GR makes perfect sense.[1]

I've argued elsewhere (Gensler 1986a and 2011a: 168–75) that we can apply GR to abortion and that GR consistency favors the belief that abortion is wrong in at least most cases. While the details here are complicated, I basically argue that most people won't be consistent if they hold that abortion is normally permissible – since they won't consent to the idea of themselves having been aborted in normal circumstances. But this argument, even if it succeeds at what it tries to do, still leaves some details fuzzy.[2]

(Q6) Can we apply the golden rule to how we treat ourselves?

The "Treat *others*" formula doesn't apply to how we treat *ourselves*. But similar and equally correct formulas do apply: "Treat your-future-self only as you're willing to have been treated by your-past-self in the same situation" and "Treat yourself only as you're willing to have others (especially those you most care about) treat themselves in the same situation." Section 2.3 called these the *future-regard* and *self-regard* principles.

---

[1] *Suzy smoking while pregnant* and *Suzy's mother smoking while pregnant* are relevantly similar actions – and so if one is permissible then so is the other. We don't need a premise about the unborn being "a human" or "a person" (which it clearly is in some senses of these ambiguous terms but not in other senses). Recall that the derivation of Gold 1 from impartiality and conscientiousness doesn't require a premise that X is human.
[2] There's controversy over whether GR applies to the unborn and to abortion. See Blumenfeld 1977, Blumenson 2000, Boonin 2003, Brugger 2009, Carter 1982, K. Chan 2004, Duxbury 2009, Gaffney 1987, Hare 1975, Meyers 2010, Sher 1977, B. Wilson 1988, and Yacasua 1974. Dr. Bernard Nathanson 1979, who had fought to legalize abortion and later directed the world's largest abortion clinic, later appealed to GR against abortion.

(Q7) Can we apply the golden rule to how we treat the dead, how we treat nations, and how we treat God?

Yes to all three. First consider the dead. To avoid complications, let's suppose that there's no afterlife. Now Henry Ford before his death donated much land to the city of Dearborn, with stipulations about its use. Suppose you're now Dearborn's mayor and want to ignore these stipulations. GR asks: "Are you now willing that if you similarly donate land with stipulations about its use, then these be similarly ignored after your death?" If you answer no, and yet you ignore these stipulations, then you violate GR.

Now consider nations. We often speak of nations as acting, having desires, having duties, and being inconsistent; I'll leave it to others to debate how or whether such talk should be analyzed. But then it seems to make sense to apply GR to nations: as a nation, we're to treat other nations only as we consent to ourselves being treated in similar circumstances.[1]

Now consider God. Augustine (400a, §3.1b) claimed that, since we want God to love us, then by GR we're to love God. This presumes the literal GR. A more sophisticated GR would have us imagine ourselves in the place of a perfect being who created and loves us, and ask: "How am I willing that I be treated by my creatures in this situation?"

9.6   Some other areas

Here are four areas of special GR urgency:

(1) *Groupism.* People often mistreat those who differ from them, in religion, race, ethnicity, sexual orientation, or whatever (ch. 3 & 8).

(2) *Family life.* Families are deteriorating fast. Statistics about divorces, abortions, and single parents are frightening. Fewer children are being brought up in an atmosphere of mutual understanding and love. Moral education is often poor (ch. 6). GR needs to permeate the family.

(3) *Treatment of animals.* Modern factory farming of animals is cruel. It treats animals who can feel pain as we'd hate to be treated ourselves, just so we can have cheap meat that makes us obese and unhealthy, while consuming resources in a way that we can't afford. When we look back at times that accepted slavery, we ask how people could have been so morally blind. When the next generation looks back at our treatment of animals, they'll ask about *our* moral blindness. What can we do about this? A useful first step would be to have an "animal-treatment facts" label on animal products (Gensler 2009c), as we now have "nutrition facts," so that we can at least know what we're doing.

---

[1] Most thinkers seem to agree that GR can apply to nations. For discussions, see Barr 1956, Berggren & Rae 2006, E. Burton 1918, Catt 1927, Durant 1969, McClure 1930, McDonald 1927, and R. Miller 2000.

(4) *Environment.* Global warming will make life much worse for future generations. We need to apply GR to future generations, to keep the earth livable for them, as we want past generations to have done for us. Again, a useful first step would be to have an "environment facts" label on what we buy, to help us realize how our choices affect the environment. We also need much clear thinking (especially on alternative energy sources) and action.

GR also applies to mundane matters about how to relate to others. When I see a PowerPoint presentation overloaded with small text that can't be read in the allotted time, I ask, "Did the presenter imagine the place of the viewer?" When a computer program crashes and I get an unintelligible error message, I ask, "Did the programmer imagine being an average computer user who reads this message?" When I get into a conversation with people who talk only about themselves and how great they are, I ask, "Would these people want to be treated this way too?" When I see family members screaming at each other, I ask, "How would this situation be changed if both sides tried to understand the other's perspective and apply GR?"

Henry Ford reportedly once said, "If there is any one secret of success, it lies in the ability to get the other person's point of view and see things from that person's angle as well as from your own." That's important in businesses, hospitals, governments, classrooms, families, sports teams, or whatever. It's also a central part of treating others as we want to be treated.

CHAPTER 10
Positive and Negative GRs

While Jesus expressed the golden rule positively, Confucius and Hillel earlier had expressed it negatively:

> Positive GR: What you want done to yourself, do to others.
> Negative GR: What you want *not* done to yourself, *don't* do to others.

The negative form is sometimes called the "silver rule."[1] Do the two forms differ in implications? If they differ, then is one better and the other perhaps flawed? And does Christianity have a positive approach to duty while Confucianism and Judaism have a negative approach? Here I'll deal with these issues.

Such issues matter in two ways. (1) Many people use GR in their lives. If one form is flawed or inferior, then people need to know this. (2) Many people see GR as part of global ethics, with diverse religions and cultures agreeing on GR (ch. 3). But if different groups accept conflicting GR forms, then this agreement is more apparent than real (Anderson 2009).

Here's an example to illustrate the problem. Over a hundred years ago, Wu Ting-Fang (1900), a diplomat from China to the U.S., wrote an open letter about how the two countries relate. He analyzed the needs and opportunities of both countries and how both sides might cooperate better for mutual advantage. Each country had to play fair, which he saw as lacking on the American side. He appealed to GR, which he saw both as part of his Confucian tradition and as the universal basis for morality and fair international relations.

Suppose there are two conflicting GR forms, with China accepting the negative GR and America accepting the positive GR. Then the appeal to a common principle would be lost. And both sides would have to appeal only to the GR form that they accept. So appeals to GR would get messy.

Here I'll consider views that say that the positive GR is better, that the forms are different but complementary, and that the negative GR is better. Then I'll argue, logically, that both forms are equivalent, and historically, that the Confucian and Jewish traditions don't have a negative ethics.

---

[1] See Matthew 7:12 and Luke 6:31 for Jesus, Analects 15:23 for Confucius (W. Chan 1963: 44), and Shabbat of the Babylonian Talmud 31a for Hillel (http://www.come-and-hear.com/shabbath /shabbath_31.html). All three used GR to sum up how we ought to live.

10.1   Positive GR is better

Some contend that the positive GR is superior.[1] On this view, morality contains DOs and DON'Ts. The DON'Ts forbid ways to harm others; we aren't to lie, cheat, steal, kill, and so on. The DOs encourage us to help others in various ways; we are to feed the poor, clothe the naked, encourage the downtrodden, and so on. In Jesus's time, the Pharisees focused on the DON'Ts. They taught a legalistic and external approach to religion and morality. As long as we didn't harm others or violate religious laws, we were doing well. The negative GR is about DON'Ts, about not harming others: since we don't want others to deceive, cheat, rob, or kill us, we aren't to do these things to others. And so the negative GR fit well the approach of the Pharisees.

Jesus was more demanding. He thought that not harming others was just the beginning. More important is to do good to others, to show love and compassion toward those in need. To express this in a dramatic way, Jesus took the standard negative GR and gave it a new, positive twist. We aren't just to avoid hurting others – treating them as we don't want to be treated. More importantly, we are to help others, showing them love and compassion – treating them as we ourselves want to be treated. Some say this shift to the positive was the most creative and original part of Jesus's moral teaching (Mould 1948).

Jesus radicalized GR. Even though his positive form differs only slightly in wording, its implications differ greatly. If you follow the positive GR, you'll move beyond the minimalist justice of not hurting others and toward a more demanding love that lavishes on others the good that we want for ourselves. Thus the positive golden rule greatly surpasses the negative rule.

10.2   Both are complementary

On this second view, the positive and negative forms are complementary. While they differ in implications, each form is equally valuable and covers an important aspect of morality.[2]

As before, the negative GR is about DON'Ts, about not harming others: since we don't want others to deceive, cheat, rob, or kill us, we aren't to do these things to others. If we were all saints, then this negative GR would be less important. But since injustice and vice are rampant in the world, it's unwise to belittle the negative GR.

---

[1] Authors preferring the positive GR include Atkinson 1982, Hale 1805, *Interpreter's Bible* 1951, Jeremias 1961, Mould 1948, Porpora 2001, Sedgwick 1993, Tasker 1906, Tillich 1955, Votaw 1904, and nine others mentioned by G. King 1928 (who rejects this view).
[2] Anderson 2009, Jeffries 1999, Jonas 1969, Kohlberg *et al.* 1990 (158), and Melé 2009 take the positive and negative GR to be distinct but complementary.

This chart shows how the two GRs cover two important parts of morality:

Negative golden rule	Positive golden rule
moral DON'Ts not doing evil to others not harming others countering vice justice	moral DOs doing good to others helping others promoting virtue love

Any morality that had just one dimension would be impoverished.

Would it be better for each religious tradition to have *both* GR forms? Ideally, yes. But a tradition might in words have just one GR form (positive or negative) but in practice apply both forms.

10.3   Negative GR is better

On this third view, the negative GR is better than the positive. Either form is workable only to the extent that people are similar in their ideals and preferences. This is more easily satisfied with the negative GR.[1]

People are fairly similar in how they want NOT to be treated. Practically no one wants to deceived, cheated, robbed, or killed. And so, following the negative GR, we shouldn't do these things to others. Because people by and large have similar dislikes, the negative GR works fairly well.

People differ much more in their likes. And so the positive GR, which has me treat others as I'd like to be treated myself, works poorly. Here are examples. I like to have people quarrel with me, let's suppose; so, following the positive GR, I quarrel with others (including those who hate quarreling). I like football; so I buy football tickets for all my friends (including those who like opera and hate football). I like broccoli; so I feed it to all my friends (including those who hate it). The positive GR is self-centered and tyrannical. It makes my personal likes into the norm of how I should treat everyone else. It ignores the fact that others may have different likes.

In addition, the positive GR can be impossible to follow. Suppose I walk down a street and pass a dozen beggars, each asking for a $50 donation to relieve their poverty. In each case, if I were in their place then I'd want to be given $50; so the positive GR tells me to give $50 to each. And suppose I keep passing more and more such people. My GR obligations will continue until I have no more money to give. Yes, it would be nice to help all the poor people in the world (since if I were in their place then I'd want to be helped). But this is

---

[1] Allinson 1982, 1992, 2003; Andrew 1986; Eisler 1947; *Jewish Encyclopedia* 1962; Kaufman 1963 (224f); Rieser 1958; L. Russell 1942; V. Smith 1946; and Tu 1981 prefer the negative GR.

impossible – I can't help them all. And so the positive GR can't really generate obligations – since if it did then it would generate so many of them that we couldn't fulfill them all. So the positive GR is unworkable.

The negative GR is practical, since we can all refrain from lying, cheating, stealing, and killing. But we can't all help everyone in need. Since we have limited time and resources, the positive GR is totally impractical.

10.4   Both are equivalent

The fourth view, which I accept, says that positive and negative GRs are logically equivalent: any action prescribed by one will be prescribed by the other.[1]

It's easy to derive the negative GR from the positive. Take this positive GR:

If you want X to <u>do A</u> to you, then <u>do A</u> to X.

We can replace "do A" with any action description, such as "omit doing B":

If you want X to <u>omit doing B</u> to you, then <u>omit doing B</u> to X.

This is equivalent to the negative GR: "If you want X not to do B to you, then don't do B to X."

Similarly, let's start with this negative GR:

If you want X not to <u>do A</u> to you, then don't <u>do A</u> to X.

Since "do A" can stand for any action, substitute "omit doing B" for it:

If you want X not to <u>omit doing B</u> to you, then don't <u>omit doing B</u> to X.

Simplifying double negations gives the positive GR: "If you want X to do B to you, then do B to X." So the positive and negative GR are logically equivalent.

Let me make the same point more concretely. A British television station created a new "ten commandments" (Spier 2005). They asked 4,000 people to suggest commandments; and they picked the 20 most popular ones. They then had 40,000 Brits rank these 20. The favorite by far was GR: "Treat others as you would be treated." Here are the other nine:

2. Take responsibility for your actions.
3. Do not kill.
4. Be honest.

[1] W. Chan 1955, Donagan 1977, Gensler 1996 (108–11), Henry 1827 (4: 63f), G. King 1928, McKenzie 1968, Nivison 1996, Pao-nan (in W. Chan 1955: 300), Reinikainen 2005, Rowley 1940, Sharp 1928 (140f, 334–43), M. Singer 1963, and Zerffi 1885 take the equivalence view.

5. Do not steal.
6. Protect and nurture children.
7. Protect the environment.
8. Look after the vulnerable.
9. Never be violent.
10. Protect your family.

Commandments 3, 5, and 9 here are negative DON'Ts, while the rest are positive DOs. But this is just a matter of wording. We could phrase them all positively if we wanted, by rewording 3, 5, and 9:

2. Take responsibility for your actions.
3. Respect life.
4. Be honest.
5. Respect another's possessions.
6. Protect and nurture children.
7. Protect the environment.
8. Look after the vulnerable.
9. Use only peaceful solutions.
10. Protect your family.

Each can be backed up by the positive GR: "As you want others to take responsibility for their actions toward you, take responsibility for your actions toward them," "As you want others to respect your life, respect their life," "As you want others to be honest toward you, be honest toward them," and so on.

Alternatively, we could express all these commandments negatively:

2. Do not shirk responsibility for your actions.
3. Do not kill.
4. Do not lie.
5. Do not steal.
6. Do not injure or neglect children.
7. Do not let the environment be injured.
8. Do not neglect the needs of the vulnerable.
9. Do not be violent.
10. Do not let your family be injured.

Each can be backed up by the negative GR: "As you want others not to shirk responsibility for their actions toward you, do not shirk responsibility for your actions toward them," "As you want others not to kill you, do not kill them," "As you want others not to lie to you, do not lie to them," and so on.

Any action can be described either positively or negatively: so *being honest* can be described as *not lying*.[1] And then the positive GR with the positive

---

[1] If you understand "being honest" as more complex than "not lying," the negative form would have to be more complex – perhaps "not either lying or saying something deceptive or otherwise withholding the truth (perhaps through silence)." My general argument would still work.

description is equivalent to the negative GR with the negative description: "As you want others to be honest toward you, be honest toward them" is equivalent to "As you want others not to lie to you, do not lie to them."

Consider "*Treat* others as you want to be *treated*." I can describe how I *treat* you by using positive or negative words: I *treat* you differently if I *smile* or if I *don't answer your hello*. It would be artificial to limit *treating* or GR just to actions described positively or negatively. The positive GR also covers the duty not to harm ("If you want others to *refrain from harming* you, then *refrain from harming* them"), as the negative GR also covers the duty to do good ("If you want others not to *refuse to do good* to you, then don't *refuse to do good* to them").

And so the positive and negative GR are logically equivalent. Both have identical logical implications. Confucius, Hillel, and Jesus didn't propose conflicting GRs; instead, they supported equivalent GRs that were worded differently. However, there may be *psychological differences* between the forms (Terry 2012: 81). Many people may be inclined to apply the positive GR more to doing good to others, and the negative GR more to not harming others. This is compatible with both forms being logically equivalent.

10.5 Defending the positive GR (technical)

We need to consider the two objections in §10.3 against the positive GR. Both objections hold equally well against the negative GR (since both forms are logically equivalent). And both objections can be overcome if we reformulate GR more carefully, following ch. 1–2. (This section is complicated; tired readers can skip to the next section.)

The first objection went:

> People differ much more in their likes [than their dislikes]. And so the positive GR, which has me treat others as I'd like to be treated myself, works poorly. Here are examples. I like to have people quarrel with me, let's suppose; so, following the positive GR, I quarrel with others (including those who hate quarreling). I like football; so I buy football tickets for all my friends (including those who like opera and hate football). I like broccoli; so I feed it to all my friends (including those who hate it).

My response has two parts. (1) The negative GR has the same problem. Suppose that I, a waiter, hate broccoli and don't want to be served it. By the negative GR, I then shouldn't serve it to you (even though you like it and ordered it). People differ widely in their dislikes (about broccoli, quarreling, football, and so on), and not just in their likes. Whenever people differ in their likes (some like X while others dislike X), they also differ in their dislikes.

(2) These absurdities come from not having a same-situation clause (§§1.3 & 2.1b). We need to ask "Am I now willing that *if I were in the same situation* then this be done to me?" (where the "same situation" includes things like whether I like broccoli). Again assume that I hate broccoli and don't want others to serve it to me. I'm clearly willing that *if I were in the same situation* as you (and thus liked broccoli and ordered it), then I be served broccoli. So GR, formulated with a same-situation clause, doesn't make my personal likes and dislikes into the norm of how I should treat everyone else.

The second objection went:

> The positive GR can be impossible to follow. Suppose I walk down a street and pass a dozen beggars, each asking for a $50 donation to relieve their poverty. In each case, if I were in their place then I'd want to be given $50; so the positive GR tells me to give $50 to each. And suppose I keep passing more and more such people. My GR obligations will continue until I have no more money to give. Yes, it would be nice to help all the poor people in the world (since if I were in their place then I'd want to be helped). But this is impossible – I can't help them all. And so the positive GR can't really generate obligations – since if it did then it would generate so many of them that we couldn't fulfill them all. So the positive GR is unworkable.

Again, my response has two parts. (1) The negative GR has the same problem. When I ask for money, I don't want to be refused; so then, by the negative GR, I shouldn't refuse others when they ask for money. So the negative GR also, taken literally, would generate so many obligations that we couldn't fulfill them all.

(2) The reasoning about GR forcing us to give to every beggar commits two fallacies (§§1.4, 1.6, & 2.4): the *soft GR fallacy* (which assumes that we should never act against what others want) and the *third-parties GR fallacy* (it follows an "Always give to beggars" policy without considering its wider impact).[1]

How should GR apply to giving money to beggars? Since this issue involves more than two people, it's more convenient to use Gold 7: "Act only as you're willing for anyone to act in the same situation, regardless of where or when you imagine yourself or others" – which has us apply Gold 1 to all affected parties. Suppose we're deciding between these policies:

A. Never do anything to help anyone else in need (including beggars).
B. Always give to beggars when they ask for money.
C. Contribute a reasonable part of your income to groups that help the needy, and encourage the state to set up efficient and fiscally responsible programs to help the needy. But in general, don't give to beggars when they ask for money. Instead, refer them to agencies that provide food and shelter.

GR consistency makes it difficult to accept A. If we accept A, then we must be

---

[1] The next paragraph is repeated in §14.3b, against Objection 9.

willing that others do nothing to help us in an imagined situation where we're in need and can't provide for ourselves. For different reasons, it would be difficult to accept B consistently – since B would lead to a huge increase in the number of beggars (especially ones who cheat people or spend what they get on alcohol or drugs) and thus an impossibly large number of obligations to give to beggars. GR consistency, when combined with knowledge and imagination, leads to something closer to C. I can hold C with GR consistency since I'm willing that I be treated according to C regardless of where I imagine myself in the situation (as beggar, or one asked for money, or whatever).

10.6 Negative traditions?

Do traditions with a negative GR, like Judaism and Confucianism, have a negative morality – emphasizing DON'Ts rather than DOs? The logical equivalence between the two forms might be thought to decide this historical point. But that would be a mistake, since different groups might be unaware of the logical equivalence[1] or might use a positive (or negative) GR form to emphasize positive (or negative) duties. So we must look at the historical data.

The historical data is clear: Judaism and Confucianism don't present a negative morality.[2] All three traditions – Christianity, Judaism, and Confucianism – have a roughly similar mix of positive and negative duties.

Jesus's Sermon on the Mount (which formulates GR positively) mixes positive and negative duties. In the part where Jesus explicitly disagrees with then-current standards (Matthew 5:21–48), he gives four DON'Ts (against anger, lust, divorce, and false oaths), one DO (love your enemies), and one norm expressed both ways ("Give to one who asks of you, and don't turn your back on one who wants to borrow" – which is about doing good, whether we say "Give" or "Don't turn your back"). So it's inaccurate to say that Jesus de-emphasized DON'Ts in favor of DOs.

Other Christian sources from early times also give a balanced mix of positive and negative duties, and often express GR negatively (for example, in the 80 AD *Didache* and in the western text of Acts 15:21 & 29), as if there's no real difference between the two forms. And Aristides the Philosopher in his second-century *Apology* defended Christianity to the Roman Emperor by mentioning a mix of positive and negative duties, and the negative GR (my italics):

---

[1] I suspect that many would think that there's a difference between the positive and negative GRs (Wattles 1996: 120) – and also between "All As are Bs" and "All non-Bs are non-As" (which are logically equivalent). Surveys about which forms are seen as logically equivalent reveal more about psychology than about logic (Gensler 2010: 377).

[2] Those who present this case for Judaism include Flusser 1968, Goldin 1946, Goldman 1995, G. King 1928, Melé 2009, and Plaks 2005. Those who present this case for Confucianism include Abbot 1870, W. Chan 1955 & 1963, Dubs 1951a & 1951b, Goldman 1995, Jochim 1980, Jung 1966 & 1969, Kim 1950, Melé 2009, and Tsai 2005.

> They [Christians] do not commit adultery nor fornication, nor bear false witness, nor covet the things of others; they honor father and mother, and love their neighbors; they judge justly, and *they never do to others what they would not wish to happen to themselves*; they appeal to those who injure them, and try to win them as friends; they are eager to do good to their enemies; they are gentle and easy to be entreated; they abstain from all unlawful conversation and from all impurity; they despise not the widow, nor oppress the orphan; and he that has, gives ungrudgingly for the maintenance of him who has not. (Swindal & Gensler 2005: 45):

As far as I can tell from my historical research, Christian thinkers paid almost no attention to the positive/negative GR difference before Hale 1805.

The Jewish tradition also has a mix of positive and negative duties. Its 613 commandments divide into 248 DOs and 365 DON'Ts. While Hillel expressed GR negatively, there's a famous story about how he helped a poor family; this is fitting, since the negative GR logically entails instances like "As you want others not to refuse you help when you're in need, do not refuse help to others in need." While the negative GR occurs in Tobit 4:15 (an ancient Jewish book not in the official Jewish scriptures), nearby verses mention positive duties to help the poor, the hungry, and the naked. Many Jewish thinkers, like Moses Maimonides, use both GR forms. And the positive "Love your neighbor as yourself" is in Leviticus 19:18, where it occurs just after a condemnation of hatred and revenge. So again we see a mix of positive and negative duties.

Confucius took the golden rule to cover all actions, positive and negative. While he formulated GR negatively, he reportedly endorsed positive GR implications (Doctrine of the Mean 13:4, W. Chan 1963: 101): we are to treat our fathers (rulers, elder brothers, friends) as we expect our sons (ministers, younger brothers, friends) to treat us. Confucius also gave a positive statement about helping others (Analects 6:28, W. Chan 1963: 31): "A man of humanity, wishing to establish his own character, also establishes the character of others, and wishing to be prominent himself, also helps others to be prominent." As you read Confucius's writings, you find a mix of positive and negative duties. And Confucius's followers Mencius (c. 372–289 BC) and Liu Pao-nan (1791–1855) expressed GR positively (ch. 5: 372 BC & 1791).

Some claim that the positive GR is unique to Christianity. But this isn't true. Bahá'í, Hinduism, Islam, Jainism, Sikhism, and Taoism had positive GRs (ch. 3), as did Confucianism and several ancient Greeks (in ch. 5, see Homer c. 700 BC, Isocrates c. 436–338 BC, Sextus c. 300 BC, and Aristeas c. 150 BC).

CHAPTER 11
More Questions

We've already discussed several questions about GR – like whether it's equivalent to "Love your neighbor as yourself" (§3.1a gave two views on this), whether it applies to how to treat animals (§9.5 Q1 said yes), and whether the positive and negative forms have the same implications (§10.4 said yes). Now we consider further questions, like whether GR gives a complete criterion of right and wrong, how it relates to sympathy and empathy, and when it was first called *golden*.

11.1 Summary of morality

(Q1) Is GR the supreme moral axiom from which all duties can be deduced?

No. On my view, *none* of our duties about concrete actions can be deduced from GR. Construed as Gold 1, GR is a consistency principle, forbidding an inconsistent combination but not telling what concrete action to do:

Gold 1 forbids an inconsistent combination:	Deductive model of GR reasoning (the *desire* wording can vary):
• I do something to another. • I'm unwilling that this be done to me in the same situation.	If you have this desire about A being done to you, then do A to X. You have this desire about A being done to you. ∴ Do A to X.

I reject the model on the right, which can lead to GR prescribing bad actions if we have flawed desires (e.g., ones that are immoral, based on an unhealthy psychological condition, or based on wrong information, §2.1d). Recall Electra, who thought severe electrical shocks were pleasant (§§1.7 & 2.1d). For her, the deductive model prescribes a bad action: since she wants to be shocked, she's to shock others. The consistency approach avoids this. While Electra satisfies GR consistency, her thinking has another defect: it's misinformed.

This Electra case shows that we can satisfy GR consistency but act wrongly. A related case shows how Electra might act rightly but violate GR consistency: here she refrains from shocking another (a right action) but she's unwilling that others refrain from shocking her in the same situation (so she violates GR consistency). So GR is neither a sufficient condition nor a necessary condition for right action. Instead, GR is a consistency norm.

Moving to the consistency model has four main advantages:

- GR doesn't tell us to do bad things if we have flawed desires.
- The consistency GR is derivable from consistency norms about impartiality and conscientiousness. (So Gold 1 is a *theorem*, not an axiom.)
- We can better explain why GR is so widely accepted: consistency norms are widely shared and are motivated by a *cognitive dissonance* drive against inconsistency that evolution built into us.
- Since the consistency GR isn't a rival to other moral principles, it easily fits into various moral philosophies (most of which already accept consistency norms).

Some may regret that GR isn't seen as the supreme moral axiom that tells us all our duties. But, sorry, this deductive-model doesn't work. And the consistency model has other advantages, as sketched above.

(Q2) Should GR replace all other moral rules (see Green 2010)?

No. Instead, GR is a consistency tool that can help guide us in our actions and in selecting moral rules. GR is especially useful when accepted norms seem questionable (for example, racist) or unclear. GR can combine with other tools of moral thinking, such as an appeal to consequences or virtue.

(Q3) In what sense is GR the summary of morality?

GR nicely captures the *spirit* behind morality. It helps us to see the point behind specific moral rules. It concretely applies ideals like fairness, concern, and impartiality. It engages our reasoning, instead of imposing an answer. It motivates us and counteracts our limited sympathies. And it doesn't assume any specific theoretical approach to ethics. If you had to give one sentence to express what morality is about, you couldn't do better than GR. In this sense, the golden rule *is* the summary of morality.

(Q4) Why is GR so important to morality and human relationships?

Humans tend to be self-centered. We often think mainly of our own good and secondarily, if at all, of the good of others. This is humanity's greatest problem. Judging from GR's omnipresence, this problem exists across different cultures and eras. GR deals with this problem, not by directly telling us what to do, but by reflecting our action toward another back to us: "How am I willing that I be treated in the same circumstances?"

We can imagine rational beings for whom GR is less important. Suppose that Martians, while otherwise like us, follow GR naturally and without struggle. But maybe they forget to get the facts about how their actions affect others – or maybe they ignore their own interests and treat themselves as doormats. We'd then expect the Martians not to emphasize GR (since they live it so completely) as much as some other norm, perhaps "Be factually informed" or "Have regard for yourself too." So GR's central importance in human life is contingent on a fact about human nature: that we tend to be self-centered.

> (Q5) Even though GR is a consistency principle and not a direct guide to action, can it still guide us on how to live and form our moral beliefs?

Yes. GR guides us indirectly, by prescribing consistency. GR pushes us to treat others according to standards that we're willing to be treated by. Since we aren't willing that people generally kill, rob, or deceive us, we won't accept that such actions are generally permissible. While GR won't always lead to moral agreement, still, when combined with knowledge and imagination, it will narrow the range of moral beliefs that people find acceptable.

GR might not bring moral agreement to people who disagree on the facts. Consider this question: Should the government give a tax cut to the rich?

- Republican Randy says yes – since this will better stimulate the economy and thus ultimately be better even for poor people.
- Democrat Dave says no – the rich will hardly notice having less to spend and the tax money can provide services that help the needy. This will better stimulate the economy and thus benefit the rich too.

Given this difference in factual beliefs, both sides can support different policies, consistent with GR. So here we need to investigate the factual beliefs in a dispassionate and non-ideological way, and try to see which side is right.

GR is less useful on issues that don't involve conflicting interests, like "What ends are ultimately worth pursuing in life?" Hedonists say only gaining pleasure and avoiding pain are ultimately worthwhile. Pluralists say many things are ultimately worthwhile – such as virtue, knowledge, pleasure, life, and freedom. GR helps less on such issues (see also §9.5 Q4).

> (Q6) Is GR conservative (traditional, right-wing) or liberal (revolutionary, left-wing)?

It's both. GR is traditional and supported by all major world religions (ch. 3). But putting GR into practice can bring revolutionary changes (like helping to end slavery, §8.5). Chapter 2 noted that GR is championed by politicians both on the right (as President George W. Bush) and on the left (as President Barack

Obama). Capitalists can say "One of the moral foundations of capitalism is the golden rule.... There is a nobility, a neighborly and brotherly love involved in dealing with others in such a way that oneself and the other are both pleased by that transaction" (Barach & Elstrott 1988: 549). Socialists can say "Socialism ... is the golden rule, not talked about, but applied" (Albert Ehrgott, quoted in R. Newton 1909: 3). All groups share GR. In the ancient world, GR supporters included kings, slaves, intellectuals, and primitives (Hertzler 1934: 434f).

> (Q7) Does GR always lead to good decisions? Would it necessarily solve all the world's problems if everyone followed GR?

No to both. GR can lead to bad decisions if we commit GR fallacies (ch. 1 & §2.4), for example, or lack knowledge. But our best hope for the world is to use GR *wisely*, which requires, among other things, knowledge, imagination, and creativity. Even then, some problems (e.g., fixing the world's ecology) might be too great for us to solve. But GR is an important part of our best shot.

> (Q8) Is the golden rule a *rule of thumb*?

A "rule of thumb" is a simple rule that gives a quick approximation. Using thumb-widths to measure inches gives a good estimate, unless we have the *fat thumb* or *skinny thumb* problem. Rulers are more precise but not always available. The literal golden rule (§2.1a) is a rule of thumb:

Pyrite 1: the literal GR	If you want X to do A to you, then do A to X.

Pyrite 1 is very simple and can give a good estimate of our duty, unless we have the *different circumstances* or *flawed desires* problem. Pyrites 2 and 3 give better results, at the cost of greater complexity.

Gold 1 is a rule not of thumb but of consistency. If we violate Gold 1, then we must change something – either our action or our desire about how we'd be treated. Gold 1 takes more time to apply (using the Kita procedure), since we must try to understand the situation and imagine ourselves in the other's place. People who find Gold 1 with Kita too complicated can fall back on the simpler literal GR (which, even for adults, has some worth as a *rule of thumb*).

> (Q9) Suppose we violate Gold 1, and thus our actions (toward another) clash with our desires (about how we be treated). How do we know which to change – the actions or the desires?

When we violate GR, usually we have fine desires but flawed actions. A rough *rule of thumb* is that, unless we have a special reason to doubt our desires, we should change how we act. Various things can lead us to reexamine our desires. For example, maybe they are criticized by others, come from bad social influences, or rest on a poor grasp of the situation. If we have some reason to think that our desires would change if we were more rational (more informed, experienced, consistent, etc.), then we need to investigate further.

(Q10) Is it difficult to live GR?

Yes. Consistency can be difficult. With limited intellectual clarity, we find logical consistency in beliefs difficult. With limited self-control, we find ends–means consistency difficult. Being self-centered, we find GR difficult.

Saints might complain that Gold 1 isn't demanding enough, that it calls us to minimal standards (about how we're *minimally willing* to be treated) rather than to heroic generosity. Saints might want to go further: to treat others with the generosity with which we *prefer* to be treated. While there's some truth in this complaint, non-saints like me find Gold 1 to be quite demanding.

GR is easier to follow if we live in a society that supports it, where people care about each other and no groups are mistreated. GR is harder to follow in a society that discourages it – for example, a corrupt society where everyone steals or where people are taught to hate another group. A prison guard in a Nazi concentration camp would find GR *very* challenging.

(Q11) Does GR force us to promote the good of others on an exactly equal basis as we promote our own good?

No. GR doesn't tell us how generous to be toward others. Instead, GR reflects the question back to us, as "How generous are we now willing that others be toward us in a similar need?" We set the standard ourselves. But we cannot set the standard too low, at least if we care about ourselves being helped when we're in need.

(Q12) Which beings can follow GR?

Rational agents can follow GR. GR forbids inconsistent action–desire combinations. A being can't follow GR if it can't act intentionally or can't consent to hypothetical actions. So the "rational agents" who can follow GR would need these abilities. Almost all adult humans would have these abilities, with few exceptions (such as those who are in a coma or severely retarded).

What about children? Older children clearly can understand and follow GR. Since growing into GR happens gradually, dating a child's grasp of GR is less clear than dating its first steps or first words. My friend Lauren Beranek told me that her three little ones started grasping GR at about two years old, when they began to see that their actions could make others sad. Zahn-Waxler *et al.* 1979 affirm this "around two years old" time and give an example about little

Todd (just under two). Todd hits Susan and makes her cry. His mother explains that he shouldn't do this, because it hurts Susan. Todd feels bad about what he did; he picks up some flower petals and brings them to Susan to comfort her and make peace. GR is forming in little Todd (§6.3).

What about animals? Higher social animals – like dogs, porpoises, and primates – at times seem to practice empathy and GR. De Waal 2005: 195 sees this in apes, dolphins, and elephants. If evolution hardwired empathy and GR into humans (§7.4), then it likely also did this with other social species. Darwin mentions animal behavior that suggests GR, like "a dog, who never passed a great friend of his, a cat which lay sick in a basket, without giving her a few licks with his tongue, the surest sign of kind feeling in a dog" (1871: 74). If higher animals can follow GR, then we should regard them, to some degree at least, as rational agents.

What about lower animals, plants, or computers – can they practice GR? While they lack the abilities needed for GR thinking, there may be something analogous going on. A computer could *simulate* following GR, if it could simulate having desires about how it's to be treated along with other required abilities. But the *duty* to follow GR would apply only to *rational agents*, which would exclude lower animals, plants, and computers.

What about Martians or rational beings on other planets, if such exist? I'd speculate that such beings would recognize and often follow GR.

(Q13) Does GR require religion?

No. GR is strong among both the religious and the non-religious, and makes sense from either perspective.

The great world religions all teach and are friendly toward GR (ch. 3). For example, Christianity sees the world as created by a loving God. Because God first loved us, as a father loves his children, we're motivated to share his love with other members of his family. Christians see the origin and destiny of the world as deeply in harmony with GR. Some (like Porpora 2001) contend that a non-religious GR is banal, because it lacks a higher moral vision and purpose. I would rather say that religion can enhance GR by giving it a deeply religious dimension (§4.2).

On the other hand, many atheists follow GR, defend it philosophically in various ways (§3.2f & ch. 12), and have deep feelings of concern for others. Some non-believers (such as Romig 1984) see GR as giving the core ethical insight of the great world religions, but without the fairy tales. Some ask, "Since we can follow GR without religion, why do we need religion?" Believers respond that religion, besides having a higher purpose than just backing up ethics, provides a richer context for GR.

(Q14) What is the "new golden rule"?

Amitai Etzioni wrote a book called *The New Golden Rule* (1996). Etzioni presents a communitarian view of society designed to balance *individual freedoms* (which he thinks are overemphasized) with *shared values*. He formulates his new GR as: "Respect and uphold society's moral order as you would have society respect and uphold your autonomy" (Etzioni 1996: xviii).

There's little discussion about why this norm is better than the old GR. GR is dismissed in two superficial sentences (Etzioni 1996: xviii), gets only two other brief mentions, and doesn't occur in the index. The 45 pages of notes mentions only one GR publication. It's disappointing that a book on shared values with "golden rule" in the title tries so little to understand humanity's greatest shared value. (See also M. Singer 2002: 290f.)

Etzioni's norm is better expressed in terms of the *golden mean*. Aristotle saw virtue as a *golden mean* of "just enough," intermediate between the twin vices of "too much" and "too little." *Courage*, for example, is to have just the right amount of fear; the twin vices to avoid are *cowardice* (too much fear) and *foolhardiness* (too little fear). Similarly, for Etzioni, a good society is one with the right balance between autonomy (individual freedoms) and society's moral order (shared values). The twin vices to avoid are *individualism* (ignoring responsibility for others) and *authoritarianism* (denying legitimate differences and forcing everyone to be the same).

I'd argue that GR, the old one but reformulated to avoid objections, can help to promote a society with a proper balance. GR is earth's most important shared value. GR respects freedom and differences between people. GR also discourages an individualism that denies responsibility for others. And GR can criticize shared values that are flawed (for example, racist or sexist).

> (Q15) Are there sayings other than GR that can lead us to have concern for others in roughly the same way?

Yes (see ch. 3 & 5), for example "Treat others as brothers and sisters of one family." Each saying has advantages and disadvantages. GR is strong:

- *religiously* (as part of all the major world religions),
- *historically* (as part of moral thinking and moral education for centuries),
- *psychologically* (its attractiveness is built into us), and
- *logically* (as a clear principle[1] that can be justified rigorously).

GR easily combines with other ways to talk about concern for others. So if we say "Treat those of other races as brothers and sisters," we could naturally add "Image yourself in their place" (a GR appeal).

---

[1] "Treat everyone as a brother or sister" can't be taken literally. If you send your brother a birthday card, should you do this to strangers? If you hate your brother, should you hate strangers? The saying is a powerful metaphor but can't be taken literally (as can Gold 1).

(Q16) What motivates us to follow GR? Is it pure concern for others? Or is it payback self-interest (we treat others well so they'll treat us well)?

Both motives are common. I may have various reasons to follow GR:

- GR promotes my self-interest (since it helps me to get respect and better treatment from others, avoid punishments and retaliations, feel better about myself, and win God's favor and rewards). And GR, in affirming the dignity and worth of others, affirms my own dignity and worth.
- GR promotes my group's interests (since it helps my group to receive better treatment from other groups).
- GR promotes cooperation and thus promotes everyone's good, mine and yours; it's a global idea of intense power to bring the world together. And so GR helps me to live out my love and concern for others.
- GR is the consistent, rational, fair, and right way to live.
- GR lives out obedience, love, and gratitude to God, who first loved us and invites us to love his creatures; it brings us closer to God and makes us more like him, who is infinite love and wisdom.
- GR is so built into me (into my culture/feelings/soul/genes/brain/etc.) that I could scarcely consider living differently.

So there are *many* reasons to follow GR.[1]

11.2   Role reversals

(Q1) Does GR use *sympathy* or *empathy*, and how do these differ?

Let me distinguish what I'll take these terms to mean:

- *Sympathy*: I have the same feelings as another (especially suffering or sorrow over a loss, and especially feelings caused in part by the other's feelings).
- *Empathy*: I imagine myself in another's place (where this *place* includes likes, dislikes, beliefs, and so on).

Sympathy by etymology means "suffer with" or "feel with." Suppose my friend Judy feels sad over her mother's death; I have *sympathy* if I feel sad too. "Sympathy" is used less often with positive feelings; but I have *sympathetic joy* if I feel joy because my friend feels joy. So sympathy is to have the same feelings as the other person, but perhaps not as intensely.

By contrast, *empathy* is the ability to put yourself in another's shoes – to imagine accurately what it would be like to be in another's situation. Empathy is understanding rather than feeling; but it's a wholistic understanding that appreciates the impact of events on another's thoughts and feelings. Again,

---

[1] See §6.4 for some reasons that people *don't* follow GR. See also §14.4 Obj. 30–31.

suppose Judy feels sad over her mother's death. I may have some empathetic understanding of Judy's situation even if I've never lost a loved one. But if I previously lost *my* mother, then I'd likely have a far greater empathetic understanding of what the death means to Judy – an understanding that would likely be difficult to put adequately into words.

For Judy, I have both sympathy and empathy. I have sympathy because I feel sad: I share her sorrow. I have empathy because I can to some degree understand what it's like to be in her situation. My sympathy is about feeling while my empathy is about understanding.

It's possible to have sympathy without empathy. My friend Dolores is crying, and so I feel sad too. But I have no idea why she's crying, and so I have little empathetic understanding of her situation.

It's also possible to have empathy without sympathy. My friend Bucky, an Ohio State fan, is sad that Michigan just beat Ohio State 45–0. I feel joy (as a Michigan fan) and don't share her sadness. So I lack sympathetic feelings. But I do have empathy. I can imagine myself in Bucky's place and understand her sadness (even though I don't feel sad myself), especially since I've felt sad in years when Michigan lost.

GR appeals to empathy – to picturing yourself in another's situation – to what I call "imagination." Empathetic understanding is a desirable prelude to the GR question: "Am I now willing that if I were in the same situation then this be done to me?" Sympathy may come into play too, but it isn't essential.

Suppose Denise is at the dentist's office. The hygienist cleaning her teeth is doing a sloppy job, poking her gums with sharp instruments, causing much pain. Imagine yourself in Denise's place. Think about this for a few seconds.... OK, when you imagined yourself in Denise's place, did you actually feel pain in your gums? No, not at all. Even if your imagination was vivid, you didn't feel gum pain. Instead, you reflected that this poking would hurt, and you may have given a pain-grunt as a signal to the hygienist. So you had an empathetic understanding of Denise's situation, which is what GR needs. But, since you didn't have gum pain, you didn't, strictly speaking, have sympathy.

When we apply GR, we imagine ourselves in the other's place (empathy). We may or may not feel what the other feels. If you imagine yourself in the place of Judy, who just lost her mother, you'll likely feel sadness (sympathy). But if you imagine yourself in the place of Denise, who's getting her gums poked, you won't feel gum pain (no sympathy). Empathy is a key element for GR (the imagination "i" in our "Kita" acronym).

> (Q2) Why don't we just formulate GR as "Before you act, apply empathy – imagine yourself in the other's place on the receiving end of the action"?

Empathy, while a desirable prelude to GR, can occur outside GR. Imagining ourselves in another's situation is a common experience. We often do it when we read or write a story, act out a part in a play, watch a movie, plan a class or an advertising campaign, or try to outsmart the opposing coach. Empathy in these cases needn't combine with GR.

Empathy, like knowledge, can be used for good or for evil. A slave owner might imagine himself in the place of his runaway slaves, in order to figure out where they'd go and thus how to catch them. A sadist might imagine himself in the place of someone being tortured, in order better to enjoy the torturing. A serial killer might attain a high empathetic understanding of his victims, in order better to trap them. These people use empathy for evil.

Bruce Maxwell 2008: 150 calls "the fallacy of the golden rule" the idea that empathetic understanding *by itself* will lead people to understand morality and care about others. Since we already have several GR fallacies (ch. 1 & §2.4), I prefer to call this the *empathy fallacy*. On the other hand, for *many* of us (but not for the slave owner, sadist, or serial killer), imagining ourselves in X's place will likely increase our motivation to follow GR toward X.[1]

(Q3) What is a *golden-rule violation* in American law?

This is when lawyers ask jurors to imagine themselves in the place of the lawyer's client; this may sway jurors in favor of the client, who may then be treated too leniently or awarded an excessive settlement. The problem here isn't GR itself but rather how jurors may misapply GR. Jurors may commit the *soft GR fallacy* by asking "If I were in the place of this defendant, would I want to be punished?" and then freeing the defendant (§§1.4 & 2.1c). Or jurors may commit the *third-parties GR fallacy* by not considering the bad effect of large settlements on third parties (§§1.6 & 2.4).[2]

(Q4) Instead of saying "Imagine yourself *in the other person's place*," could we say "Imagine yourself *being the other person*"?

We could express it this way. This leads to four-word GRs, like "Treat others as you" or "Treat everyone as me" (the TEAM acronym). Samuel "Golden Rule" Jones, who was mayor of Toledo, Ohio 1897–1904, liked to phrase GR as "Do unto others as if you were the others" (Crosby 1906: 12).

(Q5) Isn't role reversal impossible? For example, given my genetics, which can't be changed, wouldn't it be impossible for me to be a black person?

You can *imagine* yourself as a black person with different genetics; there's no logical impossibility here. It's quite common, even in cases having nothing to do with GR, to imagine ourselves in another's place. Watching a movie about Michael Jordan, for example, I might imagine myself being a black basketball

---

[1] Batson 2008 gives evidence that imagining the thoughts and feelings of a person in need tends to increase altruistic motivation, while just imagining oneself in the other's external situation doesn't. He links GR with the latter and thus sees GR as what I call *Pyrite 1b* (§14.1).

[2] See also Duxbury 2009, Goodwin 2009, Greenlee 1996, and *Virginia Law Review* 1976.

superstar. Or a slavemaster might, to catch a runaway slave, ask where he'd go if he were a black runaway slave. Humans have great imaginative powers.

(Q6) To imagine myself in X's exact place, I must imagine myself having all of X's qualities. How can I do this, since I don't know all of X's qualities?

You needn't know *all* of X's qualities (which would be impossible). Instead, you imagine yourself having those qualities that you take X to have. You fill in other details about *being in X's shoes* as best you can.

Here's a parallel. You often think about how to treat yourself, in your present situation. To do this, you needn't know *all* of your qualities (which would be impossible). Instead, you consider those qualities that you take yourself to have. You fill in other details about *being in your own shoes* as best you can.

When you don't know the specifics about the other person, you can use a reasonable default. So, given no evidence to the contrary, you'd assume that the other person isn't hard of hearing. Or, when deciding how clean to leave a restroom or campsite for the next user, you'd assume typical features for this next user, including dislike for a dirty restroom or campsite.

(Q7) Isn't it difficult to imagine in a realistic way what it's like to be in another's place, especially when this differs from your own experience?

Yes, it can be difficult, and we'll never empathize perfectly; but we can do it better if we work at it (ch. 6). The fact that we'll never do something perfectly doesn't excuse us from trying to do it as well as we reasonably can.

(Q8) Is GR the principle of *reciprocity*?

In math, x/y is the *reciprocal* of y/x: we switch the letters. So GR, which switches the parties, is often called "the principle of reciprocity." But "reciprocity" is often applied to other ideas, such as "Treat others as they treat you"; so if you help me, I *reciprocate* by returning the favor (*quid pro quo* or *do ut des* in Latin) – and if you hurt me, I *reciprocate* by taking revenge (*lex talionis*).[1] Here are further reciprocity principles:

- Start by being kind to others; thereafter, treat them as they treat you. (TIT FOR TAT, §14.3f)

---

[1] The *lex talionis* can punish evildoers in a primitive society where the state doesn't do this, and so it isn't all bad (§§8.1 & 14.3f). Reiman 1985: 121 says: "The *lex talionis* is the law enforcement arm of the golden rule, at least in the sense that if people were actually treated as they treated others, then everyone would necessarily follow the golden rule" [or would if they followed self-interest]. Apresian 2002 mentions that John Chrysostom thought that God gave us talion to discourage us from injuring others (since this would bring about our own injury). Practically speaking, we need some sort of punishment for evildoing (but moderated by GR) to promote GR among imperfect humans.

- Do good to those who do good to others and do evil to those who do evil to others. (Reward virtue and punish evildoers.)
- Return good for good; resist evil; don't do evil in return; make reparation for the harm you do. (Lawrence Becker defended this in his 1986 *Reciprocity*.)
- People in fact treat others as they've been treated. (So abused children grow up to abuse others.)

Since there are many reciprocity principles, it's confusing to call GR "*the* principle of reciprocity."[1]

11.3   Metals

(Q1) Why is GR called *golden*?

GR is called *golden* because of its great value. GR motivates us to act morally and opposes our selfishness – and it does this not by imposing external rules but by engaging our own reasoning. GR helps us to cooperate with others so that everyone benefits, and it counters hatred and divisiveness. GR is a global wisdom, common to almost every religion and culture. GR provides the best hope for achieving peace and justice. And GR does all this in an easily learnable formula. GR is truly golden – and those who follow GR have hearts of gold.

(Q2) When was GR first called *golden*?

"Golden rule" was first used for any key principle of any field. So Humfrey Baker in 1568 wrote that the mathematical *rule of three* is very useful and so "the philosophers did name it the *golden rule*."[2] The rule goes:

$$\text{If } \frac{a}{b} = \frac{c}{x} \text{, then } x = \frac{b \times c}{a}.$$

"Golden rule" occurs in a generic sense in at least sixteen other English writings of the next thirty years, referring to mathematical rules or religious ideas like "Walk according to the gospel." Edward Topsell's *Times Lamentation* (1599, p. 410f) hints at a new usage, where "golden rule" stands for "Do unto others"; he says that "Do unto others" serves well instead of other things that have been called *golden rules*. The earliest source I found that explicitly calls

---

[1] See also Chakrabarti 2012, Little & Twiss 1978: 179–206, Terry 2012 (who has many further reciprocity formulas), and Wattles 1996: 52.

[2] Writings mentioned in this paragraph are on http://eebo.chadwyck.com, which has almost everything published in English from 1477 to 1700. Earl Rivers's *Dictes and Sayings of the Philosophers* (1477) was the first book printed in England; it had "Do unto others" on page 70. Neither Rivers nor other British authors before 1599 who spoke of "Do unto others" (ch. 5: 1568 has examples) called it "golden."

"Do unto others" *golden rule* was Charles Gibbon's *The Order of Equalitie* (1604, p. 17, keeping the original spelling):

> In all Taxations euery man should remember this golden rule *To doe as he would be done to*, that is to taxe others as he would be taxed himselfe by others ... that thou wilt not haue done to thy selfe doe not to others.

This new usage caught on quickly: ten other authors before 1650 used "golden rule" for "Do unto others" (see ch. 5: 1604). It's often said that this usage started in the 18th century or the latter half of the 17th century; but we can find it much earlier, with Gibbon in 1604.

Some put the first use of "golden rule" for "Do unto others" even earlier, with Emperor Alexander Severus (222–35 AD), who was so impressed with GR that he had it inscribed on his wall in gold (France 2007: 284).

(Q3) When was GR first formulated?

In our ch. 5 chronology, the first to express GR was the fictional Fred Flintstone (c. 1,000,000 BC). Helping a stranger who was robbed and left to die, Flintstone said "I'd want him to help me." He later put GR into a formula.

Humor aside, GR's origins are hidden in the distant past. GR is likely hardwired into our genes and brain mechanisms (§7.4); so our ancestors likely used GR reasoning before they could write or speak. The first clear, written GRs go back to about 500 BC and are from Greece, Persia, India, and China – see the ch. 5 chronology. So we don't really know who first formulated or wrote down GR. But we do know that, ever since humans invented writing, similar written GRs kept popping up all over the world.

(Q4) Besides GR, are other rules named after metals or elements?

Yes. Gold, silver, and platinum have standard meanings:

- Golden rule: Treat others as you want to be treated.
- Silver rule: What you want not done to yourself, don't do to others.
- Platinum rule: Treat others as they want to be treated.

I argue that the silver rule is an equivalent way to phrase GR (§10.4) and that the platinum rule has flaws that GR can fix (§14.1).

Other metallic rules have no standard meaning. I found five different things in the literature that "iron rule" might mean. People just make something up (Sagan 1997 and Terry 2012). And so that's what I'll do here, blending ethics with chemistry. First are nine good rules:

- Calcium: Care for your future self as you want your present self to have been cared for.

- Carbon: Keep the earth livable for future generations, as we want past generations to have done for us.
- Diamond (as in "diamond ring"): Cherish spouse and family, as you want spouse and family to cherish you.
- Fluoride: Smile unto others as you want them to smile unto you.
- Phosphorus: Bring light unto others and be not discouraged by darkness.
- Potassium: How you treat others reflects what is in your heart.
- Silicon: Use technology for others, but don't let technology use you.
- Sulfur: As you want others not to stink up your world, don't stink up theirs.
- Titanium: Treat others as would Jesus (Buddha, Confucius, Moses, ...).

Here are nine less commendable rules:

- Arsenic: Kill or be killed: do others in so they won't do you in.
- Bronze: Be good to friends and bad to enemies: treat others as they treat you.
- Helium: Don't treat others; let them treat you.
- Iron: Might makes right: do unto others before they do unto you.
- Mercury: Treat others as you feel like at the moment.
- Neon: Appear unto others to follow the golden rule.
- Nickel: Treat others as most benefits you.
- Sodium: Treat others as your society says to treat them.
- Tin: Treat others who are like you as you want to be treated.

For fun, we can give element names to our pyrite rules (ch. 2). Pyrite 1 (the literal GR) is the *hydrogen rule* (too simple), Pyrite 2 (a faulty same-situation GR) is the *palladium rule* (close to platinum), and Pyrite 3 (an almost correct GR) is the *uranium rule* (works well unless others have bad desires).

CHAPTER 12
Many Philosophies

As GR is part of many religions (Chapter 3), so too GR is, or could be, part of many philosophies. The main obstacle is the belief that GR is unclear and leads to absurdities when expressed clearly; Chapters 1, 2, and 14 answer this objection. So here I'll sketch how to incorporate GR into representative theories in two areas of moral philosophy: metaethics and normative ethics.[1]

Earlier chapters discussed GR in a foundationally neutral way. We talked about how to formulate GR carefully, apply it wisely, and derive it from consistency norms about impartiality and conscientiousness. We didn't say *why* we ought to follow GR or be consistent: different philosophies can answer this differently. And we didn't specify what "consistent" here means. Section 2.7 said vaguely that a combination is *inconsistent* if it somehow doesn't fit together. Maybe the combination doesn't fit together logically (it involves a self-contradiction), or morally (it violates a duty), or religiously (it goes against God's will), or is flawed in another way. Different views can understand this differently.[2]

12.1   Metaethics

Metaethics, which is a major branch of moral philosophy, studies the nature and methodology of moral judgments. It asks questions like: What do "good" and "ought" mean? Are there objective moral truths? How can we justify or rationally defend beliefs about right and wrong?

I begin my ethics course with *cultural relativism*, which sees moral norms as social conventions. "Good" refers to what is "socially accepted" in a given society. So racism, for example, isn't good or bad objectively; instead, it's good in a society that approve of it but bad in one that disapproves. Now GR is part

---

[1] For more on these views, see Gensler 2011a (an introductory ethics textbook), Gensler *et al.* 2004 (ethics readings), and Gensler & Spurgin 2008 (an ethics encyclopedia). I'm fairly neutral on these views in this present chapter, even though I think that some of them are implausible when examined critically.

[2] While this chapter focuses on incorporating GR into various moral philosophies, it says less about how to incorporate consistency (including impartiality and conscientiousness) into these. For this, see Gensler 1996: 29–35, 56–60, & 84–8, and 2011a: 77f. And for more on incorporating GR into moral philosophies, see Gensler 1996: 131–4 & 2011a: 93–5.

of almost every culture, perhaps because a society needs it to survive and flourish. So cultural relativists of almost every culture can accept GR as a cultural convention. In addition, GR gives a way to reason about values, both within a society and between societies, and so provide a critical dimension that cultural relativism otherwise tends to lack.

Some philosophers base morality on feelings. They say that "X is good" means "I like X" (a truth-claim about our feelings, *subjectivism*) or "Hurrah for X!" (an exclamation, *emotivism*). Most such thinkers will find that they feel positively about GR and can accept it on this basis. They might feel positively about GR for various reasons, for example:

- GR promotes their own good.
- GR promotes everyone's good.
- GR is demanded by consistency.
- GR with Kita gives their feeling-based approach a more rational structure, so that not just anything goes.
- GR has an inherent emotional attractiveness for them.

Section 11.1 Q16 gives further reasons to be emotionally attracted to GR.

The *ideal-observer theory* sees moral judgments as claims about what we'd desire if we were "ideally rational" – where this means something like "consistent and informed and concerned about everyone's good." This view can accept GR and consistency as features of rational moral thinking and as norms that such thinking would endorse.

Supernaturalism (*divine-command theory*) bases ethics on God's will. Since all major theistic religions see GR as God's will (ch. 3), supernaturalists of all such religions can accept GR on this basis.

Social-contract views see morality as a social construct that people would agree to. Thomas Hobbes thinks we'd agree to GR to promote our self-interest (§7.2). John Rawls's (1971) social-contract view, which is somewhat like the ideal-observer view, suggests that we accept those principles that we'd pick for our society if we were fully rational and informed except that we didn't know our place in society (whether rich or poor, or black or white). The knowledge limitation promotes impartiality: if we don't know our race, for example, we can't manipulate the rules to favor it. Rawls's choice procedure works much like GR, since before we accept a rule we must imagine it being applied to us and be willing that it be so applied if we were in another's situation. Rawlsians can also hold that the rules we'd pick would include GR, which promotes cooperation and helps resolve conflicts.

Another option is to build GR (and perhaps impartiality and conscientiousness) into the definition of *morality*. Then any action guide that counts as a *morality* must recognize GR reasoning.

My metaethical view is a form of *intuitionism*. Intuitionism holds that there are objective, irreducible moral truths and that some of these are self-evident to a mature mind. I take the only self-evident duties to be ones about consistency (§2.7). Consistency is the first duty of a rational being; inconsistency is a defect in any area of thought or action. Our duty to be consistent is more clearly true than any premises on which it might be based. It's also presupposed by any argument; the essence of valid reasoning is that accepting the premises forces you, under pain of inconsistency, to accepting the conclusion. So our duty to be consistent is a basic presupposition of reason and a *self-evident truth* that requires no further proof or justification.

I also claim that GR *if formulated correctly* is self-evident. Most people will see the correctness of Gold 1 right away, and further investigations uncover no absurd consequences. While GR can be derived from further consistency requirements, it's clearly true in itself.

Some object that moral norms are vague and widely disputed, and hence can't be self-evident. But consistency norms are clear and have a strong consensus of support. GR is widely held too, across different religions and cultures, and can be expressed in a clear way that resists objections.

Many thinkers today, despite theoretical disagreements, share a *rationalized attitudes* approach to forming moral beliefs. To form our moral beliefs, we should, as far as practically possible, try to be informed, imaginative, consistent, concerned for people, impartial, and so on. This harmonizes well with our Kita (Know-Imagine-Test-Act) procedure, our stress on consistency, and GR. Our whole structure fits well into a rationalized attitudes approach.

Those who take this rationalized attitudes approach may differ on foundational questions. The approach works much the same, regardless of whether we base it on social conventions, emotions, God's will, a definition of morality, or objective self-evident truths.

12.2 Normative ethics

Normative ethical theory, a second major branch of moral philosophy, studies general principles about how we ought to live – or about what is right or wrong, worthwhile, virtuous, or just.

Consequentialism says we ought always to do whatever maximizes good consequences. The *utilitarianism* form of this says we ought to do whatever maximize good consequences *for everyone affected by our action*. Utilitarians (like John Stuart Mill, 1861: 22) can accept GR on the basis of the good consequences that the practice of GR brings.

Egoists say we ought to do whatever maximizes good consequences for *ourselves*. They can argue that our self-interest is best served by our living GR and promoting a society where everyone lives by GR (following Hobbes, §7.2).

Groupists say we ought to do whatever maximizes good consequences for *our group*. They can argue that their group-interest is best served by having GR widely accepted and practiced (§8.1).

Nonconsequentialism holds that some kinds of action (like breaking promises or killing the innocent) are wrong in themselves, and not just wrong because of bad consequences. Such actions may be exceptionlessly wrong, or just have some independent moral weight against them. Nonconsequentialists can accept GR and insist that GR inconsistencies are wrong in themselves, and not just wrong because of bad consequences. Similarly, consideration for others is good in itself, not just good because of its consequences.[1]

Some thinkers emphasize *virtues*, which are good habits (good character traits). A central part of being a good (virtuous) person is having consideration for others. This is the GR virtue – treating others only as we're willing to be treated in the same situation – and is sometimes called *compassion*. The opposite vice is to be *inconsiderate* or *thoughtless* or *a jerk*.

GR itself derives from the twin virtues of *impartiality* and *conscientiousness* (§§1.8 & 2.1d). *Practical wisdom* (a key virtue used to decide which other character traits are virtues) includes consideration for others (the GR virtue) as well as impartiality, conscientiousness, knowledge, and imagination.

Some thinkers emphasize *rights*. A *right* is what can justifiably be demanded of others (for example, the right not to be killed or robbed). *Legal rights* are rights legislated by a society; for example, in a given society we might have a legal right to sell our slaves. *Human rights*, on the other hand, are rights that we have, or ought to have, simply because we're human beings, and not because we belong to a specific society; for example, all people have the human right not to be enslaved. Human rights are also called "moral rights" or "natural rights." Political structures are set up, at least in part, to protect human rights. Civil laws that violate human rights are unjust and ought to be changed.

The most basic human right is the *right to equal moral consideration*. GR explains this well: "Everyone has the right to be treated by others only as these others are willing to have themselves treated in the same circumstances."

GR is an important tool for arguing about human rights and was central in the American debate about slavery (§8.5). Since GR is common to practically

---

[1] Some forms of these views conflict with consistency and GR (Gensler 2011a: 110–38): for example, an unenlightened form of egoism or groupism that violates GR instead of supporting it (§§7.2 & 8.1), an act utilitarianism that violates the rights of individuals in cruel ways for the sake of maximizing good consequences, and a nonconsequentialism with absolute principles that clash with each other and lead to inhuman results. More enlightened forms of consequentialism and nonconsequentialism are compatible with GR and the demand that we be consistent.

every religion and culture (ch. 3), it can provide common ground in global discussions about human rights.[1]

The *natural-law tradition* sees basic moral norms (called *natural laws*) as objective, from nature instead of convention, and knowable to all through human reason. Natural moral laws differ from *positive laws*, which come from human legislation, and *divine laws*, which require divine revelation.

Thomas Aquinas (1224–74) is the central natural-law thinker. He says we can learn moral norms from either human reason or religious faith; both teach many of the same ideas (like GR and the wrongness of stealing). This redundancy is useful, since those who lack the time or ability to think out moral issues using reason can just follow the Bible. Morality is part of God's plan for the world and is possible for us because God gave us an intellect (to know the basic moral norms) and a will (to choose whether to follow them). Morality's purpose is to lead us to happiness – a partial happiness here on earth and a complete happiness with God in the afterlife.

Almost every natural-law thinker accepts GR[2]; most see GR as the central norm of natural law (see the ch. 5 chronology). Aquinas, while giving more attention to "Do good and avoid evil," accepted GR and equated it with "Love your neighbor as yourself."[3]

---

[1] The Muslim thinker Abdullahi Ahmed An-Na'im 1991 & 2008 defends human rights using GR. Morsink 2009 criticizes this; but his criticism takes GR as the flawed Pyrite 3 (§2.1d).

[2] Reiner 1983: 272f claims that Christian thinkers tended to connect three doctrines: the natural moral law of the Stoics and others (accessible to everyone's reason), the moral law that Paul saw as written on everyone's heart and conscience (Romans 2:14f), and the gospel GR (Matthew 7:12). GR is seen as the core of natural law by many Christian thinkers, including Justin Martyr, Basil, Augustine, Gratian, Anselm of Canterbury, William of Champeaux, Peter Lombard, Hugh of St. Victor, John of Salisbury, Bonaventure, Duns Scotus, Luther, Calvin, and Erasmus. (See also Wattles 1996: 69, 72, 208f; du Roy 2008 & 2009; and Pennington 2008.)

[3] Summa Theologica I-II, q. 94, a. 4 and q. 99, a. 1.

CHAPTER 13
Hare and Carson

> This chapter is technical and assumes materials
> from Chapter 2 ("Harder Introduction").

This chapter discusses the GR metaethics of Richard (R.M.) Hare and Tom Carson, which are sister theories to my own.

13.1 Hare

I became a golden-rule junkie on 6 December 1968, while doing a philosophy M.A. at Wayne State University in Detroit. What started me off was a talk there by R.M. Hare (1919–2002), perhaps the most important moral philosopher of the 20th century.[1] Hare's talk featured his metaethics, his GR, and applications to moral education. It electrified my thinking. I became an immediate fan of GR, which for me took on new clarity and importance. I ran to the library to get Hare's *Freedom and Reason* (1963), which explained his view in more detail. I read his book twice the next week, trying to learn from it and poke holes in it. I liked Hare's GR insights but disliked their theoretical basis.

Hare's book begins by pointing out two features of moral thinking. (1) We are or should be *free* to form our own moral views. The facts alone don't answer moral questions, and to just copy the moral beliefs of others compromises our freedom as moral agents. (2) Forming our moral views needs to be a *rational* activity. Moral questions are important, and answering them should engage our rational powers. So moral thinking needs to be both *free* and *rational*. But these two elements are difficult to combine. Many so emphasize *freedom* that reason disappears; anything goes and all moral beliefs are equal. And many so emphasize *reason* that freedom disappears; moral axioms are provable, perhaps from religious or scientific premises, and we must accept them. Both sides leave something out.

To understand morality, Hare says, we must understand moral language. He thinks "You *ought* to do A" doesn't state a fact and so isn't true or false.

[1] Hare gave this same lecture (published in Hare 1972b: 98–116) at Oxford in 1967, at his appointment as White's Chair, perhaps the world's most prestigious chair of moral philosophy.

Instead it *prescribes*, it tells what to do, it expresses our desires, like the simple imperative "Do A." But "You *ought* to do A" is also *universalizable*: it logically commits us to making similar judgments about similar cases. So "You *ought* to do A" means something like "Do A and everyone do the same in similar cases"; it expresses a desire that a kind of act be done in the present case and in all similar cases – including ones where the parties switch places. This leads to a GR consistency condition. Suppose I hold that I *ought* to enslave you. To be consistent, I must desire that I'd be enslaved if I were in your place. If I can't desire this, then I can't consistently hold that I *ought* to enslave you.

Hare calls his view *universal prescriptivism*. Ought judgments are *universal prescriptions* – imperatives that apply to all similar cases. And permissibility judgments are *universal permissions*; if you accept "It's *all right* (permissible) for you to do A," then you must consent to the act and to all similar acts, even if you're on the receiving end of the action. Two GR consistency conditions follow (like Gold 5 & 4 of §2.3):[1]

This is logically inconsistent:	This is logically inconsistent:
• I believe I *ought* to do A to another. • I don't desire that A be done to me in the same situation.	• I believe it's *all right* for me to do A to another. • I'm not willing that A be done to me in the same situation.

These give clearer versions of the traditional golden rule.

Hare's view here is semantic. It doesn't tell us what we *ought* to do; it tells us what "ought" and "all right" mean and what we logically commit ourselves to if we use these words. We could refuse to use these words and thus avoid the game of morality. But if we want to use these moral words consistently, then we must satisfy the GR consistency conditions built into their meaning.

How does this solve Hare's initial problem? We can be *free* in our moral thinking, because our moral beliefs express how we want people to live and can't be proved or disproved from facts. But to form moral beliefs *rationally*, we need to be informed, imaginative, and consistent. A key part of being consistent is to follow the GR consistency conditions.

Hare's GR insights gave GR a new clarity and overcame the traditional objections. Hare had a same-situation clause, asked the GR question the right way, and blocked an inconsistent combination (§2.1). But I disliked three things about his theoretical framework.

(1) Hare's prescriptivism says that moral beliefs (like "Racism is wrong") aren't true or false. This violates common sense. When we deliberate about a moral issue, we want to discover the truth of the matter. We speak as if there

[1] Hare 1963 (86–111) uses the *ought* GR condition extensively. He uses the *all right* GR condition in 1963 (102, 196, 221–3), 1964 (411), and 1972a (78, 82).

are moral truths. We use words like "true," "false," "correct," "mistaken," "discover," and "know" of moral judgments – but not of imperatives. When we use such objective language, we can't substitute a universalizable prescription for an ought judgment. Suppose I say (a):

(a) I know that *you ought to do this.*
(b) I know that *do this and everyone do the same in similar cases.*

Prescriptivism says the italicized parts of (a) and (b) mean the same thing. But they don't – since (b) doesn't makes sense. So prescriptivism clashes with our moral practice.

Hare could say our moral practice is wrong when it speaks of *moral truths* or *moral knowledge.* Or he could accept such notions but water them down; maybe calling an ought belief "true" just endorses it and doesn't make an objective claim. But the presumption lies with our moral practice. So we should accept moral truths unless we have strong arguments to the contrary.

Hare says it doesn't matter that moral judgments aren't true or false. What matters is that we can refute racists and teach our children to think rationally about morality. Hare's GR helps with these areas. But his GR deals only with how to *make moral judgments* in a consistent way (and not how to *live* in a consistent way). Nazis and slave traders can escape his GR by refraining from moral judgments. Then, no matter what cruel things they do, they don't violate his GR or violate any moral truths. On Hare's view, there are no moral truths. So it isn't a moral truth that we ought to make moral judgments about our actions, that we ought to be consistent, or that we ought to follow GR. Moral truths would make GR stronger and harder to escape.

(2) Hare ties his GR to his controversial prescriptivism. This is unfortunate, since his GR insights are so important that they need to be shared with those who hold other views. Compare my Gold 1 with Hare's GR:

Gold 1	Hare's GR
Treat others only as you consent to being treated in the same situation.	You're logically inconsistent if you believe you ought to do A to another but don't prescribe that if you were in an exactly similar situation then A be done to you.
• simpler and more like the usual GR sayings • compatible with many philosophies	• about what we must do to make moral judgments consistently • tied to Hare's analysis of moral terms

I've tried to develop Hare's GR insights in a broader and stronger way that can be defended from practically any philosophical or religious view. And so my approach is compatible with the view that there are moral truths (although it doesn't force this view) and my GR can be violated even by those who refrain from making moral judgments (although it doesn't force any particular way of defending this GR – see ch. 12).

(3) The basis for Hare's system is self-contradictory, since his analysis of "ought" (which backs up his GR condition for "ought") clashes with his analysis of "all right" (which backs up his GR condition for "all right"). My argument for this (Gensler 1976 & 1996: 136–43) is technical but rigorous. Hare, in a letter to me, agreed with my argument and gave up his GR condition for "all right." This weakens his view, since now Nazis and slave traders can hold that it's *all right* for them to do nasty things to others without fearing a GR consistency challenge from his view.

There are three further differences between my view and Hare's. (1) Hare in *Freedom and Reason* does little to counter the consistent Nazi fanatic who desires that he and his family be put in concentration camps and killed if found out to be Jewish. I counter by criticizing his flawed desires (§§2.2 & 8.2). This strengthens the GR attack on racism.

(2) Hare denies the possibility of *moral weakness,* where you believe that you ought to do something, you're capable of doing it, but yet you don't do it. He thinks that if you don't act accordingly, then you don't really have an *ought* belief – you're just mouthing words. But I think such moral weakness is common. When we act against our moral beliefs, we're inconsistent; but our moral beliefs may still be genuine.

(3) Hare 1981 claims that his view about the meaning of the moral concepts necessarily leads to utilitarianism. Suppose you're deciding whether to do A, which would affect several people. You put yourself in the place of the various parties, some desiring A and some desiring not-A. Hare thinks you should sum up the desires on either side, counting stronger desires more, and go with the action that maximizes desire-satisfaction. This yields *preference utilitarianism*: we ought to do whatever maximizes the total desire-satisfaction. I disagree with this. Suppose that A maximizes the total desire-satisfaction but badly harms one person. When I put myself in the place of the parties, I may be more impressed by the great harm to the one than the slight benefits to the many. So I may universally prescribe that I ought not to do A, even though A maximizes desire-satisfaction. I don't see why consistency forces the utilitarian belief that I ought to do A.[1]

Despite these differences, I own a debt of gratitude to Hare. He opened my mind to how useful GR is and how to avoid the usual GR objections. He gave me something to build on in developing my own GR approach.

---

[1] Preference utilitarianism has strange implications. If I developed an extraordinarily strong desire, even if it was evil or ignorant, then others would be morally obliged to follow my desire. But this is implausible.

13.2   Carson

Tom Carson's *Lying and Deception* 2010: 129–56 has a GR chapter that builds
on Hare's work and mine. This is carefully argued, useful in answering GR
objections, and highly recommended.

Carson argues this way for his first GR formula:

> Consistency requires that I judge acts done to me or to people
> I love the same way I judge acts done to others, unless the
> acts differ in some morally relevant respects.
> Our attitudes must be consistent with our moral judgments.
> So if I think that it's morally permissible for someone to do
> something to me (or someone I love), then I must not object
> to her doing it to me (or someone I love).
> ∴ Consistency requires that if I think it morally permissible for
> someone to do A to another, then I must not object to some-
> one doing A to me (or someone I love) in relevantly similar
> circumstances. (Carson's GR)

Carson notes that this follows a GR argument that I've published in various
places (and now §2.1d); it's even closer to how I'd argue for Gold 4 (a GR in
§2.3 about consistently using "all right"). There are minor terminology differences between us. I speak of "impartiality" and "conscientiousness" (as forms
of *consistency*), while he speaks of "consistency." I speak of "consenting" or
"willing," while he uses "not objecting" (which at times I've used). And I use
"don't combine" while he uses "consistency requires." These differences are
minor. While Carson's GR above is about consistently using "morally permissible," he also gives other GR formulas, including ones about "morally wrong"
and "morally obligatory." Carson's GR formulas all hold on my approach. But
some GR formulas, like my Gold 1, hold on my approach but not his.

Carson argues differently for his premises. I see my impartiality and conscientiousness duties as self-evident (§§2.7 & 12.1). Understood correctly, they
have no absurd implications and are more clearly true than premises (including
ones about the meaning of the moral terms) that could be used to defend them.
They're flavors of a general consistency duty that is the first duty of a rational
being and assumed in every area of thought and action. For those who don't
like self-evident consistency duties, I suggest that practically any other
approach to ethics can justify GR and related consistency norms (ch. 12). Since
Carson gives another justification, I welcome this.

Like Hare, Carson claims that his premises are logical consistency conditions
built into our moral language. We commit a logical inconsistency if we make
conflicting evaluations about actions we claim to be relevantly similar, or if our
attitudes or actions clash with our moral judgments. Carson considers the
objection that we should change our moral language to avoid these consistency

conditions. He responds that this would cut us off from the larger moral community and detract from the purposes for which we use moral language.[1]

Compare my Gold 1 with Carson's GR:

Gold 1	Carson's GR
Treat others only as you consent to being treated in the same situation.	Consistency requires that if I think it would be morally permissible for someone to do A to another, then I must not object to someone doing A to me (or someone I love) in relevantly similar circumstances.
• simpler and more like the usual GR sayings • compatible with many philosophies	• about what we must do to make moral judgments consistently • tied to general logical claims about the moral terms

Carson's GR, like Hare's, is only about how to make moral judgments in a consistent way. Nazis and slave traders can escape his GR by refraining from moral judgments (*the amoralist strategy*). Then, no matter what cruel things they do, they don't violate his GR. But isn't it a shame to let amoral Nazis and slave traders off so easy? Shouldn't there be some suitably justified GR of Carson's system that they violate? Fortunately, this problem can be fixed in either of two ways, both consistent with Carson's metaethical framework. Fixing this problem would make Carson's approach stronger.

Carson argues that there are some *objectively true moral norms* – against some kinds of lying and deception, for example, or against Nazi racism (2010: 160f). What makes such norms objectively true is that ideally rational moral judges would agree on them. Such judges for Carson must be adequately informed (which includes empathy/imagination), consistent (which includes the GR conditions), and able to reason properly. He argues that there are objectively true norms about *lying* that even amoral business persons can violate, and objectively true norms about *racism* that even amoral Nazis can violate. Now rational moral judges (who are all GR judges) would seemingly also agree on Gold 2, which binds even amoralists: "You *ought* to treat others only as you consent to being treated in the same situation." But if rational moral judges would agree on such a GR that binds even amoralists (as they agree on other norms that bind even amoralists), then such a GR would, on Carson's approach, be an *objectively true moral norm*. Amoral Nazis and slave traders would violate this GR, even though they wouldn't violate Carson's other GRs (which apply only to those making moral judgments).

---

[1] Carson's response assumes that his two premises are logical consistency requirements and that the alternative is to have them not be requirements of any sort. But many may accept impartiality and conscientiousness requirements, but on a basis other than logical consistency.

There's also another approach. Carson gives pragmatic reasons to shun *inconsistency* and the confusion it brings (2010: 145–8): "When we vividly and concretely imagine what it would be like to be the sort of person who is not concerned about being consistent, it seems quite unattractive. There are good reasons to want to be consistent." He likewise gives pragmatic reasons to shun *amorality*, which makes us social outcasts (2010: 148–50): "A parent who was solely concerned with promoting the welfare of his child would want the child to be moral and accept moral norms." So Carson gives pragmatic reasons to shun both *inconsistency and amorality*.

Carson's GRs apply to those who want to shun *inconsistency*. He might also give GRs for those who want to shun both *inconsistency and immorality* – such as the following:

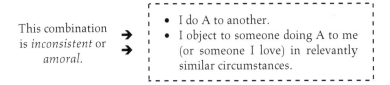

Suppose that I, as a Nazi or slave trader, do cruel things to others – but I object to someone doing the same to me in relevantly similar circumstances. There are three alternatives I might take, and each makes me inconsistent or amoral:

> I might believe that my cruel actions are *morally permissible* (then I violate Carson's original GR and am inconsistent), believe that they're *morally wrong* (then I act against my beliefs and am inconsistent by Carson's second premise), or have neither belief (then I'm amoral about my action).

If Carson went this way, he'd add a second group of GR conditions. These would say that a given combination would be either *inconsistent or amoral*. Yes, some might not care about this new group, since they don't care about being moral. But some might not care about Carson's original GRs either, since they don't care about being consistent. But most want to shun both *inconsistency and amorality*. And Carson gives pragmatic reasons to shun both.[1]

And so it would be possible, in two different ways consistent with Carson's metaethical framework, to justify a GR that's stronger in that it applies even to those who don't make moral judgments about their actions.

There's another difference between Carson's approach and mine. Hare, Carson, and I all roughly agree on these two key ideas:

1. We must make similar evaluations about similar actions.
2. We must keep our attitudes and actions in line with our moral judgments.

---

[1] Gensler 1983 goes further and argues that amoralism is inconsistent. Appealing to standard prescriptivist premises, it argues that logical consistency requires that we make moral judgments of permissibility about our actions. This argument is too technical to pursue here.

Hare bases (1) and (2) on his controversial analysis of moral judgments. Carson's view is more liberal, since it bases (1) and (2) on logical features of moral judgments that can be accepted by many views about moral judgments. My approach is even more liberal, in that it's compatible with any view that sees violations of (1) and (2) as somehow objectionable on any grounds.

Let me give two examples of views that accept (1) or (2), but not as expressing *logical features* of moral judgments (ch. 12). My first example is the emotivist Charles Stevenson; I audited the last course that he gave at the University of Michigan, where I did my doctorate. Stevenson saw the neglect of (1) ("Evaluate similar cases similarly") as a defect in his earlier work. Unlike Hare or Carson, though, he didn't see violations of (1) as logical self-contradictions. Instead, he argued that it's normally self-defeating to violate (1). Our attitudes, unless we support them with universal reasons, will receive ridicule and abuse. This violates our purpose in making ethical judgments: to express our attitudes *and influence the attitudes of others*. So Stevenson accepted (1), but not as a consistency condition built into our moral language.

Or imagine a thinker who bases moral norms on the Bible and sees moral judgments as describing God's will. This thinker might accept (1) and (2) as religious duties, on the basis of biblical verses against partiality and hypocrisy. But this thinker might not see (1) and (2) as built into our moral language and might not see violations of (1) and (2) as logical inconsistencies.

So my strategy is broader. I want to show how GR can be put into as wide a range of theoretical approaches as possible.

While I've been critical here, I don't want to leave you with a wrong impression. The GR views of Hare and Carson are sister theories of my own. The three views are similar in many ways. For example, all three see GR as a consistency condition with a same-situation clause and all three would apply GR to practical issues in rather similar ways. So these views are more alike than different.

CHAPTER 14
More Objections

> This chapter is technical and assumes materials
> from Chapter 2 ("Harder Introduction").

Chapter 2 defended GR against Objections 1–3. Chapters 7 and 8 defended GR against Objections 4–7 (about egoism and groupism). This chapter defends GR against 27 further objections, numbered 1a and 8–33.

14.1 Platinum

The Web has a GR objection that's more popular there than all others combined: that GR, in telling us to treat others as *we* want to be treated, ignores the fact that *others* may have different likes and dislikes.

Objection 1a: different likes and dislikes	If we differ from others in likes and dislikes, GR wrongly has us treat others according to *our* likes and dislikes, instead of *theirs*.

So we should move from GR ("Treat others as *you* want to be treated") to the superior *platinum rule* ("Treat others as *they* want to be treated").

I searched the Web for: "golden rule" "platinum rule" (both together, using quotes). I found hundreds of pages, most favoring platinum over gold, and I read the first fifty. As usual, the Web had a mix of wisdom and confusion. The platinum defenses were similar, except that some opposed GR (as misguided, wrong, outdated, passé, ignorant, or self-righteous) while others saw the new and improved platinum wording as expressing what the old GR meant to say.

GR allegedly stalls when we deal with those who differ from us in likes and dislikes, cultural background, or personality types. Then how *we* want to be treated is a poor indication of how we should treat *others*. We should treat others as *they* want to be treated. Following platinum is harder, since we must get to know others and apply empathy. If we have a business, gold has us treat customers as *we* want to be treated, looking at our own likes and dislikes. But platinum has us instead satisfy *their* individual needs and desires; to learn about these, we'd need to talk with customers and really listen to what they say. Platinum shows greater respect for others then does gold.

When you hear GR objections, ask "Which GR formula is criticized?" Here criticized is the *literal golden rule* (Pyrite 1): "If you want X to do A to you, then do A to X" (§§2.1a–b). Objection 1a is like our Objection 1: "If we're in *different circumstances* from the other person (for example, we have different likes and dislikes), GR can command bad actions." We gave this example. I hate broccoli but work as a waiter at a restaurant. Becky orders broccoli (which she likes). Should I serve her broccoli? Not by the literal GR, which absurdly says: "If you want Becky not to serve you broccoli, then don't serve her broccoli."

When I present GR, I often begin by giving problems with the literal GR (Pyrite 1). I sometimes wonder: Does anyone besides kindergarten students take GR so literally? Do any adults take GR as Pyrite 1? The answer is yes. To find many adults who take GR as Pyrite 1, do the Web search given above.

GR needs a same-situation clause. To apply GR, we need to know the other person's situation, which may differ from ours, with different likes, dislikes, and needs. We need to imagine ourselves in the other person's situation. And we need to ask, "How am I now willing that I'd be treated if I were in that situation?" Here I'm clearly willing that *if I were in the place of Becky (who loves broccoli and ordered it)* then I be served broccoli.

The platinum rule is another way to express flawed Pyrite 2 (§2.1c):

Pyrite 2b: platinum rule	Pyrite 2: a faulty same-situation GR
If X wants you to do A to him, then do A to him. (Treat others as they want to be treated.)	Given that if you were in X's exact place (in the reversed situation) then you'd want A done to you, then do A to X.

These two are logically equivalent[1] – since:

how X wants to be treated	=	how you'd want to be treated if you were in X's exact place	(recall that if you were in X's *exact* place then you'd have *all* of X's qualities)

Pyrite 2b and Pyrite 2, being logically equivalent, have the same problem: the other person may have flawed desires.

Platinum folks, while good at seeing problems with literal gold, are poor at seeing problems with literal platinum. Platinum, taken literally, says we should always treat others *as they want to be treated* – regardless of how foolish, evil,

---

[1] Bruton 2004, D. Locke 1981, and Whiteley 1966 also note this equivalence.

or inconsistent their wants are. Always give customers what they want? Hey, I'm a customer and want a free car. Always give students what they want? Hey, I'm a student and want an A with no work. Always give children what they want? Hey, I'm a child and want to eat only candy and never clean up after myself. Always give criminals what they want? Hey, I'm a criminal and want you to help me steal and not punish me. Always give politicians what they want? This leads to contradictions if their desires conflict (Alice wants you to vote for her and not Betty, but Betty wants you to vote for her and not Alice). Always give everyone what they want? Hey, I want you to be my slave for life. Literal platinum (Pyrite 2b) is really crazy.[1]

Our first two GR fallacies (§2.4) went as follows:

1. The *literal GR fallacy* assumes that everyone has the same likes, dislikes, and needs that we have. This assumes Pyrite 1.
2. The *soft GR fallacy* assumes that we should never act against what others want. This assumes Pyrite 2.

Platinum folks avoid the first fallacy but commit the second. So many do it that I suspect a natural progression of thinking about GR. Maybe we all start with the literal GR. Then, seeing how people differ, we move to Pyrite 2 or its platinum equivalent. If we pursue these further and uncover further problems, we may then move to Pyrite 3 or Gold 1.

I'll here mention four platinum thinkers. (1) George Bernard Shaw 1903: 217, criticizing the literal GR, says: "Do not do unto others as you would that they should do unto you. Their tastes may not be the same."

(2) Karl Popper 1996 2:386 says: "The golden rule is a good standard which can perhaps even be improved by doing unto others, where possible, as *they* want to be done by." The philosopher Popper includes "where possible," perhaps meaning "*where possible and sensible.*"

GR leads to a qualified-platinum rule. We generally want others to respect and help promote (or at least not frustrate) *our desires*. So by GR, roughly, we should respect and help promote (or at least not frustrate) *their desires*. But this needs to be qualified when others have desires that are confused, misinformed, evil, self-centered, impossible to satisfy, or otherwise flawed.

By GR, roughly, I'm to give the desires of others whatever weight I want given to *my* desires in similar circumstances. The weight I want given to my desires depends on their rationality. I want you to give little weight to my clearly confused desires – as when I order my tenth drink or tell you (by mistake) to turn right (over the cliff); I'll later thank you for disregarding such desires. But I want you to give much weight to my desires that are *rational*

[1] M. Singer 1963 and Cunningham 1998 criticize platinum in similar ways. Both say that GR normally leads us to respect (but not always follow) the desires of others. Huang 2005 supports something like the qualified-platinum rule that appears later in this section.

(informed, imaginative, consistent, and so on), even if you disagree with them; in this way you respect me as a person. So I suggest the *platinum-gold alloy rule*: give weight to another's desires to the extent that these are rational.

(3) Milton Bennett 1979, in "Overcoming the golden rule," distinguishes *sympathy* from *empathy* as follows (see also §11.2 Q1):

- *Sympathy*: I imagine myself in another's external situation (but I keep my own likes, dislikes, beliefs, and so on).
- *Empathy*: I imagine myself in another's place (which includes having the other's likes, dislikes, beliefs, and so on).

He mentions an ad in the *New Yorker* asking for contributions; it shows a poor Asian girl Tina with the words, "Tina has never had a teddy bear." Now Tina, in her culture, has no knowledge of or desire for teddy bears. But still, we're supposed to put ourselves in Tina's place in the sympathy way – in her external situation but keeping our own beliefs and desires (particularly about teddy bears) – and feel sadness over never having had a teddy bear. Along these lines, Bennett gives this *sympathy* reading of GR: "Do unto others as you imagine you would like to have done unto you in similar [external] circumstances." This suggests something between Pyrite 1 and Pyrite 2:

Pyrite 1b: switch-ing just external circumstances	Treat X in the way that, if you were in X's external situation (but keeping your own likes, dislikes, beliefs, and so on), you'd want to be treated.

Pyrite 1b has most of the same flaws as the literal GR. So it tells the broccoli-hating waiter not to serve broccoli to Becky, who loves and ordered it.[1]

Bennett gives another example. When he gets sick, he wants to be left alone; but when his wife gets sick, she wants attention. Using sympathy, he'd leave his sick wife alone (against what she wants), and she'd give her sick husband attention (against what he wants). Using empathy, he'd give his sick wife atten-tion (which she wants), and she'd leave her sick husband alone (which he wants). Bennett calls the empathy approach an *overcoming* of GR. But all it overcomes is the deficient Pyrite 1b. Gold 1 asks the empathy question: "Am I now willing that if I were in the same situation as my sick wife (who wants attention) then I be left alone?" (No, you aren't so willing.) He ends (1979: 421f): "With empathy, we might indeed be able to overcome the golden rule, putting in its place the 'platinum rule': 'Do unto others as they themselves would have done unto them.'" He seems unaware of platinum's problems.

(4) Tony Alessandra and Michael O'Connor co-authored *The Platinum Rule* (1996). While this has useful ideas, its GR criticisms target only the literal GR and its platinum rule leads to absurdities when people have flawed desires.

---

[1] I found only Hale 1805: 406 defending Pyrite 1b; D. Locke 1981 and Whiteley 1966 reject it.

14.2 Three classic objections

When I started this book, I downloaded over a thousand journal articles or book chapters to my computer. Over a hundred discussed GR objections, mostly Objections 1–3. Few authors saw that GR can be worded differently and that a strong objection to one wording might carry no weight against another.[1]

Objection 1 to Pyrite 1 was the most popular GR objection (§2.1a):

Pyrite 1: the literal GR

> If you want X
> to do A to you,
> then do A to X.

Objection 1: different circumstances

> If you're in *different circumstances* from the other person (for example, you have different likes and dislikes), GR can command bad actions.

About 40 publications mentioned GR problems like these:

- You don't speak louder to a hard-of-hearing person, because you don't want her to speak louder to you.
- You create powerful but unfriendly computer programs for beginners, because this is what you (a geek) prefer for yourself.
- You play loud rock music all night for your neighbors (who hate it), because this is what you want them to do to you.
- You shake hands with those of another culture (who hate this practice), because this is how you want them to treat you.

The pattern goes: "You do A to X, because you want X to do A to you." Pick an action that's wrong to do to X, but that (because of how you and X differ) you want done to yourself. To fix this problem, add a same-situation clause to GR.

Objection 2 to Pyrite 2 was also popular (§2.1c):

Pyrite 2: a faulty same-situation GR

> Given that if you were in X's exact place (in the reversed situation) then you'd want A done to you, then do A to X.

Objection 2: X's flawed desires

> If *X has flawed desires* (about how he wants to be treated), GR can command bad actions.

---

[1] To study GR objections, start with Bruton 2004, Cadoux 1912, Elliott 1999, Gert 1995, Hennessey & Gert 1985, Hirst 1934, Huang 2005, Kant 1785: 97, D. Locke 1981, Reilly 2006, Reinikainen 2005, L. Russell 1942, M. Singer 1963, Wattles 1996, and Weiss 1941. In August 2009, I e-mailed 41 people with a special interest in GR (including philosophers, religious thinkers, educators, and activists), asking them to feed me GR objections. I got sixty responses. Jeff Wattles sent a brief but insightful "30 objections to the golden rule"; this became one of my most prized possessions, as judged by how upset I got when I thought I lost it.

About 20 publications mentioned GR problems like these:

- You're a judge about to jail a dangerous criminal who may harm others. If you were in the criminal's place then you'd want to be set free – so set him free.
- X (who's irresponsible with money) asks you to loan her $10,000. If you were in X's place then you'd want not to be refused – so don't refuse her.
- You're a police officer about to arrest X for driving 90 mph while drunk. If you were in X's place then you'd want not to be arrested – so don't arrest her.
- You're about to flunk a student who does no work. If you were in the student's place then you'd want not to be flunked – so don't flunk the student.

The pattern goes: "If you were in X's place then you'd want A done to you – so do A to X." Pick a case where you ought to act against X's desires (and thus against the desires that you'd have if you were in X's exact place). To fix this problem, phrase GR to be about your *present desire about a hypothetical case*. Using the first example, you'd ask: "<u>Am</u> I <u>now</u> <u>willing</u> <u>that</u> <u>if</u> I were in the place of this dangerous criminal then I be sent to jail?" Yes, you should be so willing. You could add, "If I do such things, then please send me to jail too!"

Objection 3 to Pyrite 3 (and Pyrite 1) was also popular (§2.1d):

Pyrite 3: an almost correct GR	Objection 3: your flawed desires
If you want it to be that if you were in X's exact place (in the reversed situation) then A would be done to you, then do A to X.	If *you have flawed desires* about how you're to be treated, GR can command bad actions.

About 20 publications mentioned GR problems like these (the first two examples go against Pyrite 3 while the last two go against Pyrite 1):

- Suppose you want everyone to hurt you. You desire that if you were in your friend's place then you be hurt – so hurt your friend.
- You desire that if you were in your teacher's place then you be given money for a good grade – so give your teacher money for a good grade.
- You want others to get you drunk – so get them drunk.
- You want X to cooperate in sin with you – so cooperate in sin with X.

The pattern goes: "You desire that [if you were in X's place then] A be done to you – so do A to X." You pick an evil action for A. To fix this problem, give GR a *consistency form* that forbids an action–desire combination, instead of saying specifically what to do. The consistency GR doesn't tell you to do the evil action (since it doesn't say specifically what to do). A fuller solution would also criticize the flawed desire (§§2.2, 8.2, & 14.3g).

14.3   Long objections

14.3a   Competition

Objection 8: competition	If we compete successfully (in areas like sports or business) then we violate GR – since then we defeat others but don't want them to defeat us in similar circumstances.

Competition is important in life. In sports, we compete to be the starting quarterback, complete the pass, beat Ohio State, or win the gold medal. In business, we compete to win the promotion, make the sale, or have our company win. Elsewhere, we compete to gain Suzy's love, win the war, beat our friends at poker, get the highest grades, or be elected. If we win, then others lose – and if others win, then we lose. We want others not to beat us. So if we beat others, then we treat them as we want *not* to be treated. The only way to satisfy GR in competition is to lose: since we want others not to beat us, we don't beat them. GR is for losers. So GR doesn't work in areas involving competition.[1]

Which GR formula is criticized here? The target can be any of our pyrites, all of which use "want." By contrast, Gold 1 uses the weaker "consent" or "be willing." How is this difference important?

Consider that *morally legitimate competition* is done within a framework of *rules of fair play*. Football, for example, has rules. To stop the opposing quarterback from competing the pass, you can tackle him when he has the ball, grab the ball from him, or jump up to block the pass. But you suffer a penalty if you tackle him when he no longer has the ball, use excessive force, or intentionally break his leg; attempts to injure may bring a fine and ejection from the game.

Rules of fair play similarly regulate other competitive activities. Not all is fair in love or war: we don't think it fair to kill or injure your rival to gain Suzy's love, and most nations endorse the Geneva Conventions about war.

Competition serves a wider purpose, which the rules of fair play help promote. We value competition in sports because it's fun, helps us stay in shape, and teaches valuable life-skills (like discipline and teamwork). Proper background rules promote these values. In business, we value competition because it helps to bring us better and more affordable products. Practices like lying about products or burning down factories hurt legitimate competition and so go against the legal or moral rules of fair play.

How is this relevant to the competition objection? Well, in competition there's a difference between outcomes we *want or don't want* and what we

---

[1] The competition objection is difficult but gets little mention in the published literature (except Heath 2007). Jakaew Tanunath from Thailand suggested it to me, using a tennis example.

approve or disapprove of. GR is about the latter. Suppose I play for Michigan against Ohio State. The Ohio State quarterback tries to complete a pass. I want him not to succeed. I tackle him before he throws – even though I want our quarterback not to be tackled before he throws in similar circumstances. This doesn't violate our GR (see left box):

GR allows combining these:	GR forbids combining these:
• I tackle their quarterback. • I want our quarterback not to be tackled in similar circumstances.	• I tackle their quarterback. • I'm unwilling that our quarterback be tackled in similar circumstances.

The right box has the proper GR application; I should be able to satisfy this – since I should be *willing* that our quarterback be tackled in similar circumstances (fairly, according to the rules, and so on). "Willing" here is weaker than "wanting" and needn't involve favoring or advocating the act. We could also use words like *approve, allow, agree to, condone, tolerate,* or *consent* – in at least some senses of these terms.[1] So when I tackle our opponent's quarterback, I must be *willing* that our opponents do the same to us under similar circumstances – but I needn't *want* or *desire* that they do this.

Let's put this in general terms. Suppose I defeat X but I want X not to defeat me in similar circumstances. This doesn't violate our GR (see left box):

GR allows combining these:	GR forbids combining these:
• I defeat X. • I want X not to defeat me in similar circumstances.	• I defeat X. • I'm unwilling that X defeat me in similar circumstances.

The right box has the proper GR form; I should be able to satisfy this – since I should *be willing* that I be defeated in similar circumstances (fairly, according to the rules, and so on). Again, "be willing" here is weaker than "wanting" and needn't involve favoring or advocating the act. So when I defeat X, then by GR I must *be willing* that X do the same to me under similar circumstances – but I needn't *want* or *desire* that X does this. So GR applies to standards of fair play in competitive situations (and I must endorse these standards regardless of where I imagine myself in the situation). But GR doesn't prevent me from beating opponents fairly.

Why must GR be formulated in the weaker way, using "be willing" or "consent" instead of the stronger "want" or "desire"? Recall our chart in §2.1d,

---

[1] These words contrast with words like *condemning, objecting to, disapproving, forbidding, protesting, prohibiting,* and *repudiating*. I don't want our quarterback to be tackled in similar circumstances – but I wouldn't *condemn, object to*, etc. this action. See §2.7.

which shows that if you're impartial (make similar evaluations about similar acts) and conscientious (have a harmony between your moral beliefs and how you live), then you won't steal Detra's bicycle unless you're also willing that your bicycle be stolen in the same situation:

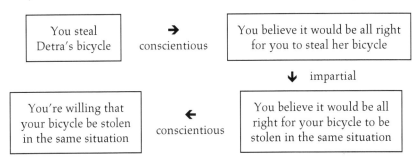

Focus on the bottom boxes: believing that the act is *all right* (permissible) commits us to *be willing* that it be done (which is weaker than *wanting* it to be done). The argument fails if we substitute "wanting" in the lower-left box:

To see why this fails, consider that we may believe that it's both permissible to do A and permissible not to do A. If permissibility committed us to wanting the act to be done, then in such cases we must both want A to be done and want A not to be done – a contradiction. (It isn't a contradiction to both be willing that A be done and be willing that A not be done.)

As we compete, GR allows us to want our opponent to lose and to beat our opponent by fair means. But GR doesn't let us use means that we don't allow our opponent in a similar situation – and we must be willing that our opponent beat us if this is done by fair means. This accords with norms that an impartial and conscientiousness being would necessarily follow.

14.3b   Over or under demanding

Objection 9: overly demanding	GR is impractical because it would force us to give to every beggar and contribute to the poor until we're equally poor ourselves.

GR makes us an easy target for anyone who asks for money. Suppose I walk down a street and pass a dozen beggars, each asking for a $50 donation to relieve their poverty. In each case, if I were in their place then I'd want to be given $50; so GR tells me to give $50 to each.[1] And suppose I keep passing more and more such people. My GR obligations will continue until I have no more money to give. Yes, it would be nice to help all the poor people in the world (since if I were in their place then I'd want to be helped). But this is impossible – I can't help them all. And so GR can't really generate obligations – since if it did then it would generate so many of them that we couldn't fulfill them all. So GR is overly demanding and thus impractical.[2]

This reasoning asks the GR question the wrong way (§2.1c). It also commits the *soft* and *third-parties* GR fallacies (§§1.4, 1.6, & 2.4).[3]

How should GR apply to giving money to beggars? Since this issue involves more than two people, it's convenient to use Gold 7: "Act only as you're willing for anyone to act in the same situation, regardless of where or when you imagine yourself or others" – which has us apply Gold 1 to all affected parties. Suppose we're deciding between these policies:

A. Never do anything to help anyone else in need (including beggars).
B. Always give to beggars when they ask for money.
C. Contribute a reasonable part of your income to groups that help the needy, and encourage the state to set up efficient and fiscally responsible programs to help the needy. But in general, don't give to beggars when they ask for money. Instead, refer them to agencies that provide food and shelter.

GR consistency makes it difficult to accept A. If we accept A, then we must be willing that others do nothing to help us in an imagined situation where we're in need and can't provide for ourselves. For different reasons, it would be difficult to accept B consistently – since B would lead to a huge increase in the number of beggars (especially ones who cheat people or spend what they get on alcohol or drugs) and thus an impossibly large number of obligations to give to beggars. GR consistency, when combined with knowledge and imagination, leads to something closer to C. I can hold C with GR consistency since I'm willing that I be treated according to C regardless of where I imagine myself in the situation (as beggar, or one asked for money, or whatever).

This answers another objection (Kant 1785: 97 and Outka 1972: 293):

Objection 10: not demanding enough	GR doesn't necessarily lead us to help others, because it lets us off if we're self-sufficient and willing to forego such help ourselves.

---

[1] The negative GR gives the same result: since I want not to be refused when I ask for money, then I shouldn't refuse others when they ask for money. See §§10.3 & 10.5.

[2] Haskell 1987 talks about this objection, which gets brief mention in Brook 1987, Brooks 1946, Double 1999, Hayes 1913, and Jonas 1969. See also §10.3 and its references.

[3] The next paragraph is repeated in §10.5, in the discussion about positive and negative GRs.

It's irrelevant that we're now self-sufficient. We must imagine ourselves in the place of the person who needs help (and isn't self-sufficient). So GR consistency makes it difficult to avoid helping others.

GR doesn't tell us how generous to be toward those in need. Instead, it reflects the question back to us: "How generous are we now willing that others be toward us if we had a similar need?" We set the standard ourselves.

14.3c   Kant's footnote

Objection 11: Kant's footnote	The trivial GR is derivable from the formula of universal law; it doesn't cover duties to oneself or benevolence to others (since many would agree not to be helped by others if they could be excused from helping others); and it forces a judge to let off a criminal without punishment.

This footnote, from Immanuel Kant's *Groundwork of the Metaphysics of Morals* (Kant 1785: 97), is the most famous GR objection. Wattles 1987: 125 (see also 83–6) noted that it "almost completely silenced a previously energetic European tradition of reflection on the golden rule for 150 years." The criminal objection is often cited against GR.[1]

Kant makes four points. (1) GR is derivable from UL (the formula of universal law). I grant this. GR (as Gold 1) is derivable from UL (taken as Gold 7 of §2.3). And both are derivable from the more basic principle that *we ought to be consistent* (taken widely to include being impartial and conscientious). But this isn't an objection to GR.

(2) GR doesn't cover duties to oneself, but UL does. I grant this, with qualifications. Duties to oneself are covered by the future-regard and self-regard principles, which are close relatives of GR and included in UL (§2.3). And GR duties to others can *indirectly* create duties to ourselves, since if we don't care about our needs we'll likely dry up and be of little use to others; we don't want others to thus hurt us through neglecting their own needs (Cadoux 1912).

(3) GR needn't lead to benevolence, since we might gladly consent that others not benefit us if we be excused from benefiting them. This is Objection 10, which we just disposed of. GR *would* lead to benevolence, since GR has us consider ourselves in the place of others, including those who aren't self-sufficient and who do need help. UL leads to benevolence in the same way.

(4) GR would force a judge to set free a dangerous criminal (since if the judge were in the criminal's place then he'd want to be set free). This is Objection 2, which we disposed of in §§2.1c & 14.2 (see also §8.5). The judge should

---

[1] Wattles 1996: 214 speculated that Kant's own formulas may have been prompted by the need to reform GR. Some consider Kant's formulas to be close to GR; treating others as ends in themselves, for example, is close to treating others only as we're willing that we be treated in the same situation. Hoche 1978 and Parfit 2011 also discuss Kant's footnote.

be able to tell the criminal: "I can send you to jail, because I'm now willing that if I were in your place (as a dangerous criminal who may harm others) then I be sent to jail."

14.3d   Assumes moral norms

Objection 12: assumes moral norms	GR, which must be seen as telling us to treat others as it's *morally proper* to desire that we be treated, presumes antecedent norms; so GR is a less important addition to other norms.

GR shouldn't ask, "How do I *desire* to be treated?" – since I may have evil desires; for example, I might desire that others help me to rob a bank. Instead, GR should ask "How would it be *right* (*morally proper*) for me to be treated?" GR thus appeals to antecedent moral standards and tells us only to be consistent in applying these standards.[1]

Which GR formula is criticized here? The target could be any of our pyrites, all of which fall to *flawed desires* Objection 2 or 3. We can fix such problems by taking GR as Gold 1, which forbids an inconsistent combination:

> - I do something to another.
> - I'm unwilling that this be done to me in the same situation.

Don't combine these.

The only antecedent norm assumed here is that we ought to be consistent. Gold 1 tests the consistency between our *action* (toward another) and our *desire* about how we'd be treated in a similar situation.

Objection 12 suggests that we take GR to mean one of these:

- If it's *morally proper* for you to desire that X do A to you in similar circumstances, then do A to X.
- If X *ought* to do A to you in similar circumstances, then do A to X.

These, while correct, are closer to impartiality than to GR. Since they assume antecedent moral norms, they're not as useful as Gold 1 in criticizing deficient moral intuitions. Dabney (1867: 196f or 124) used this objection to deflect GR criticisms of slavery. He claimed that in applying GR, instead of looking at our *desires* about ourselves being enslaved, we should appeal to *moral intuitions* about slavery – and most of his friends had pro-slavery intuitions.

---

[1] Augustine 400a & 400b, Gould 1968, Hamson 1970, Haskell 1987, Hennessey & Gert 1985, Leibniz 1704, Sidgwick 1874, and Whately 1856 raise this objection.

14.3e Contradictions

Objection 13: commands contradictions	GR can issue contradictory commands when your action affects X and Y – since you may want A done when you put yourself in X's place but want A not done when you put yourself in Y's place.

Suppose I own a store and need to hire just one worker. Alice and Betty apply, and I must choose between them. Both are qualified, but Alice more so. When I consider myself in Alice's place, I desire that I be hired instead of Betty; so GR tells me to hire Alice and not Betty. But when I consider myself in Betty's place, I desire that I be hired instead of Alice; so GR tells me to hire Betty and not Alice. So GR gives contradictory commands: "Hire Alice and not Betty" and "Hire Betty and not Alice." When our actions affect several people, who gain or lose depending on our choice, GR may give contradictory commands.[1]

Which GR formula is criticized here? The target could be any of our pyrites, all of which are if-then principles telling us exactly what to do based on what we desire about a similar action done to us (§2.1d):

Deductive model of GR reasoning (the *desire* wording can vary):

> If you have this desire about A being done to you, then do A to X.
> You have this desire about A being done to you.
> ∴ Do A to X.

Such reasoning can prescribe bad actions if we have flawed desires. It can also issue contradictory commands when our action affects more than one person. Both problems vanish if we instead take GR as Gold 1, which forbids an inconsistent combination. In our Alice-Betty case, we must satisfy GR consistency toward both parties. Gold 6 and 7 express this more clearly:

- Gold 6: Don't act in a given way toward X and Y without being willing that this act be done when you imagine yourself in X's place and being willing that this act be done when you imagine yourself in Y's place.
- Gold 7: Act only as you're willing for anyone to act in the same situation, regardless of where or when you imagine yourself or others.

To make my choice consistently, I must follow some policy that I'm willing for

---

[1] Whately 1856 and D. Locke 1981 raise this surprisingly uncommon objection. Even two-party cases can give contradictions. Suppose you're a broccoli-hating waiter and Becky orders broccoli. By Pyrite 1, you *shouldn't* serve her broccoli (since you don't want others to serve you broccoli) and you *should* serve her broccoli (since you want others to bring you what you order).

anyone to follow in that situation – regardless of which place in the situation I imagine myself in. So if I pick Alice (who's more qualified) instead of Betty, then I must be willing that I *not* be picked if I were in Betty's place.

14.3f Game theory

Objection 14: TIT FOR TAT beats GR	Game theory, using computer simulations, shows that GR is inferior to TIT FOR TAT.

Game theory is a mathematical analysis of the interacting choices of multiple agents. The usual example is the *prisoner's dilemma*. But the GR connection will be clearer if I use my own form of the dilemma (§7.2).

In the *farmer's dilemma*, two rival farming families, the Hatfields and the McCoys, can do better for themselves if they cooperate instead of pursuing their individual interests. Each family wants only to gain the most money, and each must choose between stealing and being honest. If both sides are honest, each earns $6000 from crops. If one steals and the other is honest, then the one who steals gets $8000 and the honest one gets only $1000. (Stealing and guarding crops take time away from growing crops.) If both steal, both get only $2000 worth of crops. This chart shows choices and outcomes.

Hatfields		McCoys	
honest	$6000	honest	$6000
steal	$8000	honest	$1000
honest	$1000	steal	$8000
steal	$2000	steal	$2000

You're the Hatfields. What should you do? If the McCoys are honest, you gain more by stealing ($8000 instead of $6000). If the McCoys steal, you again gain more by stealing ($2000 instead of $1000). Either way you gain more by stealing. So you steal. The McCoys reason the same way; so they steal too. So both, following the egoist strategy, steal and thus gain a poor $2000.

Each side wants to be treated honestly (and not be stolen from). So GR would say to be honest. If both sides had been honest, then each would have gained $6000. So it's better for each if both follow GR rather than both being egoistic. *GR communities outperform egoistic communities.*

Now suppose that the Hatfields follow GR (and thus are honest) while the McCoys follow egoism (and thus steal). Then the GR Hatfields get only $1000 while the egoistic McCoys get $8000. So here egoism beats GR. *Egoistic individuals outperform GR individuals.*

Robert Axelrod 1984, a political scientist at the University of Michigan, invited game-theory experts to propose strategies for playing longer matches made up of a series of prisoner-dilemma episodes. Here are some possible strategies (adapted to my farmer's dilemma):

- EGOISM: Always steal.
- GR: Always be honest.
- RANDOM: Flip a coin each time to decide whether to steal or be honest.
- ALTERNATE: Be honest the first time, then steal, then be honest, and so on.
- PERMANENT RETALIATION: Start by always being honest. If the other side steals, then switch to always stealing.
- TIT FOR TAT: Be honest the first time, then do whatever the other side did the previous time. (So retaliate if the other side steals; otherwise be honest.)

Strategies played against each other, by pairs, on a computer. The tournament's winner was TIT FOR TAT, which gained more money than any other strategy.

TIT FOR TAT won because it encouraged other programs to cooperate with it and be honest. TIT FOR TAT starts by being honest and continues being honest as long as the other side is so too. But if the other side steals, then TIT FOR TAT retaliates in the next episode by stealing. If the other side reforms and becomes honest again, then so will TIT FOR TAT. If the other side sees what is happening (and TIT FOR TAT is easy to figure out), then it realizes that it does better for itself by being honest, which also helps TIT FOR TAT.

Axelrod calls TIT FOR TAT "nice," which means it's always honest the first time; nice strategies outperform not-nice strategies. He calls TIT FOR TAT "non-envious," which means it doesn't try to earn more than its current opponent. In each match, TIT FOR TAT *never* earns more than its opponent and frequently earns less; but it does consistently well. TIT FOR TAT wins the tournament, not by trying to hurt and outscore each opponent, but by encouraging a cooperation that helps both it and its opponent. In this way, it earns the highest total over the whole tournament.

Why didn't GR win? What hurt GR was that other programs took advantage of it.[1] Axelrod 1984: 136–9 sees GR as the most widely accepted moral standard. But following GR may encourage others to take advantage of us and thus may inhibit social cooperation. TIT FOR TAT is a retaliation rule, like "An eye for an eye." This can cause problems, since it encourages endless feuds; but it punishes offenders when no central authority does this. While Axelrod thinks we can learn much from the computer tournament, he suggests that real life differs in important ways. So he doesn't say TIT FOR TAT is a better morality than GR. But doubts remain about GR.[2]

[1] If your opponent is TIT FOR TAT, then an unbending Karma governs your future: what you do to another comes back to you right away. Then following GR becomes the way to get treated as you want to be treated – the way to promote self-interest. But if your opponent is GR, paradoxically, then following EGOISM and violating GR is the way to promote self-interest.
[2] See also Arce 2004, Badcock 1986, Gauthier 1986, Heckathron 1991, Hirshleifer & Coll 1988, Kitcher 1993, Leibenstein 1982, N. Miller 1985, Trivers 1971, Tullberg 2011, and Vanberg & Congleton 1992. Nowak & Sigmund 1993 suggests a strategy to beat TIT FOR TAT.

The computer tournament is an unreal situation because it has no sanctions against stealing – no police or judicial system, no social disapproval, no pangs of conscience. In real life, you call the police when people steal from you. But imagine a primitive society with no social system to punish stealing. Here TIT FOR TAT makes sense as a substitute for punishment. Revenge gives a primitive way to discourage wrongdoing.[1]

GR in this discussion has been assumed to be Pyrite 1, the literal GR: "If you want the McCoys to be honest to you, then be honest to them."

How would a better GR apply to a series of farmer's-dilemma episodes *in a primitive society with no punishments for stealing*? Suppose we're Hatfields and we're deciding between these three policies:

1. EGOISM: Always steal.
2. LITERAL GR: Always be honest.
3. TIT FOR TAT: Be honest the first time, then do whatever the other side did the previous time.

Now GR consistency (as in Gold 7) requires that we not endorse a policy unless we're willing that it be followed regardless of where we imagine ourselves in the situation. Accepting (1) would be difficult, since we must be willing that we be stolen from continually if we were in the place of the McCoys. Accepting (2) would be difficult too, when we see that it leads to *our* being stolen from continually. Option (3) is easier to accept, once we see that it prevents stealing. Yes, (3) involves retaliation; but retaliation provides, for a society without a system of punishment, some punishment for stealing – and this may be needed to prevent a social chaos that hurts everyone. If we accept (3), as I think GR would lead us to, we should begin to set up a social organization to punish evildoers and make retaliation (which can multiply violence) obsolete.

So, while TIT FOR TAT conquers the LITERAL GR *in a primitive society with no punishments for stealing*, a more adequate GR could endorse TIT FOR TAT for such a society. Insofar as we live in a society that *does* have a workable system of punishments, this discussion has less direct application.

Axelrod 1984: 124–41 has five suggestions to promote cooperation. These are particularly relevant to groups that historically don't cooperate and don't have a system of punishment over both groups. Axelrod, writing in 1984, uses the example of the U.S. and the Soviet Union. Today, we might use Israelis and Palestinians. Here are his suggestions:

- *Enlarge the shadow of the future.* Egoism often pays short-term but not long-term. Parties need to interact multiple times, to see the benefits of cooperation and to build trust. Several small steps are better than one big step.

---

[1] But even in a primitive society, an unexpected kindness ("turning the other cheek" instead of resorting to revenge) may shock and transform the evildoer.

- *Change the payoffs*. Set up a structure (e.g., a governmental structure) to punish those who don't cooperate. (See §7.2 and Platt 1973.)
- Teach people to care about each other.
- *Teach reciprocity*. Using TIT FOR TAT, we start being nice to others, retaliate quickly when others become jerks (perhaps more by social disapproval than by doing to them what they do to us?), and forgive quickly when others reform.
- *Improve recognition abilities*. Keep track of how others behave.

I'll add another suggestion: use GR (interpreted in a better way) with Kita. Different groups need to know each other, imagine themselves in the other side's place, test for GR consistencies, and act toward others only as they're willing to be treated in the same situation (ch. 8).

14.3g   Masochists

Objection 15: masochism	GR tells a masochist, who want others to cause him pain, to cause pain to others. Thus GR can command bad actions.

Masochists enjoy pain and may want others to torture them. But then, by GR, they are to torture others. So GR can command bad actions.[1]

The GR formula criticized here is Pyrite 1, the literal GR. Masochists who apply GR in this way to a non-masochist can be criticized for committing the *literal GR fallacy* (§2.4), which assumes that everyone has the same likes and dislikes. A non-masochist doesn't enjoy pain. So masochists dealing with a non-masochist need to ask: "Am I willing that if I were in this non-masochist's place, then I be tortured?" Normally the answer will be no.[2]

Typical masochists desire physical or emotional pain because this brings satisfaction (perhaps of a sexual, religious, or athletic nature). Suppose that Rocky (a masochist) is a boxer and considers himself a "tough guy." He gets satisfaction from how much abuse he can endure, whether in the boxing ring or elsewhere. Now if Rocky were in the place of a non-masochist, he wouldn't want pain and wouldn't get satisfaction from it. So Rocky likely *won't* be willing that if he were in a non-masochist's place then he be tortured.

But suppose that Rocky isn't such a masochist. Instead, he's deranged and hates himself so much that he wants to be tortured in his present situation and

[1] For discussions of this popular objection, see Bruton 2004, Burton & Goldsby 2005, Carson 2010: 137f, Hoche 1978, M. Singer 1963, and Stanglin 2005.
[2] I'm not assuming that it's fine if a masochist inflicts pain on a fellow masochist; but inflicting pain on a non-masochist is more easily attacked by GR. The problem with causing pain to a fellow masochist is that masochism is unhealthy; we'd give it up if we better understood what leads to happy and productive lives.

in any imagined situation. So he tortures others and, yes, he's willing that he be tortured in their place. So he satisfies GR consistency. Now GR (as Gold 1) doesn't tell him to torture. GR only forbids an inconsistent combination; it doesn't command specific actions. So GR doesn't tell Rocky to torture others.

Our coal-mine and Electra cases (§2.1d) also show that we can be consistent and follow GR, but still act wrongly. This can happen if we're ignorant about how our actions affect others or if our desires are flawed. So consistency isn't enough. Sometimes other tools are needed. GR works best when combined with other factors, such as knowledge, imagination, and rationalized desires.

We can use rational means to try to counter Rocky's self-hatred. We can try to get Rocky to understand himself better (including the source of his hatred), appreciate his self-worth, and experience positive ways of living. If he develops a love for himself, then GR can extend this love-of-self to love-of-others. But even if Rocky resists having his self-hatred rationally criticized, still it's important that GR, properly formulated, doesn't tell Rocky to do bad actions.

14.4 Short objections

> Objection 16: GR may be good for personal morality, but it does nothing to change unjust social structures.

This isn't true. GR was influential in combating slavery and segregation (ch. 8) – and is important today when people think about health-care reform or helping the unemployed ("Imagine yourself as unemployed, uninsured, and in need of health care"). Many in political, interfaith, or international areas see GR as a useful tool for bringing justice and peace to the world.

> Objection 17: GR, in forcing us to be completely impartial, would destroy special loves and friendships. GR and impartiality have us treat everyone equally. This would destroy deep, important human relationships, which demand partiality (Grunebaum 1993).

Personal relationships can be destroyed by a strong impartiality that makes us weigh equally the interests of everyone, regardless of how they relate to us. But GR requires only a weak impartiality. GR lets us give greater weight to the interests of *our* relatives and friends (e.g., spending more time with them and giving them special presents), so long as we're willing that others give greater weight to the interests of *their* relatives and friends in similar cases.

> Objection 18: GR isn't an adequate moral theory, since people who apply GR can come to different moral conclusions.

While GR doesn't give a clear answer on every moral issue, it can narrow the range of moral views that people find acceptable. It can help warring parties find common ground. It can criticize inherited moral intuitions (e.g., racist or sexist ones). It can kick us in the rear when we disregard the interests of others. And it's a global wisdom, shared by diverse eras, cultures, and religions. GR is the most useful general moral norm ever conceived.

> Objection 19: GR uses an artificial imagining of ourselves in another's place. I trust my moral intuitions instead of fanciful thought experiments.

If you have solid moral intuitions, be thankful for your upbringing. Many were brought up to have a racist sense of right and wrong – so it just "feels right" to them to treat blacks or Jews badly. Should such people trust their moral intuitions *uncritically*? Surely not. But how can we be *critical* about moral intuitions? GR, when combined with factual knowledge and imagination, gives consistency tools to reinforce good moral intuitions and criticize bad ones. Historically, many who were taught racist moral intuitions later came to reject them on the basis of GR (§8.5).

Why label as "artificial" (in a derogatory way) the imagining of ourselves in another's place? This is as much a part of our nature as is reasoning about the future on the basis of the past. We imagine ourselves in the hero's place as we watch a movie, in our opponent's place as we play chess, or in our customer's place as we design a sales pitch. Human life would be impoverished if we lost the ability to imagine ourselves in another's place.

> Objection 20: We want material goods for ourselves in abundance, and so by GR should work to provide them for others. So GR would increase consumerism and bring ecological disaster. (Elliott 1999 and Cairns 2002)

This commits the *third-parties GR fallacy*. We must satisfy GR toward future generations too. *Sustainable* living, a major goal of environmentalism, requires living in a way that satisfies GR toward future generations.

> Objection 21: GR applies only between equals. (Jacks 1924)

The literal GR, when applied to unequals, can lead to absurdities like "If you don't want your children to tell you what time to go to bed, then don't tell them what time to go to bed." The same-situation clause fixes this problem. Gold 1 applies to our treatment of *everyone*, even those of a different race, gender, age, or social status from us.

> Objection 22: GR can justify mercy killing. Imagine someone trapped under a car after an accident, dying a slow and painful death, begging to be killed. You'd want to be killed in this situation; so by GR you should kill this person. (Bracewell 1941, Hare 1993a, Fergusson 1993, and Saunders 1993)

This uses flawed Pyrite 2. Properly formulated, GR doesn't justify actions – it doesn't tell what to do – it only tests our consistency. Someone against mercy killing should be able to say, consistently with GR: "I think that killing here would be wrong – and I demand that I not be killed in this situation."

> Objection 23: Adding a same-situation clause to GR won't work, since there are problems with asking: "If I were in the other's external situation, but keeping my own desires and beliefs, would I want this done to me?" – and there are problems with asking: "If I were in the other's exact place, and having the other's desires and beliefs, would I want this done to me?" (D. Locke 1981 and Whiteley 1966)

These two give Pyrite 1b and 2, and don't work. Instead ask, "Am I now willing that if I were in the same situation (including having the other's desires and beliefs) then this be done to me?" and use Gold 1. (§§2.1b–d & 14.1)

> Objection 24: There are lots of things that I'd like or wish others to do to me (e.g., give me a million dollars or kiss me erotically). GR would absurdly impose a duty on me to do these things toward others.

This objection takes GR as the literal GR. Understood as Gold 1, GR imposes on us only the duty to have a consistency between our actions toward another and our willingness to be treated likewise in the same situation.

> Objection 25: Suppose that X is dying of cancer but is ineligible to be part of an experimental program that has a tiny chance to help X to recover. GR would justify lying about X's eligibility – since we desire that if we were in X's place then doctors lie about our eligibility. However, such lying would harm others, especially by compromising the scientific integrity of the medical experiments. (Vanderpool & Weiss 1987)

This commits the *third-parties GR fallacy*. Whatever policy we decide on, we must be willing that it be followed regardless of where we imagine ourselves in the situation, including in the place of third parties who may be harmed.

> Objection 26: Empathy isn't a reliable way to know about others, since another person might react differently from how we'd react in the same situation. Thus GR reasoning is flawed. (B. Maxwell 2008)

"Knowing by empathy" involves guessing how I'd feel in similar external circumstances. For example, I guess whether you'd like a certain food by guessing whether I'd like it. It's much more accurate to just ask you, "Do you like this food?"

Empathy's main GR use isn't to *gain* knowledge about the other's situation, for there may be better ways to do this. Its main use is to help us *appreciate* what it would be like to be in the other's place (and have *their* feelings).

Objection 27: Suppose I become depressed and apathetic; so I don't care what happens to me or how I'm treated. Then, by GR, am I justified in doing just anything to others? Do all my duties disappear?

Again, GR doesn't justify actions or give you specific duties. GR only tests your consistency. So your duties don't disappear if you become completely apathetic; nor are you justified in doing just anything. Instead, in this case, GR won't be useful for you to use in thinking out moral issues – since you'd satisfy GR consistency with every possible action.

Carson 2010: 140f points out that total apathy is rare and blocks other features of moral rationality (like an empathetic understanding of another's suffering). And often a depression that brings apathy is based on a poor understanding of one's personal situation (so good aspects are ignored), and so may be dealt with in part by promoting self-understanding.

Objection 28: GR isn't a good guide, because our employer may specify so many of our duties. Someone running to catch a bus may want the driver to wait, and the driver may want someone to wait for him in such a case, but the driver has prescribed duties that must be followed. (L. Russell 1942)

In my experience, drivers typically wait a little if I'm running to catch the bus. But they won't wait for long, since then everyone is inconvenienced. I assume that bus companies let drivers wait a little. If they tell drivers not to wait at all, then drivers will have to ask: "Should I wait a little and risk getting disciplined, should I follow the rules strictly, or should I try to get the company to change its rules?" GR doesn't say exactly what to do, but instead tells us that we must follow some policy that we're willing to have followed regardless of where we imagine ourselves in the situation.

Objection 29: GR requires that, if I'm trustworthy and thus want others to trust me, then I must also trust others. But this is unrealistic, since some have proved themselves untrustworthy.

This assumes the literal GR. If someone proves untrustworthy, then GR (properly understood) lets me not trust that person; I'm willing that if I were in that person's place then I not be trusted.

Objection 30: GR is a selfish principle, since it has us treat others well so they'll treat us well. (Bultmann 1963 and Dihle 1962 – but see Kirk 2003 and Ricoeur 1990a)

Objection 31: GR is unrealistic since it appeals to a pure concern for others that's uncommon among humans.

GR doesn't say what should motivate us. People who follow GR may have various motives, including self-interest, concern for others, promoting a cooperation that helps both sides, following God's will, doing what is socially accepted, doing what accords with our feelings, or doing what is rational or consistent or right. (§11.1 Q16)

> Objection 32: "What would become of the garden if the gardener treated all weeds, slugs, birds, and trespassers as he would like to be treated, if he were in their place?" (T. Huxley 1894: 18, on GR's impracticality)

GR doesn't apply directly to how to treat weeds, since they don't think or feel (§9.5 Q1). Slugs have less intense experiences, so humane treatment is less important; some think pouring salt on slugs is crueler than stepping on them, having toads eat them, or drowning them in beer. If birds are harmful, we'd use humane ways to keep them away (e.g., a scarecrow rather than painful electrocution). Trespassers are seldom a problem. If trespassers stamp on our flowers, then we'd deal with them in humane ways, as we're willing that we or a loved one who does such things be dealt with (e.g., use a "keep out" sign or a fence or even call the police – but don't electrocute or shoot them).

> Objection 33: GR is a rule, but we need to get beyond rules.

I was once asked by Jeff Wattles, who wrote a wonderful book called *The Golden Rule*, to give a talk on GR to his church group. When I came to the room, Jeff went behind the podium and drew the window blinds. I asked him, "Jeff, why did you draw the blinds?" He said "You know, if you're sitting here, it's really glaring and distracting, because of light from the outside." To check this, I sat where the people were going to sit (putting myself in their seats). And I said, "You're right – what a nice example of the golden rule!" For Jeff, it was instinctive. I'm sure he didn't consciously apply a formula or rule. Instead, GR was built into him and how he lived.

So should we develop GR instincts but ignore GR analyses? No, not at all. There are many ways to mess up GR reasoning (many GR fallacies) – and many intellectual objections to GR (at least 34). So we need GR formulas, analyses, and books (like this one) – both to refine GR instincts and to defend them from criticisms. But still, with William James 1902: 356, we can wish for a day "with the golden rule grown natural."

Let me sum up this book by paraphrasing Hillel:

> *Treat others only as you consent to being treated in the same situation. That is my whole book. The rest is commentary.*

Bibliography

This has everything cited in the book (except for some things mentioned just in the chronology), plus a few additional items.

Http://www.jstor.org has most of the articles. You can likely get these for free if you're connected to the Web through a university.

All Web addresses in this book were checked on 16 August 2012.

Abbot, E. (1870) "On the golden rule in the Chinese classics," *Journal of the American Oriental Society* 9 (1868–71): 79f.

Adler, F. (1890) "The freedom of ethical fellowship," *Ethics* 1: 16–30.

Adler, M. (1990) *Truth in Religion*, New York: Macmillan, pp. 86–92.

Alessandra, T. and M. O'Connor (1996) *The Platinum Rule*, New York: Business Plus.

Alexander, P. (2005) "Jesus and the golden rule," in *The Historical Jesus in Recent Research*, ed. J. Dunn and S. McKnight, Winona Lake, Ind.: Eisenbrauns, pp. 489–508.

Allen, I. (1860) *Is Slavery Sanctioned by the Bible?* Boston: American Tract Society.

Allinson, R. (1982) "On the negative version of the golden rule as formulated by Confucius," *New Asia Academic Bulletin* 3: 223–32.

—— (1992) "The golden rule as the core value in Confucianism and Christianity," *Asian Philosophy* 2: 173–85.

—— (2003) "Hillel and Confucius: The proscriptive formulation of the golden rule in the Jewish and Chinese Confucian ethical traditions," *Dao: A Journal of Comparative Philosophy* 3: 29–41.

Allison, D. (1987) "The structure of the Sermon on the Mount," *Journal of Biblical Literature* 106: 423–45.

Alton, B. (1966) *An Examination of the Golden Rule*, philosophy dissertation at Stanford, http://disexpress.umi.com

American Journal of Nursing (1920) "Shall there be cots in the patients' rooms?" *American Journal of Nursing* 21: 51.

American Journal of Nursing (1953) "What's in our code?" *American Journal of Nursing* 53: 1358–60.

Ammerman, N. (1997) "Golden rule Christianity," in *Lived Religion in America*, ed. D. Hall, Princeton, N.J.: Princeton University Press, pp. 196–216.

Anderson, S. (2009) "The golden rule: Not so golden anymore," *Philosophy Now* 74: 26–9.

Andrew, E. (1986) "Simone Weil on the injustice of rights-based doctrines," *Review of Politics* 48: 60–91.

An-Na'im, A. (1991) "A kinder, gentler Islam?" *Transition* 52: 4–16.

—— (2008) *Islam and the Secular State*, Cambridge, Mass.: Harvard University Press.

Apresian, R. (2002) "Talion and the golden rule," *Russian Studies in Philosophy* 41: 46–61.

Aptheker, H. (1940) "The Quakers and Negro slavery," *Journal of Negro History* 25: 331–62.

Arce, D. (2004) "Conspicuous by its absence: Ethics and managerial economics," *Journal of Business Ethics* 54: 261–77.

Armstrong, K. (2009) *The Case for God*, New York: Alfred A. Knopf.

Aronson, E. (1969) "The theory of cognitive dissonance," in *Advances in Experimental Social Psychology*, ed. L. Berkowitz, vol. 4, London: Academic Press, pp. 1–34.

Assisi, F. (c. 1220) *Francis of Assisi: Early Documents*, 4 vols., ed. R. Armstrong, J. Hellmann, and W. Short, Hyde Park, N.Y.: New City, 1999–2002, 1: 48, 66, 68, 71, 98, 103, 134.

Atkinson, D. (1982) "The golden rule," *Expository Times* 93: 336–8.

Augustine (400a) *On the Sermon on the Mount*, bk. 2, ch. 22, http://www.newadvent.Org/fathers/16012.htm

—— (400b) *The City of God*, bk. 14, ch. 8, http://www.newadvent.org/fathers/120114.htm

—— (400c) *On Christian Doctrine*, bk. 3, ch. 14, http://www.newadvent.org/fathers/12023.htm

Aull, G. (1950) "The economics of the Bible," *Southern Economic Journal* 16: 391–9.

Axelrod, R. (1984) *The Evolution of Cooperation*, New York: Basic.

Azenabor, G. (2008) "The golden rule principle in an African ethics," *Quest: An African Journal of Philosophy* 21: 229–40.

Badcock, C. (1986) *The Problem of Altruism*, Oxford: Basil Blackwell.

Barach, J., and J. Elstrott (1988) "The transactional ethic: The ethical foundations of free enterprise reconsidered," *Journal of Business Ethics* 7: 545–51.

Barnes, E. (1998) *A Little Book of Manners: Courtesy & Kindness for Young Ladies*, Eugene, Ore.: Harvest House (also *A Little Book of Manners for Boys*). (for children)

Barr, H. (1956) "Did Jesus speak to our society?" *Journal of Bible and Religion* 24: 255–63.

Batson, C. (2008) "Moral masquerades," *Phenomenology and the Cognitive Sciences* 7: 51–66.

Bauschke, M. (2010) *Die Goldene Regel: Staunen, Verstehen, Handeln*, Berlin: Erbverlag.

Beane, A., T. Miller, and R. Spurling (2008) "The bully free program," in *School Violence and Primary Prevention*, ed. T. Miller, New York: Springer, pp. 391–405.

Becker, L. (1986) *Reciprocity*, London: Routledge & Kegan Paul.

Benedict XVI, Pope (Joseph Ratzinger) (2005) *Deus Caritas Est*, http://www.vatican.va/holy_father/benedict_xvi/encyclicals/index_en.htm

—— (2006) "Faith, reason and the university," a talk at the University of Regensburg, http://www.vatican.va/holy_father/benedict_xvi/speeches/2006/september/documents/hf_ben-xvi_spe_20060912_university-regensburg_en.html

—— (2008) *Jesus of Nazareth*, trans. A. Walker, New York: Doubleday.

Bennett, M. (1979) "Overcoming the golden rule: Sympathy and empathy," in *Communication Yearbook 3*, ed. D. Nimmo, New Brunswick, N.J.: Transaction, pp. 407–22. Also in his *Basic Concepts of Intercultural Communication*, Yarmouth, Me.: Intercultural, 1998, pp. 191–214.

Berenstain, M., S., & J. (2008) *The Berenstain Bears and the Golden Rule*, Grand Rapids, Mich.: Zondervan. (for children)

Berggren, D., and N. Rae (2006) "Jimmy Carter and George W. Bush: Faith, foreign policy, and an evangelical presidential style," *Presidential Studies Quarterly* 36: 606–32.

Betty, L. (2001) "A pragmatic argument for God's existence," *International Journal for Philosophy of Religion* 49: 69–84.

Betz, H. (1995) *The Sermon on the Mount*, Minneapolis: Fortress, pp. 508–19, 599f.

Biblical World (1917) "Religious education," *Biblical World* 49: 243–5.

Binder-Johnson, H. (1941) "The Germantown protest of 1688 against Negro slavery," *Pennsylvania Magazine of History and Biography* 65: 145–56.

Binmore, K. (2005) *Natural Justice*, New York: Oxford University Press, ch. 9.

Blumenfeld, J. (1977) "Abortion and the human brain," *Philosophical Studies* 32: 251–68.

Blumenson, E. (2000) "Who counts morally?" *Journal of Law and Religion* 14 (1999–2000): 1–40.

Boehm, C. (2009) "How the golden rule can lead to reproductive success," in Neusner & Chilton 2009, pp. 151–77.

Bono, G. and B. De Mori (2005) "Animals and their quality of life," *Veterinary Research Communications* 29 (Sup. 2): 165–8.

Boonin, D. (2003) *A Defense of Abortion*, New York: Cambridge University Press, pp. 283–97.

Boraston, G. (1684) *The Royal Law, or the Golden Rule of Justice and Charity*, London, Walter Kettilby.

Bourne, G. (1845) *A Condensed Anti-Slavery Bible Argument*, New York: S.W. Benedict.

Bracewell, B. (1941) "Pupils and parents liked our course in philosophy," *Clearing House* 15: 294–6.

Brandt, R. (1970) "Rational desires," *Proceedings and Addresses of the American Philosophical Association* 43: 43–64.

—— (1972) "Rationality, egoism, and morality," *Journal of Philosophy* 69: 681–97.

—— (1976) "The psychology of benevolence and its implications for philosophy," *Journal of Philosophy* 73: 429–53.

Brook, R. (1987) "Justice and the golden rule," *Ethics* 97: 363–73.

Brooks, L. (1946) "The school's basic challenge to crime," *Phylon* 7: 176–80.

Brugger, E. (2009) "'Other selves': Moral and legal proposals regarding the personhood of cryopreserved human embryos," *Theoretical Medicine and Bioethics* 30: 105–29.

Bruns, R. (ed.) (1977) *Am I Not a Man and a Brother: The Anti-Slavery Crusade of Revolutionary America, 1688–1788*, New York: Chelsea House.

Bruton, S. (2004) "Teaching the golden rule," *Journal of Business Ethics* 49: 179–87.

Bultmann, R. (1963) *History of the Synoptic Tradition*, trans. J. Marsh, Oxford: Blackwell, p. 103.

Burton, B., and M. Goldsby (2005) "The golden rule and business ethics," *Journal of Business Ethics* 56: 371–83.

Burton, E. (1918) "Is the golden rule workable between nations?" *Biblical World* 51: 131–41.

Cadoux, A. (1912) "The implications of the golden rule," *Ethics* 22: 272–87.

Cairns, J. (2002) "Do unto the biosphere," *Environmental Health Perspectives* 110: A66–9.

Camfield, B. (1671) *A Profitable Enquiry Into That Comprehensive Rule of Righteousness, Do As You Would Be Done By*, London: H. Eversden.

Cantor, M. (1963) "The image of the Negro in colonial literature," *New England Quarterly* 36: 452–77.

Carleton, R. (1950) "I never read fiction," *Clearing House* 25: 221–3.

Carson, T. (2001) "Deception and withholding information in sales," *Business Ethics Quarterly* 11: 275–306.

—— (2003) "A defense of the golden rule," presented at the Illinois Philosophical Association.

—— (2005) "Hare redux: The golden rule, consistency, and a theory of moral reasoning," presidential address at the Illinois Philosophical Association.

—— (2010) *Lying and Deception*, Oxford: Oxford University Press, ch. 6–10.

—— (2013) "Golden rule," in *International Encyclopedia of Ethics*, ed. Hugh LaFollette, Oxford: Wiley-Blackwell.

Carter, W. (1982) "Do zygotes become people?" *Mind* 91: 77–95.

Casanova, J. (1999) "The sacralization of the humanum: A theology for a global age," *International Journal of Politics, Culture, and Society* 13: 21–40.

Catt, C. (1927) "Elements in a constructive foreign policy," *Annals of the American Academy of Political and Social Science* 132: 187–9.

Chakrabarti, A. (2012) "A critique of pure revenge," in *Passion, Death, and Spirituality*, ed. K. Higgins and D. Sherman, New York: Springer, pp. 37–53.

Chan, K. (2004) "The golden rule and the potentiality principle," *Journal of Applied Philosophy* 21: 33–42.

Chan, W. (1955) "The evolution of the Confucian concept Jên," *Philosophy East and West* 4: 295–319.

—— (1963) *A Source Book in Chinese Philosophy*, Princeton, N.J.: Princeton University Press, pp. 27, 28, 31, 39f, 44, 101.

Chenai, M. (2008) *Recueil de textes du professeur Abdulaziz Sachedina*, Paris: Publibook, pp. 150f.

Collins, F. (2006) *The Language of God*, New York: Free Press.

Common Word (2006) "Open letter to his Holiness Pope Benedict XVI," signed by 38 Islamic leaders, http://ammanmessage.com/media/openLetter/english.pdf

—— (2009) *A Common Word Between Us and You*, Jordan: Royal Aal al-Bayt Institute for Islamic Thought, http://acommonword.com/index.php?lang=en&page=downloads

Confucius: See W. Chan 1963.

Cooper, I. (2007) *The Golden Rule*, New York: Abrams Books for Young Readers. (for children)

Cooper, N. (1994) "The intellectual virtues," *Philosophy* 69: 459–69.

Craig, W. (1994) *Reasonable Faith*, rev. ed., Wheaton, Ill.: Crossway.

Crosby, E. (1906) *Golden Rule Jones: Mayor of Toledo*, Chicago: Public.

Crothers, A. (2005) "Quaker merchants and slavery in early national Alexandria, Virginia," *Journal of the Early Republic* 25: 47–77.

Cunningham, W.P (1998) "The golden rule as universal ethical norm," *Journal of Business Ethics* 17: 105–9.

Dabney, R. (1867) *A Defense of Virginia*, New York: E.J. Hale, pp. 124 or 196f.

Dagg, J. (1860) *The Elements of Moral Science*, New York: Sheldon, pp. 356f.

Darling, S. & H. (2006) *The Golden Rule: As Expressed by Cultures Around the World*, Seattle, Wash.: Darling. (This looks like a gold ruler and has one or two rules per page.)

Darnell, R. (1967) "Morality and the ecological crisis," *BioScience* 17: 685f.

Darwin, C. (1859) *The Origin of Species*, London: John Murray.

—— (1871) *The Descent of Man*, 2 vols., London: John Murray, ch. 4–5 of Vol. 1.

Das, T. (2005) "How strong are the ethical preferences of senior business executives?" *Journal of Business Ethics* 56: 69–80.

De Waal, F. (2005) *Our Inner Ape*, New York: Penguin Group.

Didache (80 AD) In *The Apostolic Fathers*, trans. B. Ehrman, Cambridge: Harvard University Press, 2003.

Dihle, A. (1962) *Die goldene Regel*, Göttingen: Vandenhoeck & Ruprecht.

Dole, C. (1895) *The Golden Rule in Business*, New York: Thomas Y. Crowell.

Donagan, A. (1977) *The Theory of Morality*, Chicago: University of Chicago Press, pp. 57–66.

Donald, P. (2007) "Skull base surgery for malignancy: When not to operate," *Journal European Archives of Oto-Rhino-Laryngology* 264: 713–7.

Donaldson, J. (1989) *Key Issues in Business Ethics*, London: Academic Press.

Doris, D. (1978) "Teaching moral education," *Peabody Journal of Education* 56: 33–44.

Double, R. (1999) "Morality, impartiality, and what we can ask of persons," *American Philosophical Quarterly* 36: 149–58.

Douglass, F. (1855) *My Bondage and My Freedom*, New York: Miller, Orton, & Mulligan.

du Roy, O. (2008) "The golden rule as the law of nature, from Origen to Martin Luther," in Neusner & Chilton 2008, pp. 88–98.

—— (2009) *La règle d'or: Le retour d'une maxime oubliée*, Paris: Cerf.

—— (2010) A talk on the golden rule, http://freepdfhosting.com/76b9238c0c.pdf

—— (2012) *Histoire de la règle d'or*, 2 vols, Paris: Cerf.

Dubs, H. (1951a) "The development of altruism in Confucianism," *Philosophy East and West* 1: 48–55.

—— (1951b) "Confucius: His life and teaching," *Philosophy* 26: 30–6.

Dull, J., P. Mintz, L. Joyce, and C. Jannuzzi (1941) "Professional etiquette," *American Journal of Nursing* 41: 338f.

Durant, W. and A. (1969) "History and war," *Theory into Practice* 8: 56f.

Duxbury, N. (2009) "Golden rule reasoning, moral judgment, and law," *Notre Dame Law Review* 84: 1529–1605.

Dyck, A., and C. Padilla (2009) "The empathic emotions and self-love in bishop Joseph Butler and the neurosciences," *Journal of Religious Ethics* 37: 577–612.

Easton, B. (1914) "The Sermon on the Mount," *Journal of Biblical Literature* 33: 228–43.

Eddy, M. (1875) *Science and Health, with Key to the Scriptures*, Boston: Christian Science.

Edwards, J. (1791) *The Injustice and Impolicy of the Slave Trade and of the Slavery of the Africans*, 3rd ed., New Haven, Conn.: New Haven Anti-Slavery Society, 1833.

Eisler, R. (1947) "Religion for the age of reason," *Hibbert Journal* 45: 334–41.

Elliott, H. (1999) "The limits of the golden rule," *Population and Environment* 20: 561–5.

Epictetus (90 AD) *The Golden Sayings of Epictetus*, trans. H. Crossley, London: Macmillan, 1935, ch. 41, http://www.gutenberg.org/files/871

Epstein, M. (1967) *Tales of Sendebar*, Philadelphia: Jewish Publication Society, pp. 297–9.

Erikson, E. (1964) "The golden rule in the light of new insight," in his *Insight and Responsibility*, New York: W.W. Norton, pp. 217–43.

Etzioni, A. (1996) *The New Golden Rule*, New York: Basic.

Falk, R. (1999) "Hans Küng's crusade: Framing a global ethic," *International Journal of Politics, Culture, and Society* 13: 63–81.

Fansler, D. (1921) *Filipino Popular Tales*, New York: American Folk-Lore Society, pp. 271–5.

Fergusson, A. (1993) "Is medical ethics lost?" *Journal of Medical Ethics* 19: 237.

Festinger, L. (1957) *A Theory of Cognitive Dissonance*, Stanford, Calif.: Stanford University Press.

Fiske, A. (1923) "Psychology," *American Journal of Nursing* 23: 1011–4.

Fitch, J. (1725) *On Serious Piety and on the Golden Rule of Justice*, Boston: Unknown.

Flew, A. (2007) *There Is a God*, New York: HarperCollins.

Flusser, D. (1968) "A new sensitivity in Judaism and the Christian message," *Harvard Theological Review* 61: 107–27.

France, R. (2007) *The Gospel of Matthew*, Grand Rapids, Mich.: Eerdmans, pp. 283–5.

Francis: See Assisi.

Fredriksson, L., and K. Eriksson (2003) "The ethics of the caring conversation," *Nursing Ethics* 10: 138–48.

Freedman, R. (2002) *Confucius: The Golden Rule*, New York: Arthur A. Levine Books. (for children)

Frymier, J. (1969) "Teaching the young to love," *Theory into Practice* 8: 42–4.

Fulghum, R. (1990) *All I Really Need To Know I Learned In Kindergarten*, New York: Villard, pp. 6f.

Gaffney, J. (1987) *Matters of Faith and Morals*, Kansas City, Mo.: Sheed & Ward, pp. 95–7, 192–7, 202–6.

Garesché, E. (1927) "Professional honor," *American Journal of Nursing* 27: 901–4.

Garrison, W. (ed.) (1833) *The Abolitionist*, Boston: Garrison & Knapp.

Gauthier, D. (1986) *Morals by Agreement*, Oxford: Clarendon.

Gensler, H. (1976) "The prescriptivism incompleteness theorem," *Mind* 85: 589–96.

—— (1977) *The Golden Rule*, philosophy dissertation at Michigan, http://disexpress.umi.com

—— (1983) "Acting commits one to ethical beliefs," *Analysis* 43: 40–3.

—— (1985) "Ethical consistency principles," *Philosophical Quarterly* 35: 156–70.

—— (1986a) "A Kantian argument against abortion," *Philosophical Studies* 49: 83–98.

—— (1986b) "Ethics is based on rationality," *Journal of Value Inquiry* 20: 251–64.

—— (1996) *Formal Ethics*, New York: Routledge.

—— (1998) *Ethics: A Contemporary Introduction*, New York: Routledge.

—— (2009a) "Gold or fool's gold? Ridding the golden rule of absurd implications," in Neusner & Chilton 2009, pp. 131–49.

—— (2009b) "Darwin, ethics, and evolution," in *Darwin and Catholicism*, ed. L. Caruana, London: T&T Clark, pp. 121–33.

—— (2009c) "Singer's unsanctity of human life: A critique," in *Singer Under Fire*, ed. J. Schaler, Chicago: Open Court, pp. 163–84.

—— (2010) *Introduction to Logic*, 2nd ed., New York: Routledge, pp. 290–335.

—— (2011a) *Ethics: A Contemporary Introduction*, 2nd ed., New York: Routledge, ch. 7–9.

—— (2011b) "Faith, reason, and alternatives to Genesis 1:1," *Proceedings of the Jesuit Philosophical Association* 29–47, online (search for article title).

Gensler, H., and E. Spurgin (2008) *Historical Dictionary of Ethics*, Lanham, Md.: Scarecrow.

Gensler, H., E. Spurgin, and J. Swindal (eds) (2004) *Ethics: Contemporary Readings*, New York: Routledge.

Gert, B. (1995) "Morality versus slogans," in *Morality in Criminal Justice*, ed. D. Close and N. Meier, Belmont, Calif.: Wadsworth, pp. 51–60.

Gewirth, A. (1960) "'Ethics' and normative 'science,'" *Philosophical Review* 69: 311–30.

—— (1978) "The golden rule rationalized," *Midwest Studies in Philosophy* 3: 133–47. Also in his *Human Rights*, Chicago: University of Chicago Press, 1982, pp. 128–42.

Gilligan, C. (1982) *In a Different Voice*, Cambridge: Harvard University Press.

Giri, S. (2004) Review of *Botta e risposta* by A. Cattani, *Argumentation* 18: 381–6.

Glad, J. (1962) "How children may be taught tolerance and cooperation," *Marriage and Family Living* 24: 183–5.

Glenn, B. (1998) "The golden rule of grading," *Political Science and Politics* 31: 787f.

Glynn, P. (1997) *God: The Evidence*, Rocklin, Calif.: Prima.

Goldin, J. (1946) "Hillel the Elder," *Journal of Religion* 26: 263–77.

Goldman, R. (1995) "Moral leadership in society: Some parallels between the Confucian 'noble man' and the Jewish 'zaddik'," *Philosophy East and West* 45: 329–65.

Goodman, J. (1688) *The Golden Rule*, London: Samuel Roycroft.

Goodwin, J. (2009) "Actually existing rules for closing arguments," in *Pondering on Problems of Argumentation*, ed. G. van Eemeren and B. Garssen, Berlin: Springer, pp. 287–98.

Gordon, T. (1967) "Tricks of the trade," *Clearing House* 42: 184–6.

Gould, J. (1968) "Clarifying Singer's golden rule," *Crítica: Revista Hispanoamericana de Filosofía* 2: 95–101.

Graves, W. (1924) "Codes of ethics for business and commercial organization," *Ethics* 35: 41–59.

Green, S. (2010) "Golden rule ethics and the death of the criminal law's special part," *Criminal Justice Ethics* 29: 208–18.

Greene, L. (1928) "Slave-holding New England and its awakening," *Journal of Negro History* 13: 492–533.

Greenlee, M. (1996) "Echoes of the love command in the halls of justice," *Journal of Law and Religion* 12 (1995–6): 255–70.

Grimké, A. (1836) *Appeal to the Christian Women of the South*, New York: New York Anti-Slavery Society, http://utc.iath.virginia.edu/abolitn/abesaegat.html

Grimm Brothers (1812) "The old man and his grandson," http://www.gutenberg.org/ebooks/2591 (Winner 2009 is a children's version)

Grisez, G. (2011) "Health care technology and justice," in *Bioethics with Liberty and Justice*, ed. C. Tollefsen, New York: Springer, pp. 221–39.

Grunebaum, J. (1993) "Friendship, morality, and special obligation," *American Philosophical Quarterly* 30: 51–61.

Haas, P. (1988) *Morality after Auschwitz*, Philadelphia: Fortress.

Habermas, J. (1983) *Moral Consciousness and Communicative Action*, trans. C. Lenhardt and S. Nicholsen, Cambridge: MIT, 1990.

Haisch, B. (2006) *The God Theory*, San Francisco: Weiser, pp. 18–24.

Hale, M. (1805) "Of doing as we would be done unto," in *Works*, vol. 1, London: R. Wilks, pp. 378–416.

Hamilton, W. (1964) "The genetic evolution of social behavior," *Journal of Theoretical Biology* 7: 1–52.

Hamson, R. (1970) "An alternate view of management values and the Judeo-Christian ethic," *Management Science* 17: B256–8.

Hanfling, O. (1963) "Loving my neighbor, loving myself," *Philosophy* 68: 145–57.

Hare, R. (1963) *Freedom and Reason*, Oxford: Clarendon.

—— (1964) "The promising game," *Revue Internationale de Philosophie* 18: 389–412.

—— (1972a) *Applications of Moral Philosophy*, Berkeley: University of California.

—— (1972b) *Essays on Philosophical Method*, Berkeley: University of California.

—— (1975) "Abortion and the golden rule," *Philosophy and Public Affairs* 4: 201–22.

—— (1981) *Moral Thinking*, Oxford: Clarendon.

—— (1993a) "Is medical ethics lost?" *Journal of Medical Ethics* 19: 69f. (Fergusson 1993 and Saunders 1993 critique this and Hare responds on pp. 238f.)

—— (1993b) "Why I am only a demi-vegetarian," in his *Essays on Bioethics*, Oxford: Clarendon, pp. 218–35.

Harrill, J. (2000) "The use of the New Testament in the American slave controversy," *Religion and American Culture* 10: 149–86.

Hartley, H. (2002) *Manners Matter*, Uhrichsville, Ohio: Promise. (for children)

Haskell, T. (1987) "Convention and hegemonic interest in the debate over antislavery," *American Historical Review* 92: 829–78.

Hawking, S. (1998) *A Brief History of Time*, 10th anniversary edition, New York: Bantam.

Hayes, E. (1913) "Social values," *American Journal of Sociology* 18: 470–508.

Heath, J. (2007) "An adversarial ethic for business," *Journal of Business Ethics*, 72: 359–74.

Heckathron, D. (1991) "Extensions of the prisoner's dilemma paradigm," *Sociological Theory* 9: 34–52.

Hennessey, J., and B. Gert (1985) "Moral rules and moral ideals," *Journal of Business Ethics* 4: 105–15.

Henry, M. (1827) *An Exposition of the Old and New Testament*, New York: Robert Carter and Brothers.

Hertzler, J. (1934) "On golden rules," *Ethics* 44: 418–36.

Hick, J. (1977) *Evil and the God of Love*, 2nd ed., London: Macmillan.

—— (1992) "The universality of the golden rule," in *Ethics, Religion and the Good Life*, ed. J. Runzo, Louisville, Ky.: Westminster, pp. 155–66.

Hirshleifer, J., and J. Coll (1988) "What strategies can support the evolutionary emergence of cooperation?" *Journal of Conflict Resolution* 32: 367–98.

Hirst, E. (1934) "The categorical imperative and the golden rule," *Philosophy* 9: 328–35.

Hobbes, T. (1651) *Leviathan*, Oxford: Basil Blackwell, 1947.

Hoche, H. (1982) "The golden rule: New aspects of an old principle," *Contemporary German Philosophy*, ed. D. Christensen, University Park: Pennsylvania State University Press, pp. 69–90. First published in 1978, as "Die Goldene Regel: Neue Aspekte eines alten Moralprinzips," *Zeitschrift für philosophische Forschung* 32: 355–75.

Hoffman, M. (1981) "The development of empathy," in Rushton & Sorrentino 1981, pp. 41–63.

Holcomb, C. (1904) "The moral training of the young in China," *Ethics* 14: 445–68.

Holoviak, S. (1993) *Golden Rule Management*, Reading, Mass.: Addison-Wesley.

Hopkins, E. (1906) "The message of Buddhism to Christianity," *Biblical World* 28: 94–107.

Horowitz, J. (1987) "The golden rule of teaching," *Clearing House* 60: 411f.

Hoskisson, K., and D. Biskin (1979) "Analyzing and discussing children's literature using Kohlberg's stages of moral development," *Reading Teacher* 33: 141–7.

Huang, Y. (2005) "A copper rule versus the golden rule," *Philosophy East and West* 55: 394–425.

Hubbard, L. (1981) *The Way to Happiness*, Los Angeles: Bridge, ch. 19–20.

Huston, J. (2000) "Abolitionists, political economists, and capitalism," *Journal of the Early Republic* 20: 487–521.

Huxley, A. (1963) *Literature and Science*, New York: Harper & Row, p. 109.

Huxley, T. (1894) *Evolution and Ethics and Other Essays*, New York: D. Appleton, p. 18.

Interpreter's Bible (1951) "Golden rule," Nashville: Parthenon 7: 329f.

Ivanhoe, P. (1990) "Reweaving the 'one thread' of the Analects," *Philosophy East and West* 40: 17–33.

Jacks, L. (1924) "An international ethic," *Foreign Affairs* 3: 266–76.

Jackson, H. (1970) "Standards for expert scientific advice to Congress," *Operations Research* 18: 739f.

James, W. (1902) *The Varieties of Religious Experience*, New York: Longmans, Green, and Co., p. 356.

Jefferson, T. (1804) *The Life and Morals of Jesus of Nazareth*, Philadelphia: Jacob Johnson.

Jeffries, V. (1999) "The integral paradigm," *American Sociologist* 30: 36–55.

Jeremias, J. (1961) *The Sermon on the Mount*, London: Athlone.

Jewish Encyclopedia (1962) "Golden rule," New York: Ktav 6: 21f.

Jochim, C. (1980) "Ethical analysis of an ancient debate: Moists versus Confucians," *Journal of Religious Ethics* 8: 135–47.

Johnson, D. and R. (2009) "Energizing learning," *Educational Researcher* 38: 37–51.

Johnson, S. (1996) *The Book of Tibetan Elders*, New York: Riverhead.

Jonas, H. (1969) "Philosophical reflections on experimenting with human subjects," *Daedalus* 98: 219–47.

Jones, S. (1899) *The New Right*, New York: Eastern Book Concern.

Jospe, R. (1990) "Hillel's rule," *Jewish Quarterly Review* 81: 45–57.

Jung, H. (1966) "An existential and phenomenological problem of intersubjectivity," *Philosophy East and West* 16: 169–88.

—— (1969) "Confucianism and existentialism," *Philosophy and Phenomenological Research* 30: 186–202.

Kalman, I. (2005) *Bullies to Buddies*, Staten Island, N.Y.: Wisdom Pages.

Kant, I. (1785) *Groundwork of the Metaphysics of Morals*, trans. H. Paton, New York: Harper & Row, 1964, p. 97 footnote.

Katz, R. (1963) *Empathy*, London: Collier-Macmillan. (psychology)

Kaufman, W. (1963) *The Faith of a Heretic*, New York: Doubleday.

Keck, M. (1939) "Managing children," *Clearing House* 14: 83–5.

Keirstead, W. (1923) "The golden rule in business," *Journal of Religion* 3: 141–56.

Keller, L. (2009) *Do Unto Otters: A Book About Manners*, New York: Square Fish. (for children)

Kennedy, J. (1963) Speech on civil rights, 11 June, http://www.presidentialrhetoric.com /historicspeeches/kennedy/civilrightsmessage.html

Kim, K. (1950) "The meaning of negativism in oriental religions," *Journal of Bible and Religion* 18: 29–33.

King, G. (1928) "The 'negative' golden rule," *Journal of Religion* 8: 268–79 and (1935) 15: 59–62.

King, S. (1995) "It's a long way to a global ethic," *Buddhist-Christian Studies* 15: 213–9.

Kinnier, R., J. Kernes, and T. Dautheribes (2000) "A short list of universal moral values," *Counseling and Values* 45: 4–16.

Kinnier, R., K. Wilkins, D. Hauser, S. Hassert, and L. Petrolle (2011) "The main contributors to a future utopia," *Current Psychology* 30: 383–94.

Kirk, A. (2003) "'Love your enemies,' the golden rule, and ancient reciprocity (Luke 6:27–35)," *Journal of Biblical Literature* 122: 667–86.

Kitcher, P. (1993) "The evolution of human altruism," *Journal of Philosophy* 90: 497–516.

Klassen, B. (1991) *A Revolution of Values Through Religion*, Riverton, Wyo.: Creativity, http:/ /creativitymovement.net/documents/REVOLUTI.PDF

Kligler, B., and R. Lee (eds) (2004) *Integrative Medicine: Principles for Practice*, New York: McGraw-Hill.

Knight, D. (1957) *Rule Golden*, Garden City, N.Y.: Doubleday.

Kohlberg, L. (1973) "The claim to moral adequacy of the highest stage of moral judgment," *Journal of Philosophy* 70: 630–48.

—— (1979) "Justice as reversibility," in *Philosophy, Politics and Society*, 5th series, ed. P. Laslett and J. Fishkin, New Haven, Conn.: Yale University Press, pp. 257–72.

—— (1981–4) *Essays on Moral Development*, 2 vols., San Francisco: Harper & Row.

Kohlberg, L., C. Levine, and A. Hewer (1983) *Moral Stages*, Basel: Karger.

Kohlberg, L., D. Boyd, and C. Levine (1990) "The return of stage 6: Its principle and moral point of view," in *The Moral Domain*, ed. T. Wren, Cambridge: MIT, pp. 151–81.

Krebs, D. (1982) "Psychological approaches to altruism," *Ethics* 92: 447–58.

Küng, H. (1993) *Global Responsibility: In Search of a New World Ethic*, New York: Continuum.

—— (1997) "A global ethic in an age of globalization," *Business Ethics Quarterly* 7: 17–31.

—— (2000) "Global ethic: A response to my critics," *International Journal of Politics, Culture, and Society* 14: 421–8.

—— (2006) "22nd Niwano Peace Prize Commemorative Address," *Buddhist-Christian Studies* 26: 203–8.

Küng, H., and K. Kuschel (1993) *A Global Ethic: The Declaration of the Parliament of the World's Religions*, trans. J. Bowden, London: SCM Press, http://www.weltethos.org/1-pdf /10-stiftung/declaration/declaration_english.pdf

Küng, H., and W. Homolka (2009) *How to Do Good & Avoid Evil: A Global Ethic from the Sources of Judaism*, trans. J. Bowden, Woodstock, Vt.: SkyLight Paths.

Leavell, U. (1956) *Golden Rule Series*, New York: American Book Company. (for children)

Lee, C. (1995) "Unity beyond religious and ethnic conflict based on a universal declaration of a global ethic: A Buddhist perspective," *Buddhist-Christian Studies* 15: 191–7.

Lehman, D. (2007) *Adventures at Walnut Grove*, Allenton, Mich.: Lehman. (for children)

Leibenstein, H. (1982) "The prisoners' dilemma in the invisible hand," *American Economic Review* 72: 92–7.

Leibniz, G. (1704) *New Essays on Human Understanding*, trans. P. Remnant and J. Bennett, New York: Cambridge University Press, 1996, pp. 91f.

Lewis, C.I. (1955) *The Ground and Nature of the Right*, New York: Columbia University Press.

—— (1969) *Values and Imperatives*, Stanford, Calif.: Stanford University Press.

Lincoln, A. (1850s-65) *The Collected Works of Abraham Lincoln*, 8 vols., ed. R. Basler, New Brunswick, N.J.: Rutgers University Press, 1953.

Little, D., and S. Twiss (1978) *Comparative Religious Ethics*, San Francisco: Harper and Row.

Locke, D. (1981) "The principle of equal interests," *Philosophical Review* 90: 531–59.

Lowy, E. (1997) "The evolution of the golden rule," psychology dissertation at the University of Washington, http://disexpress.umi.com

MacIver, R. (1952) "The deep beauty of the golden rule," in *Moral Principles of Action*, ed. R. Anshen, New York: Harper & Brothers, pp. 39–47.

Mackarness, M. (1867) *The Golden Rule: Stories Illustrative of the Ten Commandments*, new edition, London: George Routledge and Sons.

Mackie, J. (1977) *Ethics: Inventing Right and Wrong*, London: Penguin, ch. 4.

—— (1982) *The Miracle of Theism*, New York: Oxford University Press.

Majid, A. (1998) "The politics of feminism in Islam," *Signs: Journal of Women in Culture and Society* 23: 321–61.

Manek, J. (1967) "On the mount – On the plain," *Novum Testamentum* 9: 124–31.

Maxwell, B. (2008) *Professional ethics education: Studies in compassionate empathy*, New York: Springer, ch. 4 & 7.

Maxwell, J. (2003) *There's No Such Thing as "Business" Ethics: There's Only One Rule for Making Decisions*, New York: Center Street.

Mayton, D. (2009) *Nonviolence and Peace Psychology*, New York: Springer, ch. 7.

McClure, W. (1930) "The commercial policy of the United States in the light of current world developments," *Annals of the American Academy of Political and Social Science* 150: 146–53.

McDonald, J. (1927) "Needed: A new code of international morality," *Annals of the American Academy of Political and Social Science* 132: 193–6.

McGuffey, W. (1879) *McGuffey's Fourth Eclectic Reader*, revised edition, New York: Van Antwerp, Bragg, pp. 139–43.

McKenzie, J. (1968) Comments in *The Jerome Biblical Commentary*, ed. R. Brown, J. Fitzmyer, and R. Murphy, Englewood Cliffs, N.J.: Prentice-Hall, 2: 75, 136.

Meier, J. (2009) *A Marginal Jew: Rethinking the Historical Jesus, Volume 4: Law and Love*, New Haven, Conn.: Yale University Press, pp. 551–7.

Melé, D. (2009) "Integrating personalism into virtue-based business ethics," *Journal of Business Ethics* 88: 227–44.

Meyers, C. (2010) *The Fetal Position: A Rational Approach to the Abortion Issue*, Amherst, N.Y.: Prometheus, pp. 139–57.

Michel, T. (2010) *A Christian View of Islam*, ed. I. Omar, Maryknoll, N.Y.: Orbis.

Mieder, W. (2001) "'Do unto others as you would have them do unto you': Frederick Douglass's proverbial struggle for civil rights," *Journal of American Folklore* 114: 331–57.

Mill, J.S. (1861) *Utilitarianism*, New York: Library of Liberal Arts, 1957.

Miller, N. (1985) "Nice strategies finish first: A review of *The Evolution of Cooperation*," *Politics and the Life Sciences* 4: 86–91.

Miller, R. (2000) "Humanitarian intervention, altruism, and the limits of casuistry," *Journal of Religious Ethics* 28: 3–35.

Mollenkott, V. (1987) "Human rights and the golden rule," *Christianity and Crisis* 47: 383–5. (gay rights)

Monroe, K., M. Barton, and U. Klingemann (1990) "Altruism and the theory of rational action: Rescuers of Jews in Nazi Europe," *Ethics* 101: 103–22.

Montgomery, C. (1978) "Teaching with animals," *Early Childhood Education Journal* 5: 28–31.

Morsink, J. (2009) *Inherent Human Rights*, Philadelphia: University of Pennsylvania Press, pp. 112–20.

Mould, E. (1948) Review of *An Approach to the Teaching of Jesus*, *Journal of Bible and Religion*, 16: 131f.

Mulholland, L. (1988) "Autonomy, extended sympathy, and the golden rule" in *Inquiries Into Values*, ed. S. Lee, Lewiston, N.Y.: Edwin Mellen, pp. 89–98.

Narayan, K. (1989) *Storytellers, Saints, and Scoundrels: Folk Narrative in Hindu Religious Teaching*, Philadelphia: University of Pennsylvania Press, pp. 192–200.

Nash, A. (1923) *The Golden Rule in Business*, New York: Fleming H. Revell.

Nathanson, B. (1979) *Aborting America*, Garden City, N.Y.: Doubleday, pp. 227–39.

Neusner, J., and B. Chilton (eds) (2008) *The Golden Rule: The Ethics of Reciprocity in World Religions*, New York: Continuum.

—— (2009) *The Golden Rule: Analytical Perspectives*, Lanham, Md.: University Press of America.

New Encyclopedia of Judaism (2002), ed. G. Wigoder, F. Skolnik, and S. Himelstein, New York: New York University Press, articles on "Golden rule," "Hillel," and "Love of neighbor."

New Englander (1857) "Slavery and the Bible," *New Englander* 15: 102–34.

Newton, R. (1909) "The relation of socialism to Christianity," *Christian Socialist* 6: 1–3.

Nietzsche, F. (1886) *Beyond Good and Evil*, trans. M. Faber, Oxford: Oxford University Press, 1998.

Nivison, D. (1996) "Golden rule arguments in Chinese moral philosophy," in his *The ways of Confucianism*, Chicago: Open Court, pp. 59–76.

Noble, M. (1931) *Golden Rules of World Religions*, Los Angeles: Ivan Deach.

Nowak, M., and K. Sigmund (1993) "A strategy of win-stay, lose-shift that outperforms tit-for-tat in the prisoner's dilemma game," *Nature* 364: 56–8, http://edge.org/conversation /evolution-of-cooperation-nowak has a recent account.

Nussbaum, M. (2003) "Golden rule arguments: A missing thought?" in *The Moral Circle and the Self*, ed. K. Chong, S. Tan, and C. Ten, Chicago: Open Court, pp. 3–16.

Obama, B. (2006) *The Audacity of Hope*, New York: Crown, p. 265.

Ogunyemi, Y. (2010) *The Oral Traditions in Ile-Ife: The Yoruba People and Their Book of Enlightenment*, Palo Alto, Calif.: Academica.

Ontario (1915–8) *The Golden Rule Books*, Toronto: Macmillan. (four books for children)

Outka, G. (1972) *Agape: An Ethical Analysis*, New Haven, Conn.: Yale University Press.

Panaman, R. (2008) *How to Do Animal Rights – And Win the War on Animals*, http://www .animalethics.org.uk, ch. 7.4.

Parfit, D. (2011) *On What Matters*, 2 vols, Oxford: Oxford University Press, 1: 321–30, 2: 536–8.

Penney, J.C. (1950) *Fifty Years with the Golden Rule*, New York: Harper & Brothers.

Pennington, K. (2008) "Lex naturalis and ius natural," *Jurist* 68: 569–91.

Perry, A. (1935) "The framework of the Sermon on the Mount," *Journal of Biblical Literature* 54: 103–15.

Perry, C., and W. McIntire (1994) "High school seniors' concern for others," *High School Journal* 77: 199–205.

Perry, R. (1942) "Have 'right' and 'wrong' one meaning for all mankind?" *Philosophy* 17: 378–82.

Pfaff, D. (2007) *The Neuroscience of Fair Play: Why We (Usually) Follow the Golden Rule*, New York: Dana, ch. 5.

Pfaff, D., E. Choleris, and M. Kavaliers (2008) "Brain mechanisms theoretically underlying extremes of social behaviors," in *Hormones and Social Behavior*, ed. D. Pfaff, Berlin: Springer, pp. 13–25.

Phi Delta Kappan (1948) "Will the golden rule work? A report of a class assignment in a Los Angeles high school," *Phi Delta Kappan* 30: 107f.

Philippidis, L. (1929) *Die "Goldene Regel" religionswissenschaftlich Untersucht*, Leipzig, Adolf Klein Verlag.

Piaget, J. (1948) *The Moral Judgment of the Child*, trans. M. Gabain, Glencoe, Ill.: Free Press.

Plaks, A. (2005) "Golden rule," in *Encyclopedia of Religion*, 2nd ed., ed. L. Jones, Detroit: Macmillan, 6: 3630–3.

Platt, J. (1973) "Social traps," *American Psychologist* 28: 641–51.

Popper, K. (1996) *The Open Society and Its Enemies*, 5th ed., 2 vols, Princeton, N.J.: Princeton University Press.

Porpora, D. (2001) *Landscapes of the Soul: The Loss of Moral Meaning in American Life*, New York: Oxford University Press, pp. 72, 156–65.

Post, S., (ed.) (2007) *Altruism and Health*, New York: Oxford University Press.

Raunio, A. (2001) *Summe des Christlichen Lebens: Die "Goldene Regel" als Gesetz in der Theologie Martin Luthers von 1510–1527*, Mainz, Germany: Verlag Philipp von Zabern.

Rawls, J. (1971) *A Theory of Justice*, Cambridge: Harvard University Press.

Reilly, R. (2003) "Conscience, citizenship, and global responsibilities," *Buddhist-Christian Studies* 23: 117–31.

—— (2006) "Compassion as justice," *Buddhist-Christian Studies* 26: 13–31.

—— (2008) *Ethics of Compassion*, Lanham, Md.: Lexington.

Reiman, J. (1985) "Justice, civilization, and the death penalty: Answering van den Haag," *Philosophy and Public Affairs* 14: 115–48.

Reiner, H. (1948) "Die Goldene Regel," *Zeitschrift für philosophische Forschung* 3: 74–105.

—— (1983) "The golden rule and the natural law," in his *Duty and Inclination*, trans. M. Santos, The Hague: Martinus Nijhoff, pp. 271–93. First published in 1977, as "Die Goldene Regel und das Naturrecht," *Studia Leibnitiana* 11: 231–54.

Reinikainen, J. (2005) "The golden rule and the requirement of universalizability," *Journal of Value Inquiry* 39: 155–68.

Ricoeur, P. (1990a) "The golden rule," *New Testament Studies* 36: 392–7.

—— (1990b) *Oneself as Another*, trans. K. Blamey, Chicago: University of Chicago Press, 1992.

Rieser, M. (1958) "An outline of intellectualistic ethics," *Journal of Philosophy* 55: 367–75.

Rimland, B. (1982) "The altruism paradox," *Psychological Reports* 51: 221f.

Rivers, E. (1477) *Dictes and Sayings of the Philosophers*, London: William Caxton, p. 70.

Rockhill, W. (1883) *Udânavarga: A Collection of Verses from the Buddhist Canon*, London: Kegan Paul, Trench, Trübner.

Roetz, H. (1993) *Confucian Ethics of the Axial Age*, Albany, N.Y.: SUNY Press.

Romar, E. (2002) "Virtue is good business: Confucianism as a practical business ethic," *Journal of Business Ethics* 38: 119–31.

Romig, R. (1984) *Reasonable Religion*, Buffalo, N.Y.: Prometheus.

Rosenberg, P. (2004) "Thomas Tryon and the seventeenth-century dimensions of antislavery," *William and Mary Quarterly* 61: 609–42.

Rost, H. (1986) *The Golden Rule: A Universalist Ethic*, Oxford: George Ronald.

Routley (Sylvan), R. (1973) "Is there a need for a new, an environmental, ethic?" *Proceedings of the 15th World Congress of Philosophy*, vol. 1, Sophia, Bulgaria: Sophia, pp. 205–10.

Rowley, H. (1940) "The Chinese sages and the golden rule," *Bulletin of the John Rylands Library* 24: 321–52.

Rushton, J. (1982) "Altruism and society: A social learning perspective," *Ethics* 92: 425–46.

Rushton, J., and R. Sorrentino (eds) (1981) *Altruism and Helping Behavior*, Hillsdale, N.Y.: Lawrence Erlbaum.

Russell, E. (1943) "What should I do?" *English Journal* 32: 382–6.

Russell, L. (1942) "Ideals and practice," *Philosophy* 17: 99–116.

Saeed, S. (2010) "The golden rule: An Islamic-dialogic perspective," paper at Edinburgh Festival of Spirituality of Peace, http://dialogicws.files.wordpress.com/2010/07/goldenrule_saeed1.pdf

Sagan, C. (1997) "The rules of the game," in *Billions & Billions: Thoughts on Life and Death at the Brink of the Millennium*, New York: Random House, pp. 216–30.

Saunders, P. (1993) "Is medical ethics lost?" *Journal of Medical Ethics* 19: 237f.

Schminke, M., and M. Ambrose (1997) "Asymmetric perceptions of ethical frameworks of men and women in business and nonbusiness settings," *Journal of Business Ethics* 16: 719–29.

Schnoor, L. (1953) "The attributes of an effective teacher," *Music Educators Journal* 39: 58.

Schulman, M., and E. Mekler (1994) *Bringing Up a Moral Child*, New York: Doubleday, pp. 52–117.

Sedgwick, C. (1993) "The golden rule," *Expository Times* 104: 273f.

Shanks, C. (1931) "The biblical anti-slavery argument of the decade 1830–1840," *Journal of Negro History* 16: 132–57.

Shapiro, A. (1952) "Should *The Merchant of Venice* offend Jewish students?" *National Council of Teachers of English* 41: 432f.

Sharp, F. (1928) *Ethics*, New York: Century.

Shaw, G. (1903) "Maxims for revolutionists," *Man and Superman*, New York: William H. Wise, pp. 217–29.

Sher, G. (1977) "Hare, abortion, and the golden rule," *Philosophy and Public Affairs* 6: 185–90.

Shermer, M. (2004) *The Science of Good and Evil: Why People Cheat, Gossip, Care, Share, and Follow the Golden Rule*, New York: Times.

Sidgwick, H. (1874) *The Methods of Ethics*, London: Macmillan, 1901.

Silberman, C. (1964) *Crisis in Black and White*, New York: Random House.

Singer, M. (1963) "The golden rule," *Philosophy* 38: 293–314.
—— (2001) "Golden rule," *Encyclopedia of Ethics*, http://www.credoreference.com/entry /routethics/golden_rule
—— (2002) "The golden rule," in his *The Ideal of a Rational Morality*, Oxford: Clarendon, pp. 16–9, 264–92 (the latter is Singer 1963 with further comments).
Singer, P. (1975) *Animal Liberation*, New York: Random House.
Smart, J. (1981) "Ethics and science," *Philosophy* 56: 449–65.
Smith, V. (1946) "In accentuation of the negative," *Scientific Monthly*, 63: 463–9.
Spahn, A. (2011) "And lead us (not) into persuasion...?" *Science and Engineering Ethics*, http://www.springerlink.com/content/f4441v7141711475/fulltext.pdf
Spier, R. (2005) "The British public speaks," *Science and Engineering Ethics* 11: 163–5.
Spinello, R. (2002) "The use and abuse of metatags," *Ethics and Information Technology* 4: 23–30.
—— (2005) "Competing fairly in the new economy: Lessons from the browser wars," *Journal of Business Ethics* 57: 343–61.
Stanglin, K. (2005) "The historical connection between the golden rule and the second greatest love command," *Journal of Religious Ethics* 33: 357–71.
Stilwell, B., M. Galvin, and S. Kopta (2000) *Right vs. Wrong: Raising a Child with a Conscience*, Bloomington: Indiana University Press, pp. 125–69.
Stowe, H. (1852) *Uncle Tom's Cabin*, London: Richard Bentley.
Straus, S. (1995) "Peace, culture, and education activities: A Buddhist response to the global ethic," *Buddhist-Christian Studies* 15: 199–211.
Sullivan, W., and W. Kymlicka (eds) (2007) *The Globalization of Ethics*, Cambridge: Cambridge University Press.
Suzuki, T., and P. Carus (trans.) (1906) *T'ai-Shang Kan-Ying P'ien (Treatise of the Exalted One on Response and Retribution)*, La Salle, Ill.: Open Court, http://www.sacred-texts.com/tao/ts
Swindal, J., and H. Gensler (eds) (2005) *The Sheed & Ward Anthology of Catholic Philosophy*, Lanham, Md.: Rowman & Littlefield.
Sylvan: See Routley.
Tasker, J. (1906) "Golden rule," in *A Dictionary of Christ and the Gospels*, ed. J. Hastings, Edinburgh: T. & T. Clark, 1: 653–5.
Telushkin, J. (2006–9) *A Code of Jewish Ethics*, 2 vols, New York: Bell Tower, 1:10–2, 2:9–15.
—— (2010) *Hillel: If Not Now, When?* New York: Schocken.
Terry, Q. (2012) *Golden Rules and Silver Rules of Humanity*, 5th ed., Concord, Mass.: Infinity.
Thomas, D. (2005) "Laboratory animals and the art of empathy," *Journal of Medical Ethics* 31: 197–202.
Thomas, L. (1996) "Becoming an evil society," *Political Theory* 24: 271–94.
Thompson, H. (1905) "Ethics in private practice," *American Journal of Nursing* 6: 163–6.
Thornwell, J. (1850) *The Rights and Duties of Masters*, Charleston, S.C.: Steampower Press of Walker & James.
Tillich, P. (1955) "The golden rule," *The New Being*, New York: Charles Schribner's Sons, 30–3.
Ting-Fang, W. (1900) "Mutual helpfulness between China and the United States," *North American Review* 171: 1–12.
Topel, J. (1998) "The tarnished golden rule," *Theological Studies* 59: 475–85.
Trapp, R. (1998) "The golden rule," *Grazer Philosophische Studien* 54: 139–64.
Trivers, R. (1971) "The evolution of reciprocal altruism," *Quarterly Review of Biology* 46: 35–57.
—— (1985) *Social Evolution*, Menlo Park, Calif.: Benjamin/Cummings.
—— (2002) *Natural Selection and Social Theory*, Oxford: Oxford University Press.
Troll, C. (2008) "Future Christian-Muslim engagement," paper at a Cambridge meeting between Christians and Muslims, http://chiesa.espresso.repubblica.it/articolo/208895?eng=y

Tsai, D. (2005) "The bioethical principles and Confucius' moral philosophy," *Journal of Medical Ethics* 31: 159–63.

Tsalikis, J., and M. Ortiz-Buonafina (1990) "Ethical beliefs' differences of males and females," *Journal of Business Ethics* 9: 509–17.

Tu, W. (1981) "The 'moral universal' from the perspectives of East Asian thought," *Philosophy East and West* 31: 259–67.

Tullberg, J. (2011) "The golden rule of benevolence versus the silver rule of reciprocity," *Journal of Religion and Business Ethics* 3: article 2, http://via.library.depaul.edu/jrbe/vol3/iss1/2

Vanberg, V., and R. Congleton (1992) "Rationality, morality, and exit," *American Political Science Review* 86: 418–31.

Vanderpool, H., and G. Weiss (1987) "False data and last hopes," *Hastings Center Report* 17: 16–9.

Virginia Law Review (1976) "Practice and pleading," *Virginia Law Review* 62: 1460–8.

Vogel, G. (2004) "The evolution of the golden rule," *Science* 303: 1128–31.

Votaw, C. (1904) "Sermon on the Mount," in *A Dictionary of the Bible*, ed. J. Hastings, New York: Charles Scribner's Sons, 5: 40–3.

Wallace, R. (2007) "The argument from resentment," *Proceedings of the Aristotelian Society* 62: 295–318.

Ward, D. (1932) *A More Golden Rule*, Denver: unknown.

Waterman, L. (1945) "The ethical clarity of the prophets," *Journal of Biblical Literature* 64: 297–307.

Wattles, J. (1987) "Levels of meaning in the golden rule," *Journal of Religious Ethics* 15: 106–29.

—— (1993) "Plato's brush with the golden rule," *Journal of Religious Ethics* 21: 69–85.

—— (1996) *The Golden Rule*, New York: Oxford University Press.

—— (2009) "Philosophical reflections on the golden rule," in Neusner & Chilton 2009, pp. 105–16.

Weiss, P. (1941) "The golden rule," *Journal of Philosophy* 38: 421–30.

Whately, R. (1856) *Lessons on Morality*, Cambridge, Mass.: John Bartlett, lesson 4.

Whiteley, C. (1966) "Universalisability," *Analysis* 27: 45–9.

Wierzbicka, A. (2001) *What Did Jesus Mean?* Oxford: Oxford University Press.

Wilson, A. (2007) *World Scripture and the Teachings of Sun Myung Moon*, New York: Universal Peace Federation, pp. xi, 67f. (available online, search for the title)

Wilson, B. (1988) "On a Kantian argument against abortion," *Philosophical Studies* 53: 119–30.

Wilson, D. (2003) "Evolutionary ethics," *Politics and Life Sciences* 22: 62f.

Wilson, E. (2000) *Sociobiology: The New Synthesis*, 25th anniversary ed., Cambridge: Harvard University Press.

Wilson, J. (1956) *The Culture of Ancient Egypt*, Chicago, University of Chicago Press.

Winner, R. (2009) *The Wooden Bowl, El Bol de Madera*, Goleta, Calif.: Brainstorm 3000. (for children)

Wiredu, K. (1996) *Cultural Universals and Particulars: An African Perspective*, Bloomington, Indiana University Press.

Yacasua, L. (1974) "Morality," *Phi Delta Kappan* 55: 608–10.

Zack, N. (1993) *Race and Mixed Race*, Philadelphia: Temple University Press.

Zahn-Waxler, C., M. Radke-Yarrow, and R. King (1979) "Child rearing and children's prosocial initiations toward victims of distress," *Child Development* 50: 319–30.

Zeitz, J. (2000) "The Missouri Compromise reconsidered," *Journal of the Early Republic* 20: 447–85.

Zerffi, G. (1885) "The Tchong-Yong of Confucius," *Transactions of the Royal Historical Society* 2: 254–71.

Index

These interest areas are in small caps: APPLIED ETHICS, ART, BIOLOGY, BLACK STUDIES, BUSINESS, CLASSICAL LANGUAGES, COMMUNICATIONS, COMPUTER SCIENCE, EDUCATION, ETHICAL THEORY, GAME THEORY, HISTORY, INTERCULTURAL STUDIES, LAW, LITERATURE, LOGIC, MEDICINE, POLITICAL SCIENCE, PSYCHOLOGY, RELIGION, SOCIOLOGY, SPORTS. The Bibliography isn't indexed.